Kingdom
and
Community

PRENTICE-HALL STUDIES IN RELIGION SERIES

SERIES EDITORS

John P. Reeder, Jr.
Brown University

John F. Wilson
Princeton University

JOHN G. GAGER

Princeton University

Kingdom and Community

*The Social World
of Early Christianity*

PRENTICE-HALL, INC., *Englewood Cliffs, New Jersey*

Library of Congress Cataloging in Publication Data

GAGER, JOHN G.
   Kingdom and community.

   (Prentice-Hall studies in religion series)
   Includes bibliographical references.
   1.Sociology, Christian—Early church. I.Title.
BR166.G33   270.1   74–28199
ISBN 0–13–516211–4
ISBN 0–13–516203–3 pbk.

Printed in the United States of America

10 9 8 7 6 5 4 3 2 1

PRENTICE-HALL INTERNATIONAL, INC., *London*
PRENTICE-HALL OF AUSTRALIA, PTY. LTD., *Sydney*
PRENTICE-HALL OF CANADA, LTD., *Toronto*
PRENTICE-HALL OF INDIA PRIVATE LIMITED, *New Delhi*
PRENTICE-HALL OF JAPAN, INC., *Tokyo*

Acknowledgments

The author expresses his appreciation to the following sources for permission to use the introductory quotations cited in each chapter:

CHAPTER 1: Reprinted by permission of Schocken Books Inc. and Basil Blackwell, Publisher, from *New Heaven New Earth* by Kenelm Burridge. Copyright © 1969 by Basil Blackwell.

CHAPTER 2: Reprinted by permission of the publisher, Harcourt Brace Jovanovich, Inc., and of Routledge and Kegan Paul Ltd., from *Ideology and Utopia* by Karl Mannheim.

CHAPTER 3: Reprinted by permission of the publisher, Yale University Press, from *Islam Observed* by Clifford Geertz.

CHAPTER 4: Reprinted by permission of the publisher, The Free Press, from *The Theory of Social and Economic Organization* by Max Weber. Copyright 1947 by Oxford University Press, New York, Inc.

Reprinted by permission of the publisher, Charles Scribner's Sons, and of SCM Press, Ltd., from *Theology of the New Testament* by Rudolf Bultmann.

CHAPTER 5: Reprinted by permission of the publisher, Cambridge University Press, from *Pagan and Christian in an Age of Anxiety* by E. R. Dodds.

The extracts quoted on pages 5, 90, and 95 of the text are reprinted by permission of Schocken Books Inc. and MacGibbon & Kee, from *The Trumpet Shall Sound* by Peter Worsley. Copyright © 1968 by Peter Worsley.

v

71829

Contents

Series Foreword   ix

Preface   xi

1. Introduction   1

THEOLOGY AND HISTORY IN THE STUDY OF EARLY CHRISTIANITY   *4*
RELIGION AND SOCIAL WORLDS   *9*

2. The End of Time
and the Rise of Community   19

EARLIEST CHRISTIANITY AS A MILLENARIAN MOVEMENT   *20*
Who Joined and Who Did Not?   The Prophet
Millenarian Ethics and Community   Explanations

CHRISTIAN MISSIONS AND THE THEORY OF COGNITIVE DISSONANCE   *37*
The Event of Jesus' Death
The Non-Event of the Kingdom
Conversion and Dissonance

THE ATTAINMENT OF MILLENNIAL BLISS THROUGH MYTH:
THE BOOK OF REVELATION   *49*

3. The Quest for Legitimacy
and Consolidation   66

THE QUESTION OF LEGITIMACY   *68*
Charisma, Office, and Tradition
The Canon and the Preservation of Charisma

ORTHODOXY AND HERESY   *76*
The Classical View and Its Critics
The Positive Functions of Heresy
Conclusions

4. Religion and Society
in the Early Roman Empire   93

THE ROMAN SOCIAL ORDER   *96*
Senatorial Aristocracy   Equestrian Order
Municipal Bureaucracies   Plebs   Freedman   Slaves

EARLIEST CHRISTIANITY AND THE ROMAN SOCIAL ORDER   *106*

5. The Success of Christianity   114

THE PROBLEM OF PERSPECTIVE   *115*
Some Possible Solutions

EXTERNAL FACTORS   *122*
The Empire   Church and Empire in Conflict
Diaspora Judaism

INTERNAL FACTORS   *129*

CHRISTIANITY AND ITS COMPETITORS   *132*
Mithras   Philosophical Schools
Judaism   Results

Index   149

Series Foreword

The volumes in this series are intended to contribute to the development of the study of religion. It seems to us that it is especially important that appropriately conceived and well-written materials be available for use in undergraduate and graduate instruction. Moreover, it is our hope that this series will not only be a useful teaching instrument within the formal curriculum, but will also play an important role in shaping the study of religion.

Individual volumes fall into one of three subsections in the series. One set of studies, small in number, will be concerned with theories of religion or methodological approaches to the study of religion. Our attempt will be to offer books where none are available or where the existing materials are inadequate. A second group of books, also small, will deal with general aspects of religion in various traditions. Mysticism, symbol and myth, religious ethics, and other comparable topics deserve theoretical and systematic treatments not available at present. The third section of the series consists of particular studies of various religious traditions, periods, or movements. The editors will try to identify areas of study to which sufficient attention has not been given, as well as classical subjects which deserve or even require fresh approaches.

We hope that each of the volumes in the series will be sufficiently lucid to serve as an introductory study, while also providing insights that will contribute to the work of specialists. Scholarly apparatus and bibliographies will be included to provide directions for further study. Throughout the project the editors will seek out studies which manifest unquestioned quality in scholarship and writing.

JOHN P. REEDER, JR.
Brown University

JOHN F. WILSON
Princeton University

Preface

This book has grown out of a single question, one that began to perplex me as I taught my first courses in religion: why is it that the study of early Christianity, as normally practiced, seems so different from the study of more exotic religions in Africa, Australia, and Melanesia? What appeared initially to be a simple question turned out, in fact, to be deceptively complex. A combination of theological, cultural, and historical factors has conspired to create a protected enclave for this particular religion. As a consequence, methods and techniques that are taken for granted in the treatment of other religions have been ignored or discarded in dealing with this one. Thus in pursuing an answer to my question, I became fascinated with the prospect of reexamining early Christianity in the light of modern religious movements that have flourished, so to speak, in the laboratories of sociologists and anthropologists. Increasingly, I became convinced that insights drawn from the study of these movements were not only applicable to early Christianity but also, and more significantly, that they held the promise of a genuinely new understanding of this particular religion.

Early in my musings I began to develop an awareness of the problems inherent in this sort of enterprise—our historical sources are fragmentary and woefully incomplete; theories generated by sociologists and anthropologists are themselves far from being universally accepted; and efforts to apply these theories to the facts of early Christianity regularly lead to the frustrating circumstance in which one or more facts are missing, with the result that the fit between theory and fact is often less than perfect. Despite these hazards, I have persevered in the original project on the assumption that even with partial results—and here I consoled myself with the view that at best history is an inexact science—the final outcome would more than justify the attendant risks. Before this book was completed, however, my hopes found an unexpected source of fulfillment. For in the past several years I have observed a growing

volume of studies that have corroborated and encouraged the general
thrust of my own efforts. It may be premature to speak of a new movement, but there are enough signs to warrant speaking of new beginnings
in the study of early Christianity.

Any endeavor to open new perspectives in a deeply traditional field
of scholarship is susceptible to numerous misunderstandings. Although
they may take many forms, these misunderstandings tend to cluster
around three closely related axes—first, a feeling, ranging anywhere
from vague disappointment to outright anger, that the author has committed an act of academic parricide in doubting the sufficiency of his
mentors' wisdom; second, an interpretation, or better an overinterpreta-
tion that lays greater emphasis than the author himself on the incompatibility of his own work with that of his predecessors in the field (the
author sees his relationship to previous work as a matter of both/and,
whereas his critics perceive him to be advancing a claim of either/or);
and third, a recurrent tendency to treat exploratory hypotheses as if they
were fixed dogmas. No amount of proleptic pleading will prevent these
misperceptions altogether, but a few words of caution may nonetheless
forestall the imputation of unwarranted and unintended assumptions
about the scope of this book. At this point I can do no better than to
cite the wry warning of Peter Brown in his essay, "Sorcery, Demons and
the Rise of Christianity from Late Antiquity into the Middle Ages":

> The need to link disciplines is frequently expressed among us. Discussion
> of this need takes place in an atmosphere, however, that suggests the
> observation of an African chieftain on a neighboring tribe: "They are
> our enemies. We marry them." Matchmaking must be a cautious process.
> The would-be linker of disciplines must be prepared "to sigh throughout
> the long delays of courtship": in attempts to link social and religious his-
> tory, classical and theological studies, I have observed that the unwary,
> or the precipitate, suitor has often ended up with the elderly, ugly daugh-
> ter.[1]

More than anything else, I wish to stress the experimental, almost
gamelike character of these studies. This is not to say that I have approached them with anything less than utmost seriousness or that I
have willfully ignored relevant information. Clearly I have not. But I
also recognize that in an undertaking of this sort, diligent readers will
uncover exceptions, inconsistencies, unanswered questions, and even an
occasional error. Furthermore, it is certainly to be expected that different
arguments will appeal to different readers. Partial and complete readings
of the manuscript by a variety of persons have alerted me in advance to

---

[1] *Witchcraft Accusations and Confessions,* ed. Mary Douglas (London: Tavistock
Publications, 1970), p. 17.

certain areas that are likely to be more problematic than others. Some will discover weaknesses in one or more of the theoretical models; others will propose new models as complementary or preferable to those which I have chosen to adopt. This sort of reaction I not only expect but invite. In the long run, however, I am less committed to particular models, e.g., the relevance of cognitive dissonance theories for explaining missionary activity, than I am to the more general program of a rapprochement between historians of religion and theorists in other fields. In essence, then, this book is directed neither at those who already believe in this program nor at staunch disbelievers, but at those who stand in the middle—unconvinced yet willing to explore.

Those familiar with the recent history of biblical scholarship in Germany will recall the repeated claim of each generation that it had overthrown the outmoded and unscientific work of its predecessors. Such claims seem to accompany every new wave of scholarship as it strives to establish a distinctive name for itself. I cannot insist too strongly that I do not share this view of my own work. Any attempt to reshape the study of early Christianity must inevitably—and for more than political reasons —build upon the foundations of the past several generations. The results of text, form, and redaction critics, of historians and theologians, are indispensable for any new direction. At the same time, it will be readily apparent that I cannot accept the traditional horizons of the field. As for earlier attempts to produce social histories, I have questioned the *adequacy* of their theories and methods. But I have no quarrel with their basic insight that exegetical and theological approaches have produced an incomplete picture. As for those who continue to espouse these approaches, I differ only insofar as they regard them, whether implicitly or not, as both necessary *and* sufficient. To put the matter in quite practical terms, much of this book will probably seem incomprehensible to readers with no prior knowledge of early Christianity. I have presupposed a certain amount of knowledge at every point and have deliberately not provided the neophyte with a survey of the basic "ethnographic" data. For this sort of thing the reader may wish to consult any standard introduction to the history and literature of early Christianity.

It is my pleasure to acknowledge the assistance I have received from students, colleagues, friends, and family. I have benefited from their comments and criticism even when I have chosen not to follow them. A special debt of gratitude is due to Sheldon R. Isenberg, who provided more guidance than he knows during the initial stages of this project. The coeditors of the series, John F. Wilson and John P. Reeder, have been more than generous with their time and energy.

JOHN G. GAGER
Princeton University

1

Introduction

The hypothesis that millenary activities predicate a new culture or social order coming into being . . . is a fair one. Certainly it is more scientific to regard these activities as new-cultures-in-the-making, or as attempts to make a new kind of society or moral community, rather than as oddities, diseases in the body social, or troublesome nuisances to efficient administration—though of course they may be all of these as well. Finally, of course, a millenarian movement is a new religion in the making. New assumptions are being ordered into what may become a new orthodoxy.

KENELM BURRIDGE
New Heaven, New Earth

This book is rooted in a conception of early Christianity as a social world in the making. It seeks to explore the relevance of this conception for certain basic issues—the relationship between religion and social status, the enthusiastic character of the earliest Christian communities, their gradual transformation into a formidable religious and social institution, and the emergence of Christianity as the dominant religion of the later Roman Empire. Within this general framework, the approach will be comparative and theoretical: theoretical in the sense that I will make use of explanatory models drawn from the social sciences, and comparative in that much of the evidence for these models is based on studies of non-Christian religious movements.

As outlined in the opening passage from Burridge, the treatment of new religions as new worlds coming into being has become almost a commonplace in dealing with non-Western religions and even with peripheral cults in Western societies. But with few exceptions, this perspective has not taken hold among students of early Christianity.[1] Thus it remains very much an open question for the field as a whole whether this sort of approach will prove fruitful. At the very least, however, we may be certain that its viability can never be known apart from some form of practical application. The series of studies in this book is intended to serve just this purpose—to test a variety of concepts and categories by applying them to a number of classical topics in the field. At the same time, I must emphasize that I regard my efforts as tentative in a double sense. First, any exploration of new models in a field that provides few precedents ought to proceed with caution, though not necessarily without conviction. And second, the fact that I have chosen to concentrate on the social *world* of early Christianity does not imply that the study of other social aspects, e.g., gathering the social facts and describing social institutions, is any less desirable or urgent. Nor do I mean to suggest at the outset that I have approached these studies without the benefit of previous work that has pointed in a similar direction. My dependence on the work of predecessors and contemporaries will be evident throughout. At the same time, however, it should be equally clear that the treatment of early Christianity as a social world in the making represents what T. S. Kuhn has called a paradigm-shift in a highly traditional field of scholarship. This book, together with other recent studies, advocates a new way of looking at old issues. And by implication it involves certain criticisms of old ways. For as Kuhn puts it in his analysis of paradigm-shifts in the natural sciences, changes of this sort come about only with "a growing sense . . . that an existing paradigm has ceased to function adequately in the explanation of an aspect of nature to which the paradigm itself had previously led the way."[2]

Clearly I share such "a growing sense that an existing paradigm has ceased to function adequately," and one of my primary goals is to foster a similar sense of dissatisfaction in others. In particular, I will argue that the field of early Christianity has suffered from a predominance of theological and related concerns. To quote from an unpublished paper of J. Z. Smith, "the study of early Christian materials has been characterized by an overemphasis on a literary-historical and theological point of view to the detriment of the sociological."[3] This does not mean that a theological perspective is inherently inappropriate to the subject matter of early Christianity or that theologically minded historians are the only ones with presuppositions. In terms of our immediate concerns, the inadequacy of theological paradigms is rather that they have been directly responsible for the neglect of sociological and anthropological points of view. To the extent that historians in general have stressed the particularity of historical events, they have been disinclined to make use of social scientific disciplines that by their very nature search for common patterns and principles. And when the further assumption is made, with however much sophistication, that certain events in early Christianity are not only historically distinctive but in some sense religiously unique, the aversion to the social sciences will be even more powerful.

By contrast, the rapprochement between history and the social sciences that underlies this book involves a shift of emphasis away from the particularism of most historians of early Christianity. As one observer puts it, the result is an effort "to detect the recurrent regularities of social events"[4] and hence the employment of "a comparative method —abstracting, selecting, classifying, comparing, and explicitly or implicitly testing general hypotheses."[5] In following this procedure, however, I am well aware that it is not without problems of its own. One major obstacle in applying it to a movement such as early Christianity is that the historical evidence is so diffuse and fragmentary. Obviously the data are insufficient to serve as the basis, by themselves, for generating major theories. In addition, the lack of satisfactory controls means that our conclusions regarding the degree of conformity between a given model and the Christian data must remain tentative and open to reformulation. On the other hand, the positive value of a comparative and theoretical method is precisely that it offers a source of "external controls and supplementary information by means of a more morphological analysis and more or less systematic comparison with similar movements elsewhere." [6] In other words, new "data" may come in the form of new models.

THEOLOGY AND HISTORY IN THE STUDY OF EARLY CHRISTIANITY

At this point, we need not chronicle the complicated dialectic between historical methodology and theological assumptions that has accompanied the study of early Christianity from its inception. W. G. Kümmel's *The New Testament: The History of the Investigation of Its Problems*[7] has performed this task admirably. What emerges from Kümmel's comprehensive survey and others like it is the inescapable conclusion that the history of scholarship in this area has been determined at every point by nonhistorical considerations.[8] Despite the immense body of literature on the New Testament, no one can seriously dispute P. Schubert's judgment that "more than any other special field of historical study, New Testament research has always suffered from a curious inability to be thoroughly historical in method and aim." [9] From the very beginning, when Dionysius of Alexandria (third century C.E.) disputed the Johannine authorship of Revelation in order to impugn its canonical status,[10] theological standards have been used to settle such basic questions as the selection of sources and the definition of methods. The first problem is the New Testament itself. As distinct from the individual documents that comprise it, the Christian canon is the product of theological and political conditions in the second, third, and fourth centuries. As a collection, it reflects an "orthodox" image of what Christian beginnings should have been, not a handy compendium of documents designed for later historians. And the failure to recognize this fundamental fact has led to a host of unwarranted conventions in the field: because he figures so prominently in the New Testament, Paul's significance in early Christian history has tended to be grossly overrated; early noncanonical writings have received less attention than contemporaneous writings within the canon; later canonical writings, once it was agreed that they had not been written by the apostles whose names they bear, were shunted to the periphery of scholarly concern; and to this day, Gospel parallels still list only canonical material. In other words, introductory courses, textbooks, lexicons, and histories that continue to limit themselves to the New Testament are subject to nonhistorical biases from the outset.[11] W. Wrede stated this aspect of the problem as succinctly as possible in 1897: "The expression 'New Testament theology' is wrong on both counts: the New Testament deals not so much with theology as with religion, and the reasons why 'New Testament' is an inappropriate category need not be repeated here. . . . The name that best suits the situation is 'the history of early Christian religion.' " [12] Actually, Wrede's comment raises two separate issues—the question whether and in what sense the recorded reflections of the earliest Christians can be properly called theological *and* the natural tendency of theologically minded historians to "theologize" their subject matter. With respect to the second issue, Peter Worsley notes that the same tendency occurs among students of primitive cultures. His criticism applies in our case as well:

> This over-systematization of belief is commonly accompanied by a spurious ontological "priority" or hierarchy: the assumption that general cosmological, philosophical, etc., beliefs are somehow "primary" or "higher" (and must therefore be discussed first in any academic analysis). This is a natural disease of academics, a consequence of their specialized role in the social division of labour as dealers in ideas.[13]

As a general rule, we may assume that in most new religions "only a very limited group of people . . . engages in theorizing, in the business of 'ideas' and the construction of *Weltanschauungen*." [14] In the case of small groups of intellectuals, e.g., Valentinus and his circle, a theological approach is quite appropriate, but once we begin to pay serious attention to the social constituency of the early churches, the customary overemphasis on theological matters seems quite out of place.

The other side of the matter is that new theologies have often spawned innovations in historical methodology. The rise of radical historical criticism came about not from antireligious sentiments, but as the direct result of English deism and its pursuit of "rational Christianity." [15] John Locke, in *The Reasonableness of Christianity, as Delivered by the Scriptures* (1695), put forward the view that only a thoroughly historical point of view would enable the modern believer to disentangle the universal simplicity of the original faith from the distorted ideas that appear even in the later writings of the New Testament. The same motivation is present again in the later history-of-religions school that flourished in the nineteenth and early twentieth centuries. These historians of religion firmly believed that Christianity could only be comprehended in the context of the larger Greco-Roman world, but most also believed that the comparative method would enable them to isolate certain critical ideas, usually in Jesus and Paul, that transcended both paganism and Judaism and thus guaranteed the uniqueness of Christianity.[16]

To complete the circle, we should note that opposition to the history-of-religions school likewise rested on nonhistorical considerations.[17] In 1901 Adolf Harnack spoke against a proposal to transform theological faculties into schools for the general study of religion. "Theological faculties," he insisted, "[should] remain faculties for the study of the *Christian* religion, because Christianity in its pure form is not *a* religion along with others, but *the* religion." [18] In short, the difference between Harnack and the historians of religion is relative rather than absolute. In the final analysis, the debate was more theological than historical. Both sides agreed that in the beginning Christianity offered something radically new, and both agreed that Christianity eventually became a syncretistic religion. They disagreed only with respect to the degree of this syncretism and the point at which it first took effect. Even among the historians of religion, few thought to move beyond the question of Jewish and pagan influences to the point of considering the Christian religion, from start to finish, as a typical expression of Greco-Roman piety, as one response among many to a common cultural crisis. Here the historical method reached its theological limit and could proceed no further.

Ironically, it is Kümmel himself who best exemplifies the remarkable persistence of this dilemma. After describing in masterful fashion the relentless contest between historical and theological presuppositions, he concludes his own work with this deeply ambiguous injunction:

> Yet whoever performs this profane work [sc. historical scholarship] cannot evade the word of the Johannine Christ: "My teaching is not mine, but his who sent me. If anyone wants to do His will, he will know whether this teaching is from God or whether I speak on my own authority" (John 7:16–17).[19]

By seeming to imply that the historian must somehow deal with the issue of the saying's validity or that only one who accepts it as true is in a position to properly understand it, he has cast aside the only hope of preserving the integrity of historical scholarship. And in this respect, there is still no reasonable alternative to W. Wrede's advice, given in 1897, about the independence of historical inquiry: "What the systematic theologian makes of its results, how he accommodates himself to them, is his affair." [20] This is not to say that the results of historical criticism have no bearing on theological issues—the frenzy surrounding the Dead Sea Scrolls is but one instance of their close connection. The implications of Wrede's warning are rather that a theological concern is not a prerequisite for the historian of early Christianity, that theological commitments cannot justifiably set limits to either the methods or the results of the historian's work and that exclusively theological concerns are inappropriate.

Kümmel's remark also points to the one area of study where the conflict of historical and theological loyalties has caused the greatest damage—the quest for the historical Jesus.[21] Surely no single issue has so fascinated students of early Christianity. Yet on no other issue have such prodigious efforts led to more inconclusive results. One major problem has been the extent to which religious and theological commitments have led "questers" to sacrifice methodological rigor and to minimize the difficulties inherent in the task of reconstructing the figure of Jesus. Thus Albert Schweitzer's judgment that "the historical investigation of the life of Jesus did not take its rise from a purely historical interest"[22] applies not just to the original motives for the quest but inevitably to the manner in which it has been carried out. Beyond this, the status of the New Testament as sacred Scripture, and of the Gospels within the New Testament, has long fostered a parochial attitude toward basic matters of methodology. In dealing with the oral tradition that is thought to have preceded the written Gospels, students of the Gospels have seldom looked beyond the inherited conventions of their own discipline. Anthropological studies of oral traditions in preliterate societies[23] and psychological studies of rumor formation and transmission[24] have passed largely unnoticed. And finally, the quest has tended to treat the Gospels primarily as sources of information about Jesus and only secondarily, if at all, as invaluable sources for a wide variety of early Christian communities.

In recent years there have been encouraging signs of discontent with these assumptions. In an important article on the Gospels and their sources, Helmut Koester has argued that our first approach to the Gospels, whether canonical or not, must be in terms of their respective images of Jesus.[25] Not only are the canonical Gospels not free of theological and other motives, but in Koester's words "the honor of having continued and developed the tradition about Jesus' original works and words must go to the more primitive gospel sources and to the apocryphal gospels."[26] Here the common confusion of historical (what writings qualify as sources for the quest) and theological (what writings are authoritative for the church) questions has been decisively broken. As for the oral tradition, there are scattered indications that it too may begin to receive the critical examination that it so sorely needs.[27] In 1925 O. Cullmann commented in a review of R. Bultmann's *History of the Synoptic Tradition* that

> there needs to be a special branch of sociology, devoted to the study of the laws which govern the growth of popular traditions. Form criticism will only be able to function profitably if conclusive results can be established in this area. In fact, the most serious defect in [form critical] studies which have appeared thus far is the absence of any sociological basis.[28]

Some fifty years after this warning was first issued, its pertinence may at last be understood. For apart from a consideration of its social setting, no statement about the origin and function of oral tradition in early Christianity may be accepted as valid. And in the absence of solid information about this social setting, no reconstruction of oral tradition is trustworthy.

In some respects, however, the most important recent development has been the work of redaction criticism.[29] By examining a Gospel in terms of its general structure, thematic development, and literary style, and by distinguishing insofar as possible between traditional material and its reinterpretation at the hands of the final author or editor, redaction critics have sought to sketch a picture of the beliefs and practices, the concerns and presuppositions that gave to each Gospel its final shape. If we now transpose the results of this kind of analysis into the framework of early Christianity as a new world coming into being, we may properly speak of the Gospels as religious or mythological charters. Instead of treating them exclusively as sources for the quest, we may approach them as sources for re-creating what I have called the social world of early Christianity. Furthermore, what applies to each individual Gospel is equally true of the sources behind them. During the years between the time of Jesus and the production of the written Gospels, we know that traditional material was reworked, expanded, and collated. And from the study of oral tradition in preliterate societies, we may be certain that each of these "distortions" "is in itself a piece of documentary evidence . . . and should be treated as such." [30] We also know that in the process new material was created and interpolated: eschatological prophecies, Old Testament proof texts, *ex post facto* predictions, and ethical maxims were attributed to Jesus *and thereby authorized for believers—* Jesus transmits his authority to the disciples and thus makes possible the transition from the first to the second and third generations (Matt. 16:17–20); he predicts and thus legitimizes future suffering for believers (Matt. 10:17–23); he delivers an extensive sermon that can serve as a catechism for Christian communities in handling their daily affairs (Matt. 5–7); he bests the Pharisees in debate and thus demonstrates the superiority of church over synagogue (Matt. 22–23); after his resurrection he appears to his followers in order to dispense his final wisdom, often in a mysterious language that the "world" cannot comprehend (Matt. 28:6–20; Luke 24:13–53; John 20:11–21, 25; Gospel of Thomas, etc.); and in the infancy stories and Gospels he emerges as the popular cultural hero of a broad religious movement. In other words, the various images of Jesus, whatever their relation to the historical Jesus of Nazareth, are in the first instance reflections of the communities that preserved and transmitted the Gospel traditions. Their world was projected onto the person of Jesus and thus given the highest form of legitimacy. What Schweitzer said of modern lives of Jesus applies every bit as much to the very first "lives" of Jesus—the Gospels:

> Thus each successive epoch of theology found its own thoughts in Jesus; that was, indeed, the only way it could make Him live. But it was not only each epoch that found its reflection in Jesus; each individual created Him in accordance with his own character. There is no historical task which so reveals a man's true self as the writing of a Life of Jesus.[31]

Of course this process was a dialectical one in the sense that inherited traditions tended to shape the community's view of its world, and its own experience of that world in turn influenced the shape of the tradition. Thus the Gospels and their sources are models *of* as well as models *for* their respective groups. And by charting the growth of the Gospels, from the earliest discernible sources to the later apocryphal gospels, we can trace the creation and transformation of numerous social worlds in the history of early Christianity.[32]

RELIGION AND SOCIAL WORLDS

Peter Berger defines religion as "the human enterprise by which a sacred cosmos is established." [33] By this he means to describe the phenomenon of religion as one example of his broader assertion that every human society is an "enterprise of world-building." [34] Human worlds by their very nature are social constructions.[35] Although they first confront us in objective form, our conceptions of meaning, value, goals, truth, reality, duties, social roles, etc., are not "out there" as eternal entities. They are the products of human creativity in the social order. As such, they must be constantly created, adapted, maintained, and legitimated. Without these primary processes—Berger calls them *world-construction* and *world-maintenance*—there can be no social existence whatsoever. In essence, this means that the social world in which we live determines our experience of what is real. P. Winch expresses a similar view when he proposes that language, by which he means all forms of human communication, shapes reality:

> Our idea of what belongs to the realm of reality is given for us in the language that we use. The concepts we have settle for us the form of the experience we have of the world. . . . That is not to say that our concepts may not change; but when they do, that means that our concept of the world has changed too.[36]

Religion, then, is that particular mode of world-building that seeks to ground its world in a sacred order, a realm that justifies and explains the arena of human existence in terms of the eternal nature of things. Whether this transcendent realm is the mythic world of remote ancestors, an ideal universe existing in some remote "heaven," or an order of reality utterly unlike anything known in the present, it is what gives meaning and value—whether positive or negative—to human affairs in "this world." In dealing with established religions under stable conditions, the main emphasis will be on the aspect of *world-maintenance,* i.e., the processes whereby a given social world is maintained and legitimated for those who inhabit it. But in treating new religions, the emphasis will fall on *world-construction,* i.e., the processes whereby a new world is brought into being and seeks to establish itself in competition with numerous other worlds. Only at a later time, if the movement should survive the traumatic period of its birth, will the issue of world-maintenance become relevant.

Although phrases such as "social world" and "sacred cosmos" are in some sense interchangeable, the latter is, properly speaking, a particular type of the former. My choice of "social world" represents a conscious decision to stress the processes that lead to the creation of new worlds rather than the finished products, i.e., the specifically Christian symbols, rituals, and institutions. To be precise, this is not a book about developed theologies of God or salvation in early Christianity but about the ways in which it, like other new religions, created a world so that certain ideas of God and salvation, and not others, seem peculiarly appropriate.

By adopting the perspectives of Berger, Burridge, and others, it should be apparent that I am calling into question the adequacy of certain traditional assumptions about the study of early Christianity. My view is that past failures to deal with the rise of Christianity in social terms have resulted in serious distortions of the historical realities. Despite all their talk about the need to determine the *Sitz im Leben* of a given passage (i.e., its specific setting and function in the concrete life of the community that preserved and used it), students of early Christian literature have given remarkably little attention to the social dimensions of these communities.[37] Thus the emphasis given here to the social aspect of world-construction stems from a basic conviction that the process of generating a sacred cosmos or a symbolic universe is always rooted in concrete communities of believers. This conviction takes us beyond the standard claim that religious beliefs and institutions are subject to the influence of social factors in their environment, for it makes the assertion that without a community there is no social world and without a social world there can be no community. At the same time, it should be made clear that I do not intend to produce a social history. This is not primarily a study of social teachings, social impact, social surroundings, or social institutions. Although each of these is pertinent to an understanding of what I have called the social world of early Christianity, I regard them as secondary processes that bear on but are not identical with the primary processes of world-construction and world-maintenance. All new religions, then, are directed toward the creation of new worlds: old symbols are given new meaning and new symbols come to life; new communities define themselves in opposition to previous traditions; a new order of the sacred is brought into being and perceived by the community as the source of all power and meaning; new rituals emerge to remind the community of this sacred order by creating it anew in the act of ritual celebration; mechanisms are established for preserving this new world and for adapting it to changing circumstances; and eventually an integrated world view may emerge, including systems of theology, sacred scriptures, and ecclesiastical offices whose task is to give meaning not just to the community itself but to all other worlds as well.

As indicated earlier, the promise of this paradigm is that it will make it possible to see old facts in a new light. Let me cite as an example the formation of the Christian Bible. One recurrent feature of new religions is the need to define sacred time. In historical religions, the idea of sacred time normally takes shape around those events which first brought the community into being—symbol systems express the meaning of these events, rituals revive them, institutions derive their authority from them, and the sacred scriptures preserve a record of them for each new generation. Eventually each of these facets takes on an aura of holiness by virtue of its participation in the events of sacred beginnings. From this perspective, one sees immediately that the process of forming the Christian Bible, just like the process of creating the Gospels, can become an important key to understanding the origins and permutations of sacred time throughout the early centuries of Christian history. Conflicting views of the canon thus become expressions of conflicting views of the Christian "world." And the form of the canon that finally emerged may be seen as an effort to sustain one interpretation of that world against the threat of competition from within and without. The same may also be said of scriptural exegesis, without which the sacred writings would soon have become little more than a repository of historical relics. Biblical interpretation played a critical role as the earliest believers struggled to define their new assumptions within the context of Judaism, and it continued to play this role at every stage thereafter—in the perennial disputes with Jewish opponents, in controversies among Christians themselves, and in the ceaseless task of demonstrating the relevance of the Scriptures in ever-changing historical and cultural circumstances.

The issue of the canon also suggests that the separation of world-construction from world-maintenance, while useful as an analytical tool, is impractical in fact. By this I mean that the need to justify a new world is incumbent on new religious communities from the very first. Inasmuch as new religions do not come into being *ex nihilo,* but are always in some sense heretical or revitalization movements, the task of world-construction takes the form of questioning the legitimacy of a traditional order. For this same reason, new religious communities also exemplify the precarious status of all social worlds. By revealing that the legitimacy of the old order is not, after all, inherent in the nature of the universe, they pose a tremendous threat to that order. And this unwelcome revelation explains why both sides react as they do. The old group seeks to annihilate the new one by eliminating or incorporating it (and thus removing it as a threat from the outside), and the new group draws a tight circle around itself and insists that it has broken radically with the corruptions of the previous order. In both cases, the issue at stake is nothing less than the existence of the community itself.

So much, then, for the general perspective and assumptions of the book as a whole. The question now becomes how they will work in specific cases. The method I will follow in succeeding chapters is to examine specific problems in terms of theoretical models from recent work in the social sciences. In each case the model has been formulated independently of Christian evidence. My procedure will be to test them against information based on early Christian documents. In following this course, I have taken my lead from several directions.[38] Among them, the work of S. J. Case and the "Chicago school" has been particularly important. In his chief works, *The Social Origins of Christianity*[39] and *The Social Triumph of the Ancient Church,*[40] Case endeavored, in the end unsuccessfully, to reorient the study of early Christianity toward a concern for social factors.[41] In Europe, J. Harrison,[42] E. Rohde,[43] and A. Dieterich[44] pioneered in urging the value of comparative ethnology for students of ancient religion, including Christianity. Ultimately their efforts also failed to gain a permanent hold, in part because of cultural and theological forces quite beyond their control. But beyond these extrinsic matters, it needs to be emphasized that these early initiatives suffered from a lack of theoretical sophistication. The systematic study of non-Western religions was still in its infancy—B. K. Malinowski's epoch-making essays on the Trobriand Islanders did not appear until the second decade of the twentieth century—and the fields of sociology, social psychology, and social anthropology had just begun to develop as mature disciplines. Thus, although the instincts of such figures as Case and Harrison were sound, their theoretical models were either nonexistent or inadequate. Fruitful cooperation between historians and social scientists could not occur until the social sciences themselves had reached a higher level of theoretical and empirical sophistication. A further impetus for the present undertaking has thus come from the side of more recent work in the social sciences. Social anthropologists in particular are now in the habit of appealing to the evidence of early Christianity in order to illustrate common patterns of religious behavior.[45] So far, however, specialists on the other side have been slow to exploit this initiative. At one level, this book is an attempt to explore these random observations in more systematic fashion.

But surely an undertaking of this kind demands greater justification than mere novelty or curiosity. Social scientists concerned with the study of religion may well be interested to find their hypotheses confirmed, or in some cases modified, by a detailed analysis of the data from a new direction. For students of early Christianity, however, the final test must be whether the perspective that we have adopted makes good on the claim to appreciate the genesis and growth of the Christian religion in ways that have not hitherto been possible. In general terms, my confidence that this approach will yield new insights is based on the general proposition that the starting point of any intellectual endeavor largely dictates its outcome. This means not only that the questions one asks are dictated by one's general orientation to the subject, but even more importantly that the answers one receives and thus one's understanding of the entire subject are determined by the initial questions. A theological orientation produces theological questions, which in turn give theological answers and a theological conception of the subject. This is not to say that traditional perspectives, whether theological, hermeneutical, or literary, are false or unworkable, but that they have become restrictive, imperious, and in some cases worn out by excessive use. Progress, or more modestly change, in the study of early Christianity will come about not through the discovery of new historical information, which can always be assimilated within old paradigms, but through new questions and new perspectives.

Naturally the task that I have in mind involves a number of methodological problems that no one can afford to minimize. In the first instance, I do not harbor any illusions about the scientific validity of the social scientific models utilized in these studies. The fact that I make use of certain models rather than others means only that I regard them as more fitting for the data, not that they are more "objective." In other words, the sort of analysis that I have undertaken must be as open to subsequent revision as the social sciences themselves. At the same time, however, one reason for advocating a theoretical approach lies precisely in certain differences between classical and contemporary work in the "softer" social sciences. In contrast to social theoreticians of the nineteenth century, contemporary sociologists and anthropologists are generally content with models that are less than cosmic in scope. Rather than seeking to encompass all aspects of human behavior under a single theory, they now focus on more limited areas of inquiry, e.g., social stratification, political structures, disaffected communities, and symbol systems. Furthermore, these disciplines have directed considerable energy toward testing their hypotheses through case studies, quite often involving societies outside the orbit of Western culture, e.g., the study of millenarian activities in Polynesia, Melanesia, and Africa. This latter shift is of particular significance because it offers some hope of escaping the patent circularity of previous efforts at model-building. Theories generated from the study of non-Western cultures are less vulnerable to the charge that they work in a Western context simply because they are based on a culture whose roots go back to early Christianity. Finally, contemporary social scientists have by and large given up the polemical stance that characterized the earliest attempts to interpret the history of Christianity within a theoretical framework, e.g., the Hegelian views of F. C. Baur and the "Tübingen school" [46] and the materialist interpretations of Marx, Engels, and later Marxists.[47] The hostility aroused by these efforts had the unfortunate consequence among historians of early Christianity of casting suspicion on all forms of sociological interpretation.[48] Gradually, however, this hostility has diminished as social scientists themselves have abandoned the strident reductionism of at least some of their founders.[49]

Taken together, these factors have created an atmosphere in which cooperation between historians of religion and social scientists now appears both feasible and desirable. The current interest in what I have called comparative and theoretical models, though still very much in its initial phase, marks an important shift in basic assumptions about the study of early Christianity. But we should be clear that this shift hardly betokens a paradigm-revolution. Indeed, no such revolution is possible in the historical fields that lack any concept of "normal science" and that, as one critic has put it, "must live at all times in a state that approximates 'crisis' in a developed science." [50] At most we may anticipate the emergence of a new constituency within the professional community and with it the elevation of a new paradigm to an equal status with others in the field.

NOTES

1. This void is all the more striking when one considers that a great deal of work has been done on social aspects of ancient Israel and the Old Testament. See, for example, the classic works surveyed by H. F. Hahn, *The Old Testament in Modern Research* (Philadelphia: Fortress Press, 1966), pp. 44–82, 157–84. Of the more modern literature I mention only T. Par-

SONS, *Societies. Evolutionary and Comparative Perspectives* (Englewood Cliffs, N.J.: Prentice-Hall, 1966), pp. 96–102; MARY DOUGLAS, *Purity and Danger. An Analysis of Concepts of Pollution and Taboo* (London: Penguin Books, 1966), pp. 54–72; and E. LEACH, *Genesis as Myth and Other Essays* (London: Jonathan Cape, 1969).

2. *The Structure of Scientific Revolutions* (Chicago: University of Chicago Press, 1973), p. 92.

3. "The Social Description of Early Christianity: A Working Paper," p. 1. Smith's paper was prepared for the 1973 annual meeting of the Society of Biblical Literature and the American Academy of Religion.

4. YONINA TALMON, "Pursuit of the Millennium: The Relation between Religious and Social Change," *Archives Européennes de Sociologie* 3 (1962), p. 126. Talmon's article is reprinted in *Reader in Comparative Religion: An Anthropological Approach,* ed. W. LESSA and E. VOGT, 2nd ed. (New York: Harper & Row, 1965), pp. 522–37.

5. *Ibid.*

6. *Ibid.,* p. 127.

7. Nashville: Abingdon Press, 1972.

8. See, for instance, S. NEILL, *The Interpretation of the New Testament: 1861–1961* (New York: Oxford University Press, 1966).

9. SCHUBERT, "Urgent Tasks for New Testament Research," in *The Study of the Bible Today and Tomorrow,* ed. H. R. Willoughby (Chicago: University of Chicago Press, 1947), p. 214.

10. On Dionysius see KÜMMEL, *The New Testament,* pp. 15–18.

11. Certain major exceptions to this pattern should be noted: W. BAUER's *A Greek-English Lexicon of the New Testament and Other Early Christian Literature* (Chicago: University of Chicago Press, 1957; first published in German in 1928); BAUER's *Orthodoxy and Heresy in Earliest Christianity* (Philadelphia: Fortress Press, 1971; first published in 1934); P. WENDLAND, *Die hellenistisch-römische Kultur in ihren Beziehungen zu Judentum und Christentum* (Tübingen: J. C. B. Mohr, 1912) and *Die urchristlichen Literaturformen* (Tübingen: J. C. B. Mohr, 1912); and the works of S. J. Case cited above (p. 12).

12. *Über Aufgabe und Methode der sogenannten Neutestamentlichen Theologie* (Göttingen: Vandenhoeck und Ruprecht, 1897), pp. 79f. An English translation is now available in R. MORGAN, *The Nature of New Testament Theology* (London: SCM Press, 1973), pp. 68–116.

13. *The Trumpet Shall Sound. A Study of "Cargo" Cults in Melanesia* (New York: Schocken Books, 1968), p. xxv.

14. P. BERGER and T. LUCKMANN, *The Social Construction of Reality. A Treatise in the Sociology of Knowledge* (Garden City, N.Y.: Doubleday, 1966), p. 15.

15. See KÜMMEL, *The New Testament,* pp. 51–61.

16. Kümmel comments: "It is now apparent why these theologians who consciously employed history-of-religions methodology also excepted the message of Jesus from the history-of-religions influence . . . the proof of foreign influence on early Christianity is also to serve to exclude foreign matter from the Gospel, which by these very means is preserved as 'a creative miracle' " (*The New Testament,* p. 260).

17. See, for instance, the question posed by R. Bultmann, himself an early advocate of the school: "Today we can ask whether this intention [of the history-of-religions school] can do justice to the New Testament, and whether we are not rather to turn back again to the old question about the *theology* of the New Testament." His words appear in the introduction to W. BOUSSET, *Kyrios Christos* (Nashville: Abingdon Press, 1970), p. 9.

18. From an address entitled "Die Aufgabe der Theologischen Fakultäten und die allgemeine Religionsgeschichte" (the translation is from KÜMMEL, *The New Testament,* p. 310).

19. KÜMMEL, *The New Testament,* p. 406.

20. *Op. cit.* (above p. 15, n. 12), p. 9; the translation is from KÜMMEL, *The New Testament,* p. 304. For a similar statement see K. STENDAHL, "Biblical Theology," *Interpreter's Dictionary of the Bible* (Nashville: Abingdon Press, 1962), vol. 1, pp. 418–32.

21. For a more thorough discussion of my views on this issue see my article, "The Gospels and Jesus: Some Doubts about Method," *Journal of Religion* 54 (1974), pp. 244–72.

22. *The Quest of the Historical Jesus* (New York: Macmillan, 1959), p. 4. On the subject as a whole see VAN HARVEY, *The Historian and the Believer* (New York: Macmillan, 1966).

23. See J. VANSINA, *Oral Tradition. A Study in Historical Methodology* (Chicago: Aldine, 1965).

24. See G. ALLPORT and L. POSTMAN, *The Psychology of Rumor* (New York: Henry Holt, 1947), and T. SHIBUTANI, *Improvised News. A Sociological Study of Rumor* (New York: Bobbs-Merrill, 1966).

25. "One Jesus and Four Primitive Gospels," in *Trajectories through Early Christianity,* by J. M. ROBINSON and H. KOESTER (Philadelphia: Fortress Press, 1971), pp. 158–204.

26. "One Jesus," p. 203.

27. See the article of E. L. ABEL, "The Psychology of Memory and Rumor Transmission and Their Bearing on Theories of Oral Transmission in Early Christianity," *Journal of Religion* 51 (1971), pp. 270–81. See also the controversy over B. GERHARDSSON's *Memory and Manuscript. Oral Tradition and Written Transmission in Rabbinic Judaism and Early Christianity* (Lund: C. W. K. Gleerup, 1961). Among the numerous responses to Gerhardsson, see M. SMITH, "A Comparison of Early Christian and Early Rabbinic Tradition," *Journal of Biblical Literature* 82 (1963), pp. 169–76.

28. "Les récentes études sur la formation de la tradition évangélique," *Revue d'histoire et de philosophie religieuses* 5 (1925), p. 573 (my translation).

29. Some of the more important studies include N. PERRIN, *What Is Redaction Criticism?* (Philadelphia: Fortress Press, 1969); W. MARXSEN, *Mark, the Evangelist* (Nashville: Abingdon Press, 1969); J. M. ROBINSON, *The Problem of History in Mark* (London: SCM Press, 1957); G. BORNKAMM, G. BARTH, and H. J. HELD, *Tradition and Interpretation in Matthew* (Philadelphia: Westminster Press, 1963); and H. CONZELMANN, *The Theology of St. Luke* (New York: Harper & Row, 1960). Of the somewhat older, pioneering literature see R. H. LIGHTFOOT, *History and Interpretation in the Gospels* (New York: Harper and Bros., no date; the book represents the

Bampton Lectures of 1934), and H. J. CADBURY, *The Making of Luke-Acts* (London: SPCK, 1958).

30. VANSINA, *Oral Tradition,* p. 112.

31. SCHWEITZER, *Quest,* p. 4.

32. For an excellent example of this kind of approach see W. A. MEEKS, "The Man from Heaven in Johannine Sectarianism," *Journal of Biblical Literature* 91 (1972), pp. 44–72. Meeks remarks that "it is astonishing that attempts to solve the Johannine puzzle have almost totally ignored the question of what *social* function the myths may have had. . . . I shall argue that one function of the 'symbolic universe' communicated in this remarkable body of literature was to make sense of all these aspects of the group's history" (pp. 49f.).

33. *The Sacred Canopy. Elements of a Sociological Theory of Religion* (Garden City, N.Y.: Doubleday, 1969), p. 25. For a similar definition and approach, see R. BELLAH, "Religious Evolution," *American Sociological Review* 29 (1964), pp. 358–74 (reprinted in Bellah's volume of collected essays, *Beyond Belief. Essays on Religion in a Post-Traditional World* [New York: Harper & Row, 1970], pp. 20–45, and in *Reader in Comparative Religion,* ed. Lessa and Vogt, pp. 73–87). See also C. GEERTZ, "Religion as a Cultural System," in *Anthropological Approaches to the Study of Religion,* ed. M. Banton (London: Tavistock Publications, 1966), pp. 1–46 (an abridged version of Geertz' article is reprinted in *Reader in Comparative Religion,* pp. 204–16).

34. *Sacred Canopy,* p. 3.

35. Compare BERGER and LUCKMANN, *The Social Construction of Reality, passim.*

36. *The Idea of a Social Science and Its Relation to Philosophy* (New York: Humanities Press, 1971), p. 15.

37. In his paper cited earlier (p. 15, n. 3), Smith comments that "we have been seduced into a *Sitz im Leben* that lacks a concrete (i.e., non-theological) 'seat' and offers only the most abstract understanding of 'life' " (p. 1).

38. Of the more recent literature, E. R. DODDS, *Pagan and Christian in an Age of Anxiety. Some Aspects of Religious Experience from Marcus Aurelius to Constantine* (Cambridge: The University Press, 1965) has exercised the greatest influence on my own thinking, although his work has stressed psychological rather than sociological issues.

39. Chicago: University of Chicago Press, 1923.

40. London: George Allen and Unwin, 1934.

41. Two further examples of the "Chicago school" are F. J. FOAKES JACKSON and K. LAKE, ed., *The Beginnings of Christianity,* 5 vols. (London: Macmillan, 1920–33); and D. W. RIDDLE, *The Martyrs. A Study in Social Control* (Chicago: University of Chicago Press, 1931).

42. In particular, *Prolegomena to the Study of Greek Religion* (Cambridge: The University Press, 1922) and *Themis: A Study of the Social Origins of Greek Religion* (Cambridge: The University Press, 1927). Harrison was quite deliberate in her use of theories borrowed from anthropology (Durkheim and Lévy-Bruhl) and philosophy (Bergson). For a discussion of her work, together with others of her time, see G. S. KIRK, *Myth. Its*

Meaning and Functions in Ancient and Other Cultures (Berkeley: University of California Press, 1973), pp. 2–5.

43. *Psyche. The Cult of Souls and Belief in Immortality among the Greeks,* 2 vols. (New York: Harper & Row, 1966; first published in 1890).

44. *Eine Mithrasliturgie* (Berlin: Teubner, 1923).

45. See, for example, the figures discussed in Chapter 2, below. In addition, the work of MARY DOUGLAS should prove increasingly fruitful to students of early Christianity; see her "Social Preconditions of Enthusiasm and Heterodoxy," in *Forms of Symbolic Action* (Proceedings of the 1969 Annual Spring Meeting of the American Ethnological Society), ed. R. F. SPENCER (Seattle: University of Washington Press, 1969), pp. 69–80; and *Natural Symbols* (New York: Vintage Books, 1973).

46. On the "Tübingen school" and its impact see W. G. KÜMMEL, *The New Testament*, pp. 127–46.

47. The most important essays on early Christianity are contained in the volume, *Marx and Engels on Religion,* introduction by REINHOLD NIEBUHR (New York: Schocken Books, 1967). Of the later Marxist interpreters, K. KAUTSKY, *Foundations of Christianity* (New York: S. A. Russell, 1953), is the best known.

48. One of the few historians even to mention Max Weber is H. VON CAMPENHAUSEN in his *Ecclesiastical Authority and Spiritual Power in the Church of the First Three Centuries* (Stanford, Calif.: Stanford University Press, 1969). In a footnote on the first page, he cites Weber's work on organizations and charisma, but dismisses it with the comment that "the categories are developed in too schematic a manner to be useful as they stand for throwing light on early Christian situations."

49. For a discussion of the theoretical issues involved in joining sociological and theological perspectives see P. BERGER, *Sacred Canopy*, pp. 179–85. Berger's main contention is that "sociological theory must, by its own logic, view religion as a human projection, and by the same logic can have nothing to say about the possibility that this projection may refer to something other than the being of its projector" (p. 180).

50. D. A. HOLLINGER, "T. S. Kuhn's Theory of Science and Its Implications for History," *American Historical Review* 78 (1973), p. 386.

2

The End of Time
and the Rise of Community

*From one point of view, the whole history of the comparative study
of religion from the time Robertson-Smith [1846–94] undertook his
investigation into the rites of the ancient Semites (and was dismissed
from Oxford as a heretic for his pains) can be looked at as but a cir-
cuitous, even devious, approach to a rational analysis of our own
situation, an evaluation of our own religious traditions while seeming to evaluate only those of exotic others.*

CLIFFORD GEERTZ
Islam Observed

EARLIEST CHRISTIANITY
AS A MILLENARIAN MOVEMENT [1]

A curious irony emerges from the titles of two important works in the field of social anthropology. Peter Worsley entitles his study of cargo cults in Melanesia, *The Trumpet Shall Sound*,[2] and Kenelm Burridge's work on millenarian activities bears the title, *New Heaven, New Earth*.[3] Both titles are direct quotations from the New Testament, yet neither author mentions early Christianity except in passing. Indeed, one searches the abundant literature on millenarian movements almost in vain in an effort to ascertain whether anthropologists regard early Christianity as fully, substantially, or tangentially related to millenarian activities in more exotic parts of the world. Occasionally connections are made, but they are rarely supported by argument. A. F. C. Wallace remarks that "both Christianity and Mohammedanism . . . originated as revitalization movements." [4] Norman Cohn notes that "for many of its early adherents Christianity was just such a [millenarian] movement." [5] And Yonina Talmon, in her survey of studies in the area, comments that "Christianity itself originally derived its initial élan from radical millenarism." [6] Apart from their brevity and lack of substantiation, what unites these statements is the assumption that early Christianity was self-evidently a millenarian movement and that it has been a prime cause (through the dissemination of the Bible) of subsequent movements not only in the West but in Africa, South America, and Oceania as well. Now I have not the slightest interest in challenging these assumptions. On the contrary, I intend to do what these authors themselves, perhaps out of professional modesty, have not done: to ask whether recent theories of millenarian movements apply to Christianity and, if so, in what respects. But to do only this would be of interest primarily to social anthropologists, for its results would tend either to confirm or modify their own theories. What is more interesting and important for us is the other side of the question, to wit, whether the application of these comparative theories will lead in some areas to a new understanding of early Christianity.

Recent discussions of millenarian movements have focused on two fundamental issues: *descriptions* of the cults themselves—constituencies, leaders, beliefs, history, and environment—with an emphasis on isolating common elements in different cults; and *explanations* of their similarities and underlying causes. Although the two issues are by no means identical, they are inevitably interrelated. Our description of a cult will always constitute a provisional, and often a final explanation of it; conversely, our prior notion of what constitutes an adequate explanation will influence our selection of its salient features. Still the two are not the same, and we stand a better chance of doing justice to both if we treat them separately.

On the matter of explanation, I. C. Jarvie isolates four basic traits as common to all such cults: the promise of heaven on earth—soon; the overthrow or reversal of the present social order; a terrific release of emotional energy; and a brief life span of the movement itself.[7] To these we need add only a fifth, namely, the central role of a messianic, prophetic, or charismatic leader. Without further argument at this point, we will take it as given that earliest Christianity meets these criteria and thus deserves to be designated a millenarian movement. But we must confront one apparent difficulty at the outset—the last of Jarvie's four traits. If a brief life span is fundamentally inherent in such a movement, what are we to make of Christianity's obvious and, from the perspective of this chapter, somewhat embarrassing longevity? In fact, there is really no problem at all. Any cult that survives the failure of its initial prophecy must necessarily modify or scrap its beliefs about the future. In so doing it ceases to be millenarian in the proper sense. This is more than a deft juggling of words and will have important consequences in the course of our discussion. Initially, it means that Christianity survived, but *not* as a millenarian cult. This is not to say that this primitive impulse lost all influence in later times—the Montanist movement around 150 c.e. is bold evidence to the contrary—but that by definition no millenarian cult can long survive in its original form.

From this brief digression we return to the five basic criteria noted above. The advantage of beginning here is that they will enable us to generate a series of specific questions to serve as guidelines for our inquiry. The questions themselves are formulated by Jarvie with reference to cargo cults in Melanesia, but their relevance for early Christianity will become apparent as we proceed:[8]

> Why do certain people join? What are their situation and aims?
> Why do certain people not join, and what about their situation?
> What is the role, character, and significance of prophets in different cults?
> Why and how do myths and beliefs about the millennium arise? What are they about?
> Why do these cults grow and decline so fast? Why do they fail, and

under what circumstances do they become "passive," "mystical," or disappear altogether?

To what can we attribute the similarities of such movements—cultural
diffusion, similar circumstances, or a combination of these and other
factors?

What consequences and motives, obvious as well as hidden, are involved
for those who join?

Now it should be clear from the start that the application of these
questions to historical movements raises special problems. The surviving
sources are always selective and incomplete, and there is no opportunity
for direct interrogation of participants. Insiders seldom speak openly of
their reasons for joining, and when they do their views of the past are
conditioned by their new situation. Outsiders are rarely heard at all.
Thus our method will of necessity remain somewhat circular. To quote
one participant in a discussion of millenarian movements, we must "take
the evidence of the movement itself as grounds for inference about the
relationship of the movement to society, and the psychology of the members." [9] The basic point I wish to make is that without the use of a theoretical framework, it will be impossible to draw these wider inferences
"about the relationship of the movement to society, and the psychology
of the members." If we eschew this course, the only other alternatives are
to refrain from dealing with broader issues altogether or else to treat
them in a thoroughly haphazard manner.

One final word of caution. For the early Christians, the figure of
Jesus stood at the center of their world. In speaking of that world, it is
impossible to avoid speaking about him. But our present concern is not
with the historical Jesus, i.e., with what he "really" said and did. Thus
when we refer to Jesus' words and actions in what follows, we do not
mean to imply that they are to be taken as authentic. Instead we will be
focusing on *images of Jesus* in the literature of early Christianity. Often
these images will correspond to real moments in the life of Jesus, but
for present purposes this correspondence is not germane. Our chief concern will be to emphasize the extent to which the role of Jesus as portrayed in the Gospels conforms to the role of the millenarian prophet as
one who articulates aspirations in such a way that a visible movement
will erupt from a bed of amorphous discontent.

Who Joined and Who Did Not?

"I am quite unrepentant, therefore, about cleaving to my basic
assumption that the *millenarian movements that have been historically
important* . . . are movements of the disinherited." [10] As it stands,
Worsley's pronouncement hardly seems questionable; yet it falls short

of providing a complete explanation even of the social and economic factors behind millenarian cults. There are, to be succinct, many more deprived persons than members of millenarian cults. Thus we must ask further whether certain kinds of deprivation, or certain degrees, are most likely to eventuate in concrete actions. To what extent, then, and in what respects can we speak of earliest Christianity as a community of the disinherited?

In *political* matters, the whole of Jewish Palestine was subjugated to Roman authority in the person of a resident governor (procurator or prefect). And if Josephus' account is to be believed, their behavior was a major factor leading up to the revolt against Rome in 66–73 c.e. Thus while some benefited from the Roman presence, many others resented it to the point of open resistance. One center of this resistance was Galilee, the native territory of Jesus and many of his early followers. The first sign of overt hostility, coinciding with the appointment of the first procurator (Coponius) in 6 c.e., was initiated by "a Galilean, named Judas [who] incited his countrymen to revolt, upbraiding them as cowards for consenting to pay tribute to Rome and tolerating mortal masters. . . ."[11] So important was this group of Judas' followers that Josephus presents them as "the fourth philosophy of the Jews," despite his blatant hostility toward them.[12] Again, in his detailed account of his own role as Jewish military governor of Galilee during the revolt against Rome, Josephus chronicles the militant activities of a group that seems to have suspected him of collaboration with the enemy.[13] And finally, the Zealots themselves, who are related generically to these and other movements in Jewish Palestine under Roman rule but may not have become an organized party until some time in the 60s, played a prominent role in the final battle with the Roman armies.[14] That Judas and similar figures couched their political message in an apocalyptic medium seems likely;[15] in any case, the parallel with certain Melanesian prophets, urging local villagers to withhold duty payments and work assignments from their colonial masters, is evident. In short, a premillenarian mood of political alienation and active resistance was abroad in Palestine during and beyond the time of Jesus' activity there. This is not to say that Jesus himself belonged to any of these groups, for the sources will not support such a claim.[16] Still he was probably regarded as such, or at least as a political agitator, by Rome—crucifixion was reserved for political crimes committed by non-Roman citizens. And there are indications that some of his own followers saw in him the fulfillment of their political dreams. One of them bore the name Simon the Zealot, and a remarkable passage in Luke 24:21 reports the following lament of two disciples after Jesus' death: "We had hoped that he was the one to redeem [i.e., purify, liberate, and restore] Israel."

Closely related to political alienation is the question of *money*. Burridge, for instance, stresses that money "seems to be the most *frequent* and *convenient* axis on which millenarian movements turn." [17] Money, like cargo, represents wealth, power, and above all a symbolic measure of human worth. Thus, the introduction of money into a previously un-monied culture (the Melanesian situation depicted by Burridge and others), or the hoarding and control of money by a colonial power in a monied land (the situation of Palestine under Roman rule), creates a crisis not just of finance but of human dignity as well. This is obvious in the case of the Zealots and other radical groups who refused to pay Roman taxes, and it appears also in the violent popular reaction against Pontius Pilate's use of sacred Jewish funds to construct an aqueduct.[18] In this regard, the economic pronouncements in early Christian literature reveal both the economic status of believers[19] and the deeper symbolic associations of money:

> "It is easier for a camel to go through the eye of a needle than for a rich man to enter the kingdom of God."
>
> Mark 10:25; cf. Matt. 19:24; Luke 18:25

> "Blessed are you poor . . ."
>
> Luke 6:20; cf. Matt. 5:3

> Come now, you rich, weep and howl for the miseries that are coming upon you. Your riches have rotted and your garments are moth-eaten. Your gold and silver have rusted, and their rust will be evidence against you and will eat your flesh like fire.
>
> James 5:1–3

Given these sayings, there can be no mistaking a clearly formulated ethic of poverty, an ethic with deep roots in Jewish tradition.[20] They reflect the fact that early believers came primarily from disadvantaged groups and that in return they were rewarded with the promise that poverty, not wealth, was the key to the kingdom. Here the symbolic value of money is paramount. But unlike the Melanesian, who expected the prophet to deliver the cargo that had been diverted by immoral Euro-peans, the early Christian did not anticipate eternal financial benefits in the age to come. The difference is that the Melanesian native, previously unfamiliar with money, accepts this new measure of dignity and seeks, through the symbol of cargo, to make it his own. In a monied economy, however, millenarian movements normally treat wealth as an irreversible symbol of corruption and decay. To quote Burridge:

> The millenarian situation in the traditionally moneyed community reveals attempts to re-order what seems to have become an unmanageable

manyness into sharply contrasted contraries. Life is so multifaceted, so to speak, that it becomes almost impossible to exercise that basic moral capacity, the discrimination between right and wrong. The solution to this is a reformulation into contraries.[21]

And:

Millenarists find in the closed community the soil in which virtues can flower, and in the relatively open society that jungle of opportunity where vices proliferate like weeds. . . . Money as an abstract, factorial and quantitative system must be opposed to the qualities that measure the stature of man.[22]

Thus the complexities of moral judgments that typify a complex society are resolved into a series of binary oppositions: poor-rich, good-evil, pious-hypocrite, elect-damned. And a final reckoning is proclaimed for the near future.

To a degree we have already touched on the matter of *social status* in our brief discussion of money, but no treatment of social questions in Jewish Palestine is possible apart from their *religious* setting.[23] Even in a "secular" society, social standing is never determined exclusively by objective factors such as wealth, education, and kinship. It is also a matter of agreement among the various parties that social classes exist, that they are defined by specific criteria and not others, and that certain individuals meet these criteria. And in a society where religious issues count heavily, other measures of social status may play a secondary role. Our question then is this: What groups in Jewish Palestine would have been most attracted to a millenarian movement, and what evidence do early Christian documents provide concerning the prior religious and social standing of the earliest converts?

The evidence from recent work on millenarian movements shows that new converts come from those who feel disadvantaged in some significant way. Early Christianity is no exception. Apart from Paul, no Pharisee is known to have embraced the new faith.[24] Not a single high priest is mentioned as a convert. Acts 6:7, to be sure, reports that "a great many of the priests were obedient to the faith," but even if the report is accurate it is unlikely that any of them were of the higher orders. If we are to credit the account in Acts as anything other than the author's normal tendency toward exaggeration, the converted priests probably came from the large number of poor and powerless priests of the lower orders who, according to Josephus, engaged in open conflict with the high priest in Jerusalem.[25] With respect to the Essenes, there is no evidence, nor indeed would one expect such, that they became followers of Jesus.[26]

Thus far we may conclude that early converts did not represent the established sectors of Jewish society. We are supported in this not only by theoretical considerations and by the silence of Christian sources, but by positive evidence as well. The frequent and bitter controversies between Jesus and the Pharisees as pictured in the Gospels leave no doubt that the latter numbered Jesus and his disciples among the impure outsiders (*am ha-areṣ*). The points at issue between them are numerous and quite specific: Jesus keeps company with unclean persons, i.e., "tax collectors and sinners" (Mark 2:13–17; cf. Matt. 9:9–13; Luke 5:27–32); Jesus does not fast as do the Pharisees (Mark 2:18–22; cf. Matt. 9:14–17; Luke 5:33–39); Jesus violates the sanctity of the Sabbath by preparing food (Mark 2:23–28; cf. Matt. 12:1–8; Luke 6:1–5) and by performing healings (Mark 2:1–6; cf. Matt. 12:9–14; John 9:13–17); and finally Jesus fails to observe the practice of ritual hand-washing before meals (Mark 7:1–23; cf. Matt. 15:1–20; Luke 11:37–41).[27] In response to these charges, Jesus issues a withering condemnation of the Pharisees for their alleged hypocrisy in all matters of piety (Matt. 23:1–35; cf. Mark 12:37–40; Luke 11:42–52). What is this catalogue of charge and countercharge but an expression of the resentment, with its peculiar mixture of religious and social factors, between Pharisees and *am ha-areṣ*, a resentment that is amply attested in rabbinic sources themselves?[28]

> Hillel [died c. 10 B.C.E.] said: "No rude man [*bor*] fears to sin, and no *am ha-areṣ* is pious."
>
> Mishnah, *Aboth* 2.6

And,

> And R. Akiba [c. 90–135 C.E.] said: "When I was an *am ha-areṣ*, I used to say, 'I wish I had one of those scholars, and I would bite him like an ass.'" His disciples said, "You mean like a dog." He replied, "An ass's bite breaks the bone; a dog's does not."
>
> Talmud Bab., *Pes.* 49b[29]

In considering these passages, however, we must keep in mind the time during which the Gospels took their final form, i.e., between 70 and 90 C.E. Although tensions between Jesus and the Pharisees may well go back to Jesus' lifetime, in their final form the sayings reflect the situation in the latter part of the first century when two important developments had taken place. First, the Pharisees and their successors had emerged as the dominant group within Palestinian Judaism, and, second, there was "competition between the Pharisees and the Christian missionaries for the loyalty of the mass of Jews."[30] From this point on, to be an *am ha-areṣ* would have serious consequences, for the rabbis now exercised considerable control over political and religious institutions.[31] From the perspective of this later period, what we see in this material from the Gospels is a classic form of protest in which the outsider-insider distinction is simply reversed. The two groups remain in an antithetical relationship, but the value-scale has been inverted.[32] On this point the Christian sources speak with unmistakable clarity:

> "But many that are first will be last, and the last first."
>
> Mark 10:31; cf. Matt. 19:30; Luke 13:30

> "Truly, I say to you [the chief priests and elders of the people], the tax collectors and harlots go into the kingdom of God before you."
>
> Matt. 21:31

> "Blessed are you poor, for yours is the kingdom of God."
>
> Luke 6:20-23; cf. Matt. 5:3-12

Those who previously held no status or value now claim the exclusive privilege of both.

In the preceding discussion we have argued that the situation of the earliest Christian communities is best described as one of deprivation. But recent work on millenarian movements has suggested that *relative* rather than absolute deprivation most often characterizes premillenarian conditions. Defined as an *"uneven relation between expectation and the means of satisfaction,"* [33] this condition frequently emerges when new hopes arise but for some reason remain unfulfilled. This concept of relative deprivation sheds light on several important aspects of earliest Christianity. First, it stresses the need to locate it within the tradition of apocalyptic Judaism, which in itself represents a paradigm case of great expectations followed by repeated disappointments. The succession of millenarian prophets who accompanied the political subjugation of Palestine, from the Seleucids to the Romans, is not at all unlike the series of prophets who have been a constant companion of European control in Oceania and Africa. At the same time, the concept of relative deprivation highlights the *prepolitical* character of all millenarian cults, including Christianity.[34] This is not to say that Christianity was intentionally political, but that it arose among those who were without political organization and experience and that it had far-reaching political consequences. Despite protests to the contrary, the churches from the very beginning presented Rome with a serious political problem. Christians were constantly amazed to find themselves cast as enemies of the

Roman order, but in retrospect we must admit that it was the Romans who had the more realistic insight. Finally, the concept reinforces the impression, given initially by the Christian sources and supported by further indications that the *am ha-areş* were by no means limited to the poor and ignorant, that the earliest believers did not necessarily come from the lowest social and economic strata.[35] Thus we are forced to conclude that the ideology of poverty does more than simply mirror social reality. It exaggerates and idealizes this reality. Again, this is typical of millenarian movements where, as Burridge suggests, "a scheme of binary contraries is required if those who join are to be sharply distinguished from those who do not." [36]

The Prophet

Thus far we have been dealing with premillennial murmurings. There are many such situations in which millenarian *movements* do not arise. In every case, the decisive factor would appear to be the prophet. But we must be careful not to confuse description with explanation. The fact that there can be no cult without a prophet does not justify a premature conclusion that the prophet is the primary cause of the cult. Yonina Talmon remarks, for instance, that "in many cases leaders function as a symbolic focus of identification rather than as sources of authority and initiative." She adds that their symbolic function is apparent in the common phenomenon that "death, imprisonment, or mysterious absence have increased their stature and enhanced their authority." [37] To what extent these qualifications are appropriate for Jesus or other prophetic figures (e.g., Paul) is difficult to say. Certainly the Gospels and the later christological controversies treated the figure of Jesus as a malleable symbol through which they expressed their own distinctive concerns, and this was certainly true from the first. On the second point, there can be no doubt that for both Paul and Jesus, death and imprisonment served to enhance their status and authority among their followers. In any case, we will surely be closer to the truth if we regard the symbolic and initiatory functions of prophets as complements rather than as alternatives.

It has also been customary to explain the authority of prophets in terms of "charisma." Frequently this has been understood to mean certain types of personality, so that it has been thought possible to delineate a more or less objective profile of charismatic figures.[38] Against this objectivist definition, Worsley proposes an interactionist model:

> To the sociologist, charisma . . . can only be that which is recognized,
> by believers and followers, as "charismatic" in the behaviour of those they

treat as charismatic. Charisma is thus a function of recognition: the
prophet without honour cannot be a charismatic prophet. Charisma,
therefore, sociologically viewed, is a social relationship, not an attribute
of individual personality or a mystical quality.[39]

By redirecting our attention to the obvious datum that notions of authority are socially and culturally determined, Worsley's redefinition
makes it possible for us to speak about Jesus as a charismatic prophet
even in the absence of certain knowledge about his personality.[40] This is
most important in that it opens an avenue beyond the inevitable scep-
ticism with regard to Jesus' biography. For by concentrating on his
standing among believers we will in effect be dealing with a fundamental
aspect of his charisma.

In his discussion of prophetic activity Burridge proposes two com-
ponents as indispensable: first,

> where two groups or categories of persons share the same values or
> assumptions, but only one of these groups or categories has access to the
> rewards or benefits implied in the shared values, then the *guru* or prophet
> is generated, new assumptions enter the arena, a new group or category
> of persons may come into being.[41]

and, second,

> he [the prophet] either symbolizes the new man in himself, or he is the
> vehicle by means of which the lineaments of the new man may
> become known.[42]

The first statement reveals Burridge's understanding of what millenarian
movements are really about—moral regeneration.[43] They arise whenever
new measures of value and integrity challenge traditional assumptions
(the classic colonial situation of Oceania and Africa), or whenever two
groups share the same value but only one of these groups has access to
the rewards associated with these values (the situation of the earliest
Jewish converts).[44] Thus we have further specified a premillenarian situation as the quest within a common religious tradition for new definitions
of power, value, and truth as well as new paths of access ("redemptive
media") to them. It is the role of the prophet to articulate these new
assumptions.[45]

In this respect, Jesus' activities in the Gospels reflect a perfect
image of the millenarian prophet, for he combines criticism of the old
with a vision of the new. With the Pharisees, his polemic touches on
nearly every point of their program, but the fundamental issues concern
control over "redemptive media"—authority to interpret Scripture as
divine revelation and authority to settle the terms of membership in the

redeemed community. On the latter point, the solution was, in effect, to reverse the categories of insider-outsider. The pious suddenly become hypocrites, while "tax collectors and sinners" emerge as the chosen few. On the issue of authority and rules for interpreting Scripture, Jesus again reacts in prophetic fashion by dismissing out of hand the established criteria—elaborate rules of exegesis, recognized status in a legitimate line of scholarly succession, and appeal to extrabiblical tradition.[46] And he does so not by rejecting the basic source of authority, the Law of Moses, but by interpreting it in direct, inspired fashion.[47] This is most clearly expressed in the series of pronouncements (Matt. 5:21–48) in which he opposes his own authority ("But I say to you . . .") to that of the tradition ("You have heard that it was said to the men of old . . ."). And the same stance is taken on numerous other occasions. When accused of violating Sabbath regulations, he cites nothing but his own authority in defense of his new interpretation (Mark 2:25–27; cf. Matt. 12:3–8; Luke 6:3–5); when charged with blasphemy for pronouncing forgiveness of sins, an act otherwise reserved to God alone, he responds simply that he, the Son of man, has been given authority to forgive sins (Mark 2:5–11; cf. Matt. 9:2–6; Luke 5:20–24); when asked to demonstrate his legitimacy through signs and proofs, his outright refusal reflects a sovereign sense of transcendence over traditional criteria of legitimacy (Mark 8:11–12); and when the chief priest, scribes, and elders ask him openly, "By what authority are you doing these things, or who gave you authority to do them?," his clever counterquestion confounds them, but the answer is evident—directly from heaven (Mark 11:27–33; cf. Matt. 21:23–27; Luke 20:1–8). Nowhere is this image of Jesus more apparent than in two programmatic statements at the beginning of Mark's Gospel, where the crowds are made to wonder at his prophetic character:

> And they were astonished at this teaching, for he taught them as one who had authority, and not as the scribes.
>
> Mark 1:22; cf. Matt. 7:29; Luke 4:32

> And they were all amazed, so that they questioned themselves, saying, "What is this? A new teaching?"
>
> Mark 1:27; cf. Luke 4:36

In each of these illustrations, the immediacy of prophetic charisma functions to neutralize traditional canons of authority. In short, they offer new formulations of redemptive media.

The evidence for Jesus' attack on the second front, namely, the priestly aristocracy and the temple cult, is less extensive but nonetheless prominent. Here again the position of Jesus was not unique, for discontent and dispute about control of the temple were endemic at the time. Though the high priests held direct power over the performance of the rituals, Pharisaic legislation had probably made inroads into regulations governing them.[48] A different form of the same problem is evident with the Essenes, whose origins went back to a struggle for control of the priesthood in the Maccabean period. As a result of this struggle, the ousted group (the precursors of the Essenes) held the new incumbents to be illegitimate and the temple itself to be defiled.[49] Similarly, when the Zealots seized control of Jerusalem in 67 c.e., one of their first acts was to occupy the temple and appoint their own line of high priests.[50] In this context, the statements attributed to Jesus about the temple are very much in line with what one would expect from a millenarian prophet. The central passage is the scene of Jesus overturning tables in the temple and expelling the money-changers (Mark 11:15–19; cf. Matt. 21:12–13; Luke 19:45–48). This is a typical feat of prophetic authority—purifying the sacred place, fallen into corrupt and impure hands—and the quotations from Isa. 56:7 and Jer. 7:11 merely serve to reinforce this aspect by presenting the event as a deliberate fulfillment of scriptural prophecy. So also with the predictions concerning the destruction of the temple:

> "This fellow said,
> 'I am able to destroy the temple of God, and to build it in three days.' "
>
> Matt. 26:61 [51]

> "Destroy this temple, and in three days I will raise it up."
>
> John 2:19

When read in the light of the scene in the temple, these words imply not that Jesus sought to do away with it altogether, but that its original purity could only be restored through a radical act of destruction and rebuilding.

As in the case of his attitude toward the authority of the Pharisees, Jesus' actions with respect to the temple make sense only within the conditions that we set forth at the outset—a prophet arises to articulate new assumptions in a situation where two groups share common values but only one of these groups has access to the rewards implied in them. Interestingly, both aspects of these new assumptions are brought together in a statement about Jesus attributed to one of his earliest disciples:

> "This man [Stephen] never ceases to speak words against this *holy place* and the *law:* for we heard him say that this Jesus of Nazareth will destroy this place and will change the customs which Moses delivered to us."
>
> Acts 6:14

The fact that the words are actually spoken by an antagonist corroborates our view that the new assumptions formulated by Jesus centered on the fundamental redemptive media of his time—the temple and the interpretation of Torah.

At this point we may return briefly to the second of Burridge's statements regarding prophetic charisma—that the prophet must also symbolize in himself the contours of the new man. Not only must he comprehend the present crisis and proclaim the promise of a new order, he must in some sense embody that order in the present. In part, this happens through the creation of a new community, through sacramental rites, and through the imposition of rigorous moral standards, all of which anticipate actual conditions of the new order. Each of these is present in early Christian communities and will concern us later on. In addition, however, the role of Jesus as the new man shows up with particular force in two Gospel sayings:

> "For whoever is ashamed of me and of my words in this adulterous and sinful generation, of him will the Son of man also be ashamed when he comes in the glory of his Father with the holy angels."
>
> Mark 8:38; cf. Matt. 16:27; Luke 9:26
>
> "And I tell you, every one who acknowledges me before men, the Son of man will acknowledge before the angels of God; but he who denies me before men will be denied before the angels of God."
>
> Luke 12:8f.; cf. Matt. 10:32f.[52]

Although the second saying shows none of the explicitly apocalyptic focus of the first, and thus is probably a later version, both illustrate Burridge's point. For Jesus here presents himself as *the* measure of redemption: as men relate to him now in the final days of this age, precisely so will the Son of man relate to them in the millennium proper.

Millenarian Ethics and Community

The pursuit of the millennium is a characteristically communal venture. And within the community its most prominent feature, perhaps even its basic drive, is moral regeneration. If we look back to the first generations from the perspective of the third, fourth, and fifth centuries, we cannot help but be struck by the relative absence of specifically theological reflection on the one hand and the tremendous emphasis on community and ethics on the other. One way to characterize, and also to explain this difference, is to state that in the first generations Christianity was a millenarian movement and that in later centuries it was not.

In *The Ritual Process*,[53] Victor Turner argues that liminality, or the status of being an outsider, and *communitas* are necessary correlates, and that millenarian movements offer a striking expression of the phenomenon. For liminal groups or persons in a premillenarian situation, community is the only alternative to continued existence within the frustrating confines of the social structure.[54] Thus the intense preoccupation with the unity and stability of Christian congregations, a motif that pervades all of early Christian literature, is more than an effort to defend apostolic prerogatives or to ensure the survival of a movement. It is an effort to preserve the only meaningful form of social existence for a liminal community (so regarded by Jews and pagans alike) constituted primarily by liminal persons. Furthermore, Turner's enumeration of the properties of liminal and millenarian groups bears directly on specific attributes of early Christian communities:

> homogeneity, equality, anonymity, absence of property (. . . for property rights are linked with structural distinctions both vertical and horizontal), reduction of all to the same status, the wearing of uniform apparel (sometimes for both sexes), sexual continence (or its antithesis, sexual community, both continence and sexual community liquidate marriage and the family, which legitimate structural status), minimization of sex distinctions. . . .[55]

Without claiming that all these attributes are equally applicable, I would contend that together they enable us to appreciate certain features as essential, inseparable aspects of primitive Christian millenarianism—specifically, the abolition or minimization of status distinctions and the absence of fixed structure. Eventually, of course, the churches established their own status distinctions and their own structure, but by that time they were no longer either liminal or millenarian.

Initially, one can see both aspects in the opening phrases of Paul's letters. All of them are addressed to the entire local congregation, and in none of them does he single out special leaders.[56] More generally, the earliest Christian documents are remarkable for their neglect of questions concerning leadership within individual communities. If we concentrate on Paul's letters, the synoptic Gospels, and the Gospel of John, it would be virtually impossible to define any kind of communal structure. Now it would appear that this silence is not accidental, that it embodies a stage of antistructure to be found in all millenarian movements. The same tendency is reflected in the common self-designation of Christians as "brothers"—again no accident, for this particular kinship term excludes hierarchical relationships. Similarly, when Paul argues at length with the Corinthians that the emergence of status distinction among them is contradictory to the very nature of Christian community (1 Cor. chapters 10–13), he is attempting to restore a millenarian sense of fraternal equality. Even Jesus contends with the issue when he intervenes in a dispute among the disciples as to which of them enjoyed the greatest stature (Matthew adds "in the kingdom of heaven").[57] From our present perspective, it comes as no surprise that he deals with the dispute by taking a child, who neither knows nor creates status, as a model for membership in the redeemed community (Mark 9:33–37; cf. Matt. 18:1–5; Luke 9:46–48).

In other areas, we find similar tendencies to minimize or even abolish traditional status distinctions. Wealth, as we have seen, is rejected as a measure of human worth. Normal duties, such as burying the dead, are discarded (Matt. 8:22; cf. Luke 9:60). Kinship ties are scorned:

> "If any one comes to me and does not hate his father and mother and wife and children . . . he cannot be my disciple."
>
> Luke 14:26 [58]

> And they said to him, "Your mother and your brothers are outside, asking for you." And he replied, "Who are my mother and brothers?" And looking around on those who sat about him, he said, "Here are my mother and brothers. Whoever does the will of God is my brother, and sister, and mother."
>
> Mark 3:31–35; cf. Matt. 12:46–50 [59]

Property, at least in Luke's account of the primitive community in Jerusalem, is held in common (Acts 4:32–5:11). And although Luke's description is generally dismissed as a form of idealizing, it is nonetheless significant that he chose to emphasize this particular trait as central to the earliest believers.

Finally, distinctions between the sexes were minimized in a variety of ways, some of them no doubt quite unconscious. Turner's observation —that sexual continence, like sexual liberality, has the effect of neutralizing marriage and family and thus of abolishing sexual subordination—sheds new light on the numerous exhortations to continence in early Christian literature.[60] A curious passage in the Gospels suggests that a further impetus in this direction may have come from a desire to anticipate the millennium, in which there would be no sexual differentiation at all, by ignoring sexuality in the present. To a trick question posed by the Sadducees, Jesus replies, "For when they rise from the dead, they neither marry nor are given in marriage, but are like angels in heaven [i.e., either asexual or bisexual]" (Mark 12:25; cf. Matt. 22:30). But it is Paul who gives the most forthright expression to this view:

> There is neither Jew nor Greek, there is neither slave nor free, there is neither male nor female; for you are all one in Christ Jesus.
>
> Gal. 3:28

Whether he meant these words as a description of the kingdom soon to come or as applying already in the present, we must read them as the prototype of all millenarian ethics.[61] In light of Paul's radical stance, as expressed in this and other passages,[62] it may seem ironic that mainstream Christianity chose finally to exclude women from all important cultic roles and in the process often cited the authority of Paul.[63] But to say that the churches failed to translate his program into reality is merely to belabor the obvious. For millenarian movements fail by definition, and those that survive do so under substantially new circumstances. In the long run, it fell to the "heresies," notably Montanism with its prominent prophetesses and Marcionism where marriage was prohibited and women shared in a wide range of cultic roles, to carry forward the primitive ideal.[64]

Thus far we have seen a constant tension in the early sources between radical (millenarian) and moderate (institutional) precepts. The major source of this tension lies in the fact that the sources themselves span several generations and thus cover the time of initial apocalyptic excitement as well as the first phases of consolidation.[65] This gradual metamorphosis from enthusiastic beginnings to a new settled stage raises one final issue: the growth of a new morality. Burridge proposes the formula: old rules–no rules–new rules.[66] We have seen this pattern repeatedly on matters of ritual observance and the like. Old practices are overthrown, only to be followed quickly by new ones, many of which bear a striking resemblance to the old ones.[67] Perhaps the best example of this process is again the figure of Paul. Speaking of him directly, Burridge remarks that

> Saint Paul's strictures on the sexual activities of his fellow Christians reveal not so much the prig as an awareness of what was involved in becoming free after moral awareness has cramped instinctual behaviour. In emphasizing a freedom of the spirit . . . and propagating rules for the guidance of the flesh, he drew an implicit distinction between the two expressions of "no rules." [68]

Indeed a significant catchword of Paul's teaching in all of his letters is freedom and release from burden, specifically from the Law of Moses. "For freedom Christ has set you free; stand fast therefore, and do not submit again to a yoke of slavery" (Gal. 5:1). And the release of emotional energy so characteristic of the phase of "no rules" is amply attested in Paul's correspondence with the Corinthians: visions, revelations, wisdom, healings, miracles, prophecy, speaking in tongues, and interpreting tongues. Among the same Corinthians, some had apparently expressed their new freedom by flaunting accepted sexual strictures.[69] Paul's attitude on these matters, as Burridge notes, is that to indulge the flesh is the very opposite of freedom, a new form of slavery. Thus he excoriates a believer who was living with his father's wife (1 Cor. 5:1–2). On the other hand, he is quite willing to countenance an equally extreme form of sexual liberation in which a man and woman would live together as virgins (1 Cor. 7:36–38).

But there is another side to Paul's guidelines on these matters. It is quite clear from several passages that however much the Corinthians pointed to the apostle himself as the basis for their practices, Paul rejected them as contrary to his gospel. The difference may be, as some have suggested, that the Corinthians and certain of the later Gnostic groups believed that the End had already come and with it the abolition of distinctions, sexual and otherwise, characteristic of the old order. For Paul, however, the End had not yet come.[70] Thus he clearly illustrates the stage of "no rules" in some respects, but he also prefigures the transition from "no rules" to "new rules" in others. Or perhaps one should say that he reflects the tension between "old rules" and "no rules"; in either case the practical results would be the same. His insistence on a distinction between freedom of the spirit and domination of the flesh falls within the phase of "no rules," but in his treatment of other problems he imposes limitations on this freedom. And in doing so he appeals to another millenarian principle, the well-being of the community.

> "All things are lawful," but not all things are helpful.
> "All things are lawful," but not all things build up.
>
> 1 Cor. 10:23 [71]

In other words, if there is conflict between individual freedom with respect to previous taboos (in this case, reluctance about eating meat sacrificed before pagan idols and later sold in the market) and potentially divisive consequences of exercising this freedom, Paul subordinates the freedom of the individual to the unity of the congregation.[72] In the process, the transition from "no rules" to "new rules" becomes evident, and with it the gradual demise of Christianity as a millenarian movement.

Explanations

In an effort to present a reasonable case for understanding early Christianity as a millenarian movement, I have deliberately chosen to rely on the work of Burridge. Unlike other theoretical models, his has the double advantage of taking such movements at face value (e.g., their longing for "cargo") while at the same time doing justice to other, half-articulated longings.[73] It accounts for their occurrence among the disinherited without reducing them to material factors. Similarly, it explains the central role of the prophet but stops short of treating him as a sufficient condition. For just as there are more disinherited persons than members of movements, so are there more prophets than cults. Coincidentally, Burridge's work makes it possible, although Weber's would have worked just as well, to dismiss the recent contention of G. A. Wells, based largely on the paucity of reliable facts about Jesus, that "Christian origins can be accounted for, with reasonable plausibility, without recourse to a historical Jesus." [74] And finally, his model casts in a new light the peculiar emphasis on ethics and community in the early church. In commenting on Burridge's earlier work, *Mambu,* Worsley remarks, with a hint of criticism, on "his almost rhapsodic celebration of brotherhood." [75] But in this case it fits. What Burridge fails to explain, only because he does not address the issue, is why some millenarian movements disappear completely after the first rush of enthusiasm, whereas others persist in different forms. Eventually, then, we must ask ourselves this question: What went wrong with early Christianity so that it not only survived the failure of its initial prophecies but did so in spectacular fashion?

CHRISTIAN MISSIONS AND THE THEORY OF COGNITIVE DISSONANCE

Despite uncertainty about numerous aspects of primitive Christianity, the sources are unanimous in reporting certain basic traits. Among these is an enthusiastic dedication to missionary activity.[76] There was, to be sure, a protracted and often bitter debate about whether the mission should focus exclusively on Jews ("Go nowhere among the Gentiles, and enter no town of the Samaritans, but go rather to the lost sheep of the house of Israel"—Matt. 10:5f.; cf. also the story of the Syrophoenician woman in Matt. 15:21–28) or should include Gentiles as well ("Go therefore and make disciples of all nations . . ."—Matt. 28:19!). Even among those who advocated a universal calling, there was disagreement about the conditions under which Gentiles could embrace the faith. Should they assume the full burden of the Mosaic Law ("But some believers who belonged to the party of the Pharisees rose up, and said, 'It is necessary to circumcise them, and to charge them to keep the law of Moses.' "—Acts 15:5) or just a partial burden (Acts 15:19f.)? Still others, like Paul, maintained that allegiance to the Christ meant freedom from the Law altogether (Galatians, *passim*). But transcending these disagreements was a consensus that a primary obligation of the community as a whole was to proclaim the gospel of Christ in the world. More than any other cult in the Roman Empire, Christianity was a missionary faith and, of course, owed its ultimate status in the empire to the success of its mission.

The fact of Christian mission is plain enough, but the underlying issue of what motivated it is far from clear. Indeed, the issue has seldom even been raised. In his classic work on *The Mission and Expansion of Christianity in the First Three Centuries,* Adolf Harnack deals systematically with every issue *except* that of motivation.[77] Almost in passing, he remarks that the churches inherited their missionary zeal from Judaism.[78] Just a few pages later he strikes a somewhat different note in suggesting that missions arose as a response to the death of Jesus and as an expression of their hope in the coming of the kingdom in the near future.[79] But why, one is tempted to ask, should the death of Jesus and the expectation of the kingdom have led to mission? More recent studies have also taken up the matter of motivation but have succeeded merely in proliferating the number of explanations: words of Jesus, a sense of responsibility for the unevangelized world, the experience of Jesus' resurrection, etc. Of these perhaps the most common explanation is that the enthusiastic anticipation of the End was the fundamental motivation for early Christian missions. F. Hahn locates the initial impetus in Jesus' own command to proclaim the message of the kingdom (Mark 6:7–13; Luke 9:1–6, etc.), and adds that the events of Jesus' death and resurrection "awoke in the whole of the primitive Church a white-hot expectation of its [the kingdom's] imminence, and now [it] had to be made known afresh to men." [80] Similarly, O. Cullmann has argued that early Christian eschatology, rather than paralyzing the communities, turned it outward toward the world.[81] In particular, he points to Mark 13:10 ("And the gospel must first be preached to all nations.") as evidence for the connection between mission and eschatology.[82]

Undeniably the missionary zeal of the early churches was related to their eschatological consciousness. But this statement alone hardly settles the matter, for it still leaves the basic questions unanswered. Why, for instance, did the churches ignore those sayings in the Gospels that limited the mission to Israel? Why did they attach such importance precisely to missionary commands? Or, to put the matter somewhat differently, why did the communities that eventually produced the Gospels choose to represent and emphasize Jesus' role as initiator of missions? What precisely is the connection between missionary action and eschatological awareness? Why did missions persist long after most Christians had ceased regarding the kingdom as imminent? Why is it that certain Jewish communities in this period (e.g., the Essenes at Qumran), who also understood themselves to be living in the last days, did not undertake vigorous missions? Or, on a more general level, why is it that in the case of early Christianity expectation of the End did not lead, as often happens, to an isolationist or quietist stance toward the outside world? In short, explanations that appeal to eschatology as the basic motivation for missions are not really causal explanations at all. They simply note that the early communities were both eschatological and missionary and then proceed to assume that the one must have caused the other. *Post hoc ergo propter hoc.*

Rather than abandon the connection between eschatology and missions, I would contend that the precise nature of their connection can be understood by appealing to the theory of cognitive dissonance, as developed by L. Festinger and others. As presented in *When Prophecy Fails. A Social and Psychological Study of a Modern Group That Predicted the Destruction of the World,*[83] the theory states that under certain conditions a religious community whose fundamental beliefs are disconfirmed by events in the world will not necessarily collapse and disband. Instead it may undertake zealous missionary activity as a response to its sense of cognitive dissonance, i.e., a condition of distress and doubt stemming from the disconfirmation of an important belief. The critical element of the theory is that "the presence of dissonance gives rise to pressures to reduce or eliminate the dissonance. The strength of the pressures to reduce the dissonance is a function of the magnitude of the dissonance." [84] Among the various techniques for reducing dissonance, Festinger et al. argue that proselytism is one of the most common and effective. Rationalization, i.e., revisions of the original belief or of views about the disconfirming event, will also operate, but proselytism almost always occurs. The assumption, often unconscious, is that *"if more and more people can be persuaded that the system of belief is correct, then clearly it must, after all, be correct."* [85] Thus, the authors argue, we find the apparent paradox that an increase in proselytizing normally follows disconfirmation.

To support and illustrate the theory of cognitive dissonance, the authors devote the bulk of *When Prophecy Fails* to a group (Lake City) in the 1950s that had predicted the destruction of the world on a given December 21 and that had made extensive preparations for the occasion. The most striking feature of the group is that when December 21 had come and gone, i.e., when the central belief of the group had been unequivocally disconfirmed, the members responded not by disbanding but by intensifying their previous low level of proselytizing. Eventually the group broke up as the result of a number of factors (legal action and ineffective proselytism), but its initial response to disconfirmation aptly substantiates the basic theory. Other examples illustrate the same sequence: the Millerite movement in the Northeastern United States of the 1840s; the messianic fervor surrounding Sabbatai Zevi in the Near

East between 1640 and 1670; and finally the origins of Christianity. Although the authors regard early Christianity as the best historical illustration, they finally conclude that it cannot, because of uncertainty on one or two issues, serve by itself to validate the theory. But once the theory has been established through other, more controlled movements, should we not reexamine its relevance as a tool for investigating the source of missionary activities in earliest Christianity?

At the outset, *When Prophecy Fails* stipulates five conditions that must be present before one can expect disconfirmation to produce increased proselytism:[86]

1. A belief must be held with deep conviction and it must have some relevance to action, that is, to what the believer does or how he behaves.
2. The person holding the belief must have committed himself to it; that is, for the sake of his belief, he must have taken some important action that is difficult to undo. In general, the more important such actions are, and the more difficult they are to undo, the greater is the individual's commitment to the belief.
3. The belief must be sufficiently specific and sufficiently concerned with the real world so that events may unequivocally refute the belief.
4. Such undeniable disconfirmatory evidence must occur and must be recognized by the individual holding the belief. . . .
5. The believer must have social support. . . . If [however] the believer is a member of a group of convinced persons who can support one another, we would expect the belief to be maintained and the believers to attempt to proselytize or to persuade nonmembers that the belief is correct.

There is little need to argue that early Christianity meets the first, second, and fifth conditions. The conviction with which early Christians held to their beliefs was greeted by many pagans with a mixture of admiration (for their remarkable tenacity) and contempt (for the unworthiness of the beliefs themselves).[87] The decision to embrace the faith in the first decades often entailed the irrevocable loss of family, friends, and social status. And it is clear that missionary activities flourished primarily *after* the death of Jesus. Questions do arise, however, concerning the third and fourth conditions. Can we locate important beliefs that were specific enough to be disconfirmed by events in the world, and is there any evidence that believers regarded such events as having occurred? To answer these questions I propose to consider two critical moments in the early history of the movement, in fact the same two moments mentioned earlier by Harnack—the death of Jesus and the expectation of the kingdom.[88]

The Event of Jesus' Death

On the matter of Jesus' death, we must be able to demonstrate that it was regarded by his followers as in some sense disconfirming beliefs and hopes that they had attached to him during his lifetime. And as a subsidiary issue, our case will be strengthened if there are also indications that his death continued to disconfirm belief for a period of time thereafter.

There is no doubt that the crucifixion of Jesus constituted a major obstacle to the conversion of many Jews. Paul says as much in 1 Cor. 1:23 ("but we preach Christ crucified, a stumbling block to Jews and folly to Gentiles"), and his assertion is supported by an examination of Jewish messianic expectations prior to the time of Jesus. There are no signs that any group of Jews awaited a suffering Messiah, let alone one who would be crucified by Rome.[89] In other words, insofar as the followers of Jesus shared the messianic views of their time, they were unprepared for the death of the one whom they believed to be the fulfillment of their messianic dreams. But a problem arises precisely at this point: how far did Jesus' followers adhere to traditional messianic formulations? Jesus himself is portrayed in the Gospels as predicting his future suffering and death (Matt. 16:21—"From that time on Jesus began to show his disciples that he must go to Jerusalem and suffer many things from the elders and chief priests and scribes, and be killed, and on the third day be raised.").[90] "If this view is maintained," comment the authors of *When Prophecy Fails,* "then the crucifixion, far from being a disconfirmation, was indeed a confirmation of a prediction and the subsequent proselytizing of the apostles would stand as a counterexample to our hypotheses." [91] But the difficulties raised by this text are actually less severe than the authors recognize. There are two possible views about the origin of these predictions. Either they were created after the event in order to lend supportive meaning to the otherwise disconfirmatory event of the crucifixion[92]—in which case the text must be read as *sustaining* the theory—or they originated with Jesus himself. Even in the second case, however, there is firm evidence that the prediction was not accepted or understood by the disciples and that Jesus' death still came as a rude shock to them.

The passages in question (Mark 8:27–33; 9:30–32; 10:33–34), when read as a whole, tend to support rather than contradict the theory of dissonance. The first section (Mark 8:27–29) culminates in Peter's confession, "You are the Christ [i.e., the Messiah]," in which Peter clearly represents the universal belief of early Christians. The confession is then followed by Jesus' command to remain silent about this (8:30) and by his teaching that he (Matt. 16:21), or the Son of man (Mark 8:31), must suffer and die. To this Peter responds with dismay, presumably at the prediction of suffering and death—Matt. 16:22 makes this explicit: "God for-

41

bid, Lord! This shall never happen to you."—thus expressing his inability to comprehend or accept the notion of a suffering Messiah. And finally, Jesus turns on Peter angrily, calling him Satan and questioning even his loyalty to God, again presumably for his failure to understand the need for suffering and death. Here again, Peter must be seen as representing more than his own personal views. To summarize: Whether or not this scene actually occurred in Jesus' lifetime, it conveys the clear sense that the death of Jesus was a problem for his followers from the beginning and that its problematic character persisted thereafter, no doubt reinforced by Jews who maintained that a crucified Messiah was a contradiction in terms.

The relevance of this passage for the theory of dissonance is twofold. In the first place, it obviously springs from a sense of doubt and distress about Jesus' death, and in the second place, it represents the process of rationalization that, according to Festinger et al., normally accompanies proselytism. And on this particular issue, it is still possible to trace the process of rationalization whereby the early church sought to persuade others and itself that Jesus' death was both necessary and beneficial. The Gospel of Luke records a rather striking conversation between two disciples and the resurrected Jesus, whom the disciples do not recognize: "But we had hoped that he was the one to redeem Israel. Yes, and besides all this, it is now the third day since this [the crucifixion] happened." (Luke 24:21). To this expression of disappointment, Jesus replies, "O foolish men, and slow of heart to believe all that the prophets have spoken! Was it not necessary that the Christ should suffer these things and enter into his glory?" (Luke 24:25). In what we may call the first stage, we find the risen Jesus himself claiming that his death was both necessary and in accordance with the Scriptures as properly, i.e., in a Christian context, interpreted. Much the same view is expressed by Paul when he affirms that "Christ died for our sins in accordance with the scriptures . . . that he was raised on the third day in accordance with the scriptures . . ." (1 Cor. 15:3f.). Although neither Luke nor Paul cites a specific passage from Scripture, both reflect a situation in which an effort has been made to turn the disconfirmatory evidence of Scripture (traditional interpretations had not produced the idea of a suffering Messiah) into supporting evidence (correct interpretation showed that such was precisely what had been intended from the beginning).[93] A final stage appears in those Gospel passages in which Jesus predicts, *before* the event and in detail, the necessity of his suffering and death (Mark 8:31, etc.).

It would appear, then, that we are justified in maintaining that the death of Jesus created a sense of cognitive dissonance, in that it seemed to disconfirm the belief that Jesus was the Messiah. Even the event of the resurrection, which the Gospels present as having surprised the disciples every bit as much as the death, seems not to have eradicated these doubts. Thus according to the theory, we may understand the zeal with which Jesus' followers pursued their mission as part of an effort to reduce dissonance, not just in the early years but for a considerable time thereafter. Initially, it might seem reasonable to suppose that Jesus' death was most problematic for converts from Judaism, but there is good reason to believe Paul when he reports that the crucified Christ was "a stumbling block to Jews and folly to Gentiles." [94] Long after Paul's time, Lucian[95] and Celsus[96] continued to mock Christians for their faith in a crucified Savior, whereas Justin Martyr raises the question, surely not a rhetorical one, "Why should we believe that a crucified man is the first-born of the unbegotten god . . . ?" [97]

The Non-Event of the Kingdom

We may now return to the issue raised at the start of our discussion, that is, the connection between mission and eschatology. Specifically, can we now envisage the continuing mission as deriving, at least in part, from disappointment and despair over the delay of the kingdom? In different terms, were the eschatological hopes of early Christians "sufficiently specific and concerned with the real world so that unequivocal disproof or disconfirmation is possible," and are there intimations that believers sensed such disconfirmation "in the form of the nonoccurrence of a predicted event within the time limits set for its occurrence"? [98]

Recent scholarship has given affirmative answers to both questions.[99] The earliest Christian communities stood in the mainstream of Jewish apocalyptic thinking. With but one possible exception (the Gospel of John), the earliest ascertainable traditions, i.e., the Gospel sources and the letters of Paul, present a unified picture. The kingdom would happen in the near future; and it would happen as an event in history, indeed as the final event of history in its present mode. The resurrection, the act of divine judgment, and the transformation of the physical and political orders—all were understood to be specific and unmistakable events in the real world. In this respect, Paul's description of the eschatological drama in 1 Thess. 4:16f. ("For the Lord himself will descend from heaven with a cry of command, with the archangel's call, and with the sound of the trumpet of God . . .") may be taken as typical expressions of widely shared beliefs. Whether or not Jesus himself first announced the imminent arrival of the kingdom has been a much debated matter. I am inclined to the view that Jesus shared and thus prompted the belief that the kingdom was imminent,[100] but I am even more certain that our picture of primitive Christian eschatology does not hinge on an answer to the question of Jesus' predictions about his death. As with these predictions, the texts that portray the kingdom as an event in the near future (Mark 1:15; 14:25; 11:12–14, etc.) can have only two possible sources—Jesus or the earliest Christians. Thus even if it should prove methodologically impossible to assign them with certitude to Jesus, the only alternative is the early community.[101] And from that point on, they were transmitted and received *as words of Jesus.* In either case, the structure of the problem remains unchanged: a specific and important prediction that is liable to disconfirmation.

In the final analysis, however, the surest testimony on this issue is expression of concern about the delay of the kingdom in Christian texts themselves. In 1 Clement 23:3–5 (written around 96 c.e.), the author speaks openly of such concern:[102]

> Let that Scripture be far from us which says: "Wretched are the double-minded, those who doubt in their soul and say, 'We have heard these things even in our fathers' times, and see, we have grown old and none of this has happened.' " [103]

2 Peter 3:3–9 (probably written around 125 c.e.) reflects a similar situation:

> First of all you must understand this, that scoffers will come in the last days . . . saying, "Where is the promise of his coming? For ever since the fathers fell asleep, all things have continued as they were from the beginning of creation." . . . But do not ignore this one fact, beloved, that with the Lord one day is as a thousand years, and a thousand years as one day. The Lord is not slow about his promise as some count slowness. . . .

Both passages reveal that the traditional chronology of the kingdom was under attack, whether by outsiders (i.e., Jewish antagonists) or by Christian revisionists (e.g., Hymenaeus and Philetus who are anathematized by the author of 2 Tim. 2:18 for "holding that the resurrection is past already"). Paul, too, confronts the issue in 1 Thess. 4:13–5:11, where the concern appears to have arisen quite apart from any outside instigation:

> But we would not have you ignorant, brethren, concerning those who are asleep [i.e., have died], that you may not grieve as others do who have no hope. . . . For this we declare to you by the word of the Lord, that we who are alive, who are left until the coming of the Lord, shall not precede those who have fallen asleep. . . .

This passage is especially revealing because it points to the specific occasion for the concern, namely, the death of some believers. In other words, the kingdom had been expected before any believers, or at least the first generation, would die, and Paul is forced to remind his readers that the coming event of the resurrection was the positive assurance that those who had died would not miss "the coming of the Lord." Finally, of the many passages in the synoptic Gospels, one will serve to complete our survey.[104] The prediction in Matt. 10:23 ("Truly, I say to you, you will not have gone through all the towns of Israel, before the Son of man comes.") has been variously interpreted as an authentic saying of Jesus and thus a primary *source* of later concern about the delay, or as a product of the early tradition, a word of consolation spoken in the name of Jesus, and thus a *response* to the delay.[105] Both, of course, are possible. But once again either view leads to the same consequences, for the saying entered the tradition *as a word of Jesus* at an early stage. As those who had known Jesus began to die, this saying and others like it (esp. Mark 9:1— ". . . There are some standing here who will not taste death before they see the kingdom of God come with power.") become a source for concern rather than an attempt to assuage it. In fact, it seems quite likely that the anxiety reflected in later texts (e.g., 2 Peter and 1 Clement), arose from the fact that specific prophecies like that of Mark 9:1 had been unequivocally disconfirmed. Thus we should probably conceive of the response to the delay in at least two stages: an initial disappointment among the earliest believers who had expected the end in the immediate future, a disappointment that evoked consolation in the form of sayings like Mark 9:1; and a subsequent disappointment among those who had expected the end within the first generation of the faithful, a disappointment that produced consolatory sayings (e.g., Mark 13:10—"And the gospel must first be preached to all nations") as well as more systematic efforts to de-eschatologize the Christian message.[106] The success of these efforts may be seen in the fact that by the year 150 c.e. not only was Christianity no longer an eschatological community, but, as the reaction to the apocalyptic fervor of Montanism clearly reveals, that it had come to regard eschatological movements as a serious threat. Toward the end of the first century Christians could still pray, "Thy kingdom come" (Matt. 6:10). But at the end of the second century, Tertullian tells us that Christians prayed "for the emperors, for their deputies and all in authority, for the welfare of the world, *and for the delay of the final consummation*" (*Apol.* 39.2; cf. 32.1)!

At this point it is obvious that Festinger and his colleagues' discreet glance at early Christianity is far more significant than they have recognized.[107] We may now formulate their position as follows: Rationalization in connection with important beliefs, specifically the death of Jesus and the delay of the kingdom, represents an effort to reduce doubt and despair and thus is evidence of cognitive dissonance. When, in addition, missionary activity is regularly associated with the same beliefs, it can and must be interpreted as a further attempt to reduce dissonance. In contrast to O. Cullmann, who rejects the notion that mission was "something which has been substituted for the unrealized hope of the kingdom" and who insists that "if this were true, then the Church has carried on its mission because it has been obliged to renounce eschatology," [108] it now becomes possible to reverse Cullmann's terms and to conclude that the church initially carried on its mission *in an effort to maintain* its eschatology. The strength of this factor in relation to other motivating forces is beyond final determination. Here we must rest content with the general principle that as other factors, such as commands of Jesus or influence from Judaism, are minimized, the factor of cognitive dissonance must be maximized.

One final question: Does our discussion suggest the need for any modification in the theory itself? Festinger et al. set out from the observation that disconfirmation of important beliefs produces a sense of disappointment, ranging from doubt to despair, as well as pressures to reduce this disappointment. One method for reducing it is to give up the belief; but in other circumstances, as they say, "it may even be less painful to tolerate the dissonance than to discard the belief." [109] In other words, individuals find it easier to maintain a disconfirmed belief when there is group reinforcement. Thus "the other circumstances" must include loyalty to the group itself, so that it becomes less painful to maintain a disconfirmed belief than to abandon one's loyalty to the group. The authors point in this direction when they admit that "there is a limit beyond which belief will not stand disconfirmation." [110] Our examination of early Christianity suggests that this outer limit is not absolute but is rather a function of (1) the extent to which individual members have transferred former loyalties and identities (family, friends, religion, profession) to the new group; and (2) the extent to which the group itself succeeds in retaining and sustaining these new loyalties.

This last point is of particular importance because it has been questioned in a follow-up study to *When Prophecy Fails*, entitled "Prophecy Fails Again: A Report of a Failure to Replicate." [111] The authors, Jane Allyn Hardyck and Marcia Braden, examined a Pentecostal community (True Word) that appeared to meet the five conditions. But the group did not turn to proselytism following its prediction of nuclear destruction on a given date. This result led the authors to propose two revisions in the theory itself: first, "that the more social support an individual receives above the minimum he needs to maintain his belief, the less he will have to proselytize"; [112] and, second, "that if a group is receiving considerable ridicule from nonmembers, one way of reducing dissonance that would be apparent to them would be to convince these 'unbelievers' that the group is right." [113] The second proposal obviously reinforces our own analysis of early Christianity and requires no further analysis. As for the first proposal it would appear that either the theory itself needs modification or that the type of social support was different in the two cases (Lake City and True Word). There is, in fact, one significant and perhaps decisive difference between early Christian communities and the Lake City group on the one hand and the True Word group on the other. Hardyck and Braden note that "many members of the True Word group had worked together for several years" [114] and that their prophet, Mrs. Shepard, had been proclaiming her prophecy for nearly four years before the final deadline was set.[115] In other words, the fact that the identity of individuals with the group as well as their breaking of old loyalties had long been established suggests that the prophecy was less important to the members than the existence of the group itself. For the earliest Christians, however, as well as for the Lake City group, the prophet and the message were recent, the movement was new, and between them prophet and prophecy were the basic occasion for the coalescence of the groups. This situation, in which the creation of the group and the subsequently disconfirmed belief are inseparable, seems a likely explanation for the presence of proselytism in the one case and its absence in the other.

Thus we may summarize the proposed modifications in the theory of dissonance as follows:

1. Proselytism as a means of reducing cognitive dissonance will appear primarily in new groups, like early Christianity, whose existence has been occasioned by or associated with a belief that is subsequently disconfirmed.
2. Public ridicule at the time of disconfirmation may play an important role in turning such a group toward missionary activity.
3. The limit beyond which belief will not withstand disconfirmation is a function of the degree to which identification with the group supplants the original belief as the basic motivation for adherence to the group.

To these we may add one further point. Festinger mentions, though he does not emphasize the fact that rationalization always accompanies proselytism in the period following disconfirmation—the timetable was wrong; the event really did occur in some unexpected and imperceptible fashion; the disconfirming event, when properly understood, turns out to be confirmatory after all, etc. Thus the total process of adjustment includes a social (proselytism) as well as an intellectual (rationalization) component. And insofar as rationalization occurs, it will inevitably alter the shape of the original belief, whether by setting a new deadline, by recasting it in more general terms, or by relegating it to a lower rank within the total nexus of the group's beliefs and practices. In other words, what at first appeared to be a paradox in our explanation of early Christianity—that its status as a millenarian movement enables us to understand both its failure, in the sense that all such movements fail, *and* its success, in the sense that its very failure became the occasion for the intense missionary activity that ensured its ultimate survival—turns out not to be a paradox at all.

Conversion and Dissonance[116]

In the preceding discussion I have attempted to reinforce Festinger's proposal that cognitive dissonance associated with the disconfirmation of important beliefs was one among several factors behind missionary activity. Beyond this, there is a quite different area, not considered by Festinger, in which dissonance theory can be related to missions. In *A Theory of Cognitive Dissonance,* Festinger deals with dissonance in relation to the general question of decisions and their consequences.[117] Briefly, he notes that dissonance is an inevitable consequence of decisions and that the magnitude of dissonance, and thus of pressures to reduce it, depends on two elements—the importance of the decision and the initial attractiveness of the unchosen or rejected alternative. Successful reduction of dissonance, he maintains, will tend to increase confidence in the decision taken *and* to intensify the attractiveness of the chosen alternative in contrast to the rejected one.[118] These are familiar stages in the process of rationalization. What Festinger does not consider is the further possibility that attempts to diminish postdecision dissonance may also, as in the case of disconfirmed beliefs, lead to or reinforce an inclination to proselytism.

The relevance of these propositions for the question of conversion is readily apparent. Without pursuing the matter in detail, let me suggest several ways in which efforts to reduce postconversion dissonance may have influenced the experience of early Christians. In the case of Paul, for instance, one is tempted to say that his effort to play down the status and significance of the Mosaic Law (e.g., Gal. chapters 3–4) is an attempt to diminish the attractiveness of the rejected alternative. More generally, the recurrent polemic against pagan cults may express the need of pagan converts to reduce dissonance by emphasizing the discrepancy between rejected and chosen alternatives. The intensive commitment which so often characterizes new converts should also be seen in the same light. Finally, proselytism itself, again among recent converts, would serve to reduce dissonance, not only by stressing the incompatibility of the two alternatives but also by assuming, in Festinger's words, that "if more and more people can be persuaded that the system of belief is correct, then clearly it must, after all, be correct." [119]

Two words of caution are in order before completing this brief aside. First, I do not wish to claim that cognitive dissonance is the single explanation for either missionary activity or polemic against Judaism and paganism. Several factors were involved, and dissonance must be counted among them. Second, dissonance theory will apply only in those cases that involve conversion as defined above, i.e., a decision between incompatible and attractive alternatives. *In this sense,* not all early believers would qualify as converts. Paul would, of course, and he behaves accordingly. But for those who did not see Christianity as a choice between incommensurables, e.g., for those "Jewish Christians" who disagreed violently with Paul as to the status of the Law, one would have to speak of conversion, if at all, in a different manner. The same would be true of "pagan Christians" who saw in Christianity the fulfillment of Greek wisdom rather than its antithesis. This particular result points forward to the discussion of orthodoxy and heresy. The harsh attitude of emergent orthodoxy toward both "Jewish Christianity" and syncretistic Gnosticism can thus be viewed as a process of emphasizing the discrepancy between chosen and rejected alternatives.[120] These movements were threatening precisely because they diminished this discrepancy and thereby increased dissonance for those who had made the decision to convert.

THE ATTAINMENT OF MILLENNIAL BLISS THROUGH MYTH: THE BOOK OF REVELATION

Thus far we have followed the lead of recent anthropologists in assuming that millenarian movements fail because they do not achieve their stated goal—the millennium. In an obvious sense, of course, this judgment is true. But at the same time certain aspects of these cults have already suggested that they may indeed reach the millennium in other, less obvious, ways. To begin with, there is the undeniable continuity of the group and its individual members. The failure of fundamental prophecies always produces some defections, but the remarkable fact that the majority remains should prompt us to ask whether the millennium has in some sense come to life in the experience of the community as a whole. Undoubtedly, rationalization and missionary activity are factors that facilitate continued adherence to the group, but insofar as millennial dreams remain alive they are probably understood to have been at least partially fulfilled. What interests us at present is the mode of their fulfillment. Some of the standard forms are sacraments, meditation, asceticism, and mystical visions. In these instances, the attainment of millennial bliss is largely individual. Other forms encompass the entire community. M. Simon remarks of Qumran "that the whole organization of the Essene sect is a prefiguration of the coming kingdom." [121] In similar fashion, we have argued that various elements of early Christian ethics can best be understood as efforts to capture in the present the conditions of the future —the self-designation of Christians as brothers and sisters; the abolition, at least in theory, of premillennial distinctions between male and female, Jew and Greek, slave and free; and the denigration in some quarters of marriage and sex. Beyond these modes of apprehending the future, I would contend that the Book of Revelation, as an expression of apocalyptic mythology, offers a third and largely unexamined form of anticipating the End.

In approaching this particular book, however, we must be conscious of its fate in Western history, for it has probably alienated more readers than it has enchanted. One common solution to the enigmatic character of the book has been to treat it as a kind of literary puzzle, either by seeing it as a collage of prophetic sayings drawn from Daniel, Ezekiel, Zechariah, and others, or by attempting to decipher its historical and political code.[122] More recently attention has turned from individual symbols and passages to the structure of the writing as a whole. Here, it is thought, lies the key to its interpretation. The obvious advantage of this approach is that it accepts the work for what it is, an irreducibly mythological and tightly structured product of literary creativity. To be sure, there has been nothing even approaching unanimity on specific details of structure. Austin Farrer's tantalizingly complex analysis in *A Rebirth of Images. The Making of Saint John's Apocalypse*[123] and J. W. Bowman's theatrical interpretation,[124] complete with settings and props borrowed from the Greco-Roman stage, have little in common beyond a sense that the key to understanding lies in structure. Still, this common ground is important and offers the only substantial basis for further work.

My own approach presupposes both the importance of structure and the indispensability of myth in locating the author's method and message. In addition, however, I assign both structure and myth to a specific role in relation to the concrete situation (persecution and martyrdom) and purpose (consolation) of the book as a whole. Whatever its date and location, the writing inescapably presupposes a situation in which believers had experienced suffering and death at the hands of Rome. This is the crisis in which John offers his unique message of consolation—consolation not simply as the promise of a happy fate for the martyr in the near future but through the mythological enactment of that future in the present. In a word, through "the suppression of time." Though the phrase itself is borrowed from Claude Lévi-Strauss's *The Raw and the Cooked*,[125] the idea of overcoming time by various means is by no means a novel one.

Both Lévi-Strauss[126] and Mircea Eliade[127] have suggested that psychoanalysis represents a secular counterpart of the same phenomenon. And
it is at the point of this analogy between ancient myth and ritual on the
one hand and modern psychoanalysis on the other that the structure of
the Book of Revelation enters the picture. For I intend to argue that the
writing is a form of therapy, much like the technique of psychoanalysis,
whose ultimate goal is to transcend the time between a real present and a
mythical future. In this analogy, the relationship between myth and audience parallels the relationship between analyst and patient; both serve as
vehicles for suppressing time. In his essay on "The Effectiveness of Symbols," Lévi-Strauss recognizes the differences between the two cases, but
insists on a fundamental similarity: the therapeutic value of myth and
psychoanalysis lies in their unique ability to manipulate symbols and in
so doing to change reality.

One basic function of myth is to overcome unwelcome contradictions between hope and reality, between what ought to be and what is,
between an ideal past or future and a flawed present. Clearly, the hearers
(Rev. 1:3) of the book were caught in such a predicament. The occasion
was persecution at the hands of the church's enemies, but the real crisis
lay in the unbearable and irreconcilable tensions created by persecution.
On the one hand was the belief that, as Christians, they were the chosen
people of God, protected by him and assured of eternal life in his kingdom. On the other hand was the overwhelming experience of suffering,
deprivation, and death at the hands of those whom they most despised.
Although the precise date of the book is uncertain,[128] it probably dates
from the very end of the first century. We know from one of Pliny's letters
to the emperor Trajan (*Epistle* 10, dating from 112 c.e.) that Christian
communities in Asia Minor were being persecuted by Roman officials in
the years between 90 and 110 c.e.[129] What we learn from the book itself
is the depth and intensity of the Christian reaction to persecution.

In speaking of medieval millenarian movements, Cohn likens their
view of the world to a form of paranoia:

> The megalomaniac view of oneself as the elect, wholly good, abominably
> persecuted yet assured of ultimate triumph; the attribution of gigantic
> and demonic powers to the adversary . . . these attitudes are symptoms
> which together constitute the unmistakable syndrome of paranoia. But a
> paranoiac delusion does not cease to be so because it is shared by so
> many individuals, nor yet because those individuals have real and ample
> grounds for regarding themselves as victims of oppression.[130]

Whether or not we accept Cohn's comparison of apocalyptic mentality
and group paranoia, his language conveys a sense of the internal crisis
that confronted the author and his audience. I emphasize this point be-

cause it explains why a simple message of consolation, encouraging believers to stand firm and reiterating earlier promises, would have been inadequate to the needs of the occasion. Indeed, these traditional hopes and promises were very much a part of the crisis, for their credibility had been called into question by the fact of persecution, and simply to repeat them would have been to compound the agony. Instead the writer offers a Christian myth, using as building blocks the full supply of Jewish and Christian symbols. And he structures these symbols so as to reflect the bifurcated experience of believers under persecution. Much attention has been given to the obvious role of the number seven in the framework of the work as a whole: seven sections, each with seven parts; seven opening letters; seven trumpets; seven seals; etc. Equally important, however, because it closely mirrors the crisis to which the book is directed, is the separation of all symbols into two distinct categories: symbols of oppression and despair (beasts, plagues, Babylon, Satan, etc.) *and* symbols of hope and victory (Lamb, elders, book of life, New Jerusalem, etc.). There is no middle ground, no possibility of mediation or reconciliation between the two poles. The absence, even the unacceptability of any common ground between worship of the beast and loyalty to the Lamb, is symbolically represented in the last of the letters to the seven churches:

> "I know your works: you are neither cold nor hot. Would that you were cold or hot! So, because you are lukewarm, and neither cold nor hot, I will spew you out of my mouth."

Rev. 3:15–16

As we have seen in our earlier discussion of millenarian movements, the category of lukewarmness has no meaning whatsoever in an apocalyptic setting where good and evil are completely unambiguous and totally opposed.[131] Thus it can only be spit out at the very beginning and eliminated from the subsequent drama.

At this point we must return to the overall structure of the work, for it is here that the two patterns (sevens and twos) meet to create a "machine" for transcending time. Contrary to initial impressions, the distribution of the two groups of symbols is not random; it follows a definite and recurring order from start to finish. There is a clear pattern of alternation between them, like the periodic crests and hollows of a continuous wave. This pattern is initiated in the opening letters (chapters 2–3): in three of the letters the writer follows praise with blame (2:2f.; 2:13; 2:19); in two he creates a dramatic tension between being dead and being alive (2:9; 3:1); and in the final letter he stresses the point through his rejection of those who are lukewarm. But the main force of the movement takes shape in the seven visions that stretch from 4:1 to 22:5. Schematically, these visions can be arranged as follows:

VICTORY/HOPE	OPPRESSION/DESPAIR
4:1–5:14 throne and Lamb	
	6:1–17 first six seals

7:1–8:4
    multitude of the faithful and
    seventh seal	

	8:5–9:21 first six trumpets
10:1–11:1 dramatic interlude in heaven	
	11:2–14 attack of the beasts
11:15–19 seventh trumpet	
	12:1–17 the dragon assaults the woman
	13:1–18 the beast with horns
14:1–7 Mount Zion and Lamb	
	14:8–15:1 destruction and judgment
15:2–8 martyrs worship God	
	16:1–20 seven bowls of wrath
	17:1–18:24 fall of Babylon
19:1–16 worship in heaven	
	19:17–20:15 final judgment

21:1–22:5
    new heaven, new earth,
    new Jerusalem	

Several aspects of this rhythmic oscillation need to be underlined. In the first place, the pattern of recurrent crests and hollows breaks the pattern of sevens at three points: at 6:17 where the opening of the sixth seal is followed not by the seventh seal but rather by a vision of the one hundred and forty-four thousand who bear the seal of God (7:1–17); again at 9:21 where the sixth trumpet gives way not to the seventh but to a dramatic interlude in which the final outcome is revealed to John alone (10:1–11); and, finally, at 15:1 where the seven angels with the seven plagues are introduced but followed immediately by a vision of those who have conquered the beast (15:2–4).[132] In the first two instances, an almost perfect series of seven disasters is broken by a vision of final glory; and in the third, the seven plagues are presented as symbols of penultimate rather than ultimate truth. By thus substituting a dynamic for a static relationship between oppression and hope, these broken series serve to undermine any tendency among the audience to treat them as a permanent, unbearable contradictions. The glimpse of final victory in each case shatters the anticipation of perfect despair and points to an experience of exultation not just in the future but in the immediacy of the myth itself. Thus the dominant structural feature of the book is not the pattern of sevens, but the simpler and more immediate pattern of oscillating oppositions. A second observation concerns chapter 10, which falls roughly midway in the book. Properly speaking, chapter 10 ought to be bracketed as a moment of dramatic suspense, for it promises but then withholds the final revelation. At the same time, the scene in 10:8–10 provides an indispensable clue to the author's hidden design. His symbolic gesture of eating the scroll, coming as it does after the dramatic announcement of "the mystery of God" in 10:1–7, intimates that the path to understanding the work lies not in deciphering specific symbols or external events but rather in digesting the myth as a whole. Finally, we should note the relative imbalance between crests and hollows before and after chapter 10. In chapters 4–9 there is a rough equilibrium between symbols of hope (4:1–5:14; 7:1–8:4) and those of despair (6:1–17; 8:5–9:21), whereas after chapter 10 symbols of hope are in relative decline. But within the schema outlined above, this decline may be regarded as a deliberately dramatic preparation for the climactic visions of 21:1–22:5, which crown the story:

> Then I saw a new heaven and a new earth. . . . And night shall be no more; they need no light of lamp or sun, for the Lord God will be their light, and they shall reign for ever and ever.

To appreciate the therapeutic function of this final episode we must return to Lévi-Strauss's comparison of myth and psychoanalysis. In most cases the key to successful analysis lies in the dynamics of transference, through which the patient comes to experience repressed memories, relationships and instincts from the past—Lévi-Strauss likens them to a myth[133]—as alive in the present.[134] Through transference the therapist becomes a contemporaneous gateway for past events as they are recovered and rehearsed in a series of therapeutic encounters. Similarly, the therapeutic value of the myth rests on its periodic structure.[135] The audience's ability to identify with it depends on its wavelike character, which in turn expresses the contradictory experience of faith under persecution. And if we have sustained our analysis thus far, the triumphant visions of 21:1–22:5 represent both the suppression of time and the dissolution of contradictions. Their role is not just to illustrate what lies in the future but to transcend the time separating present from future, to make possible an experience of millennial bliss as living reality. Just as the therapeutic situation is the machine through which the patient comes to experience the *past* as present, so the myth is the machine through which the believing community comes to experience the *future* as present. In psychoanalytic terms, this appears as the phenomenon of abreaction, in which the patient reacts momentarily—in anger, fear, love, dependence, or whatever—to the therapist as he once related to parents, siblings, etc. The therapeutic function of myth could thus be called a form of abreaction.[136] And what unites the two techniques is a common view—one is tempted to label it as primitive—that knowledge can change the world. In comparing shamanism and psychoanalysis, Lévi-Strauss remarks that,

> in both cases also, the conflicts and resistances are resolved, not because of the knowledge, real or alleged, which the sick woman acquires of them, but because this knowledge makes possible *a specific experience, in the course of which conflicts materialize in an order and on a level permitting their free development and leading to their resolution.*[137]

To be sure, there is one major difference in the forms of this resolution, in that psychoanalysis leads to an integration of the conflicting poles, whereas the apocalyptic solution envisages the complete eradication of one pole. Apart from this difference of form, however, the process is essentially the same. Again in Lévi-Strauss's words,

> the effectiveness of symbols would consist precisely in the "inductive property," by which homologous structures, built out of different materials at different levels of life—organic processes, unconscious mind, rational thought—are related to one another.[138]

If Lévi-Strauss and others are right in proposing that changes at one level of reality or consciousness, say mythological, can induce homologous changes at other levels, say in one's perception of time, then we must revise our earlier assumption that millenarian movements always fail to attain the millennium. This is not to deny that the overcoming of time, whether through myth, abreaction, music, or poetic metaphor, is anything but transitory. The real world, in the form of persecution, reasserted itself with dogged persistence for Christian communities. But in an apocalyptic setting, where the goal is to support the community for a short time before the End, this ephemeral experience of the future might have been sufficient. For hearers of this book, even a fleeting experience of the millennium may have provided the energy needed to withstand the wrath of the beast.

Finally, we must consider the specific setting in which the book would have been able to exercise its therapeutic function. From the opening verses we know that it was meant to be read aloud before a gathered community: "Blessed is he who reads aloud the words of the prophecy, and blessed are those who hear . . ." (1:3). We also know that it was customary in communal assemblies to read aloud from early Christian writings (Col. 4.16; 1 Thess. 5:27). Thus the intended setting for reading the book was collective rather than private. Furthermore, to an extent shared by no other primitive Christian document, the book's language, content, and structure is thoroughly liturgical; at one level it is little more than a compilation of prayers, benedictions, and hymns. Whether these liturgical fragments are the creations of the author himself or whether, as seems more likely, they reflect liturgical practice in Asia Minor,[139] they reinforce the view that the book was meant to be read before the community gathered for the purpose of worship. What role it may have played in the liturgy is more difficult to ascertain. The one undeniable fact is that the attention of the community, and thus of its worship, was entirely on the imminent End. "The time is near" (1:3) and "Amen, come Lord Jesus" (22:20) frame the work as a whole as much as they express the mood of its hearers. What other elements entered the liturgy must remain unknown, although it seems probable that the Lord's Supper would have been celebrated. If so, it no doubt took the primitive form of an eschatological sacrament in which, according to Schweitzer and others, the meal anticipated the return of Jesus and the messianic feast with him in the immediate future.[140] More importantly, we do not know whether the reading was completed in a single session, in which case reading the book would have been the chief ritual of the liturgy, or whether it was done in portions over a period of consecutive daily or weekly gatherings. At most, we may assume that the book would have achieved its maximum effectiveness if read in a compressed period of time. In any case, we know that it was not written for posterity nor as a permanent contribution to Christian worship. For it was the fervent hope of writer and hearer alike that there would be no need to hear these words on more than one or two occasions.

NOTES

1. On the subject of this chapter as a whole see S. R. ISENBERG, "Millenarism in Greco-Roman Palestine," *Religion* 4 (1974) pp. 26–46. Throughout this chapter I will use the terms "millennial" and "millenarian" in the extended sense of movements that expect a new order of reality in the near future; my use bears no relation to the narrower sense of a thousand-year reign that is to occur in the indefinite future.

2. See above, p. 15, n. 13.

3. See below, n. 6.

4. "Revitalization Movements," *American Anthropologist* 58 (1956), p. 267.

5. "Medieval Millenarism: Its Bearing on the Comparative Study of Millenarian Movements," in *Millennial Dreams in Action. Studies in Revolutionary Religious Movements,* ed. SYLVIA THRUPP (New York: Schocken Books, 1970), p. 33. See also COHN's larger work, *The Pursuit of the Millennium. Revolutionary Messianism in Medieval and Reformation Europe and Its Bearing on Modern Totalitarian Movements* (New York: Harper & Row, 1961), pp. 1–13.

6. TALMON, "Pursuit of the Millennium" (above, p. 15, n. 4), p. 139. Compare also I. C. JARVIE, *The Revolution in Anthropology* (Chicago: Henry Regnery, 1967), p. 52.

7. JARVIE, *Revolution,* p. 51.

8. *Ibid.,* pp. 68–73. For a similar list of questions, also designed for fieldwork, see R. K. MERTON, *On Theoretical Sociology* (New York: Free Press, 1967), pp. 109–14.

9. H. KAMINSKY, "The Problem of Explanation," in *Millenial Dreams* (above, n. 5), p. 215.

10. WORSLEY, *Trumpet Shall Sound,* p. xlii.

11. JOSEPHUS, *War* 2.118.

12. JOSEPHUS, *Antiquities* 18.23f.

13. So JOSEPHUS, *War* 2.594: "He [John of Gischala] had been spreading the calumny that Josephus was about to betray the country to the Romans. . . ."

14. On the Zealots in general see W. FARMER, *Maccabees, Zealots and Josephus* (New York: Columbia University Press, 1956); M. HENGEL, *Die Zeloten* (Leiden: Brill, 1961); S. G. F. BRANDON, *Jesus and the Zealots* (New York: Charles Scribner's Sons, 1967); S. APPLEBAUM, "The Zealots: The Case for Revaluation," *Journal of Roman Studies* 61 (1971), pp. 153–70; and M. SMITH, "Zealots and Sicarii. Their Origins and Relations," *Harvard Theological Review* 64 (1971), pp. 1–19. Smith in particular argues that

the Zealots became an organized party only in 67–68 C.E.; according to this reconstruction, any attempt to associate Jesus with the Zealots would represent anachronistic reasoning.

15. Recent literature on the Zealots and similar movements in first-century Palestine is virtually unanimous in affirming that their nationalism was closely tied to apocalyptic expectations. Although this connection seems entirely plausible, it must be noted that Josephus, our chief source of information, presents them as secular groups with no religious program. In support of the modern interpretation we may point out that in his description of John the Baptist (*Antiquities* 18.116–19) and the Essenes (*ibid.* 18.18–22), both of whom we know to have been thoroughly apocalyptic, Josephus makes no mention at all of this aspect of their beliefs.

16. On this issue see BRANDON, *Jesus and the Zealots,* pp. 322–58; O. CULLMANN, *The State in the New Testament* (New York: Charles Scribner's Sons, 1956), pp. 8–23; and *Jesus and the Revolutionaries* (New York: Harper & Row, 1970).

17. *New Heaven,* p. 146 (his emphasis).

18. JOSEPHUS, *War* 2.175–77.

19. In general see F. C. GRANT, *The Economic Background of the Gospels* (Oxford: Oxford University Press, 1926).

20. For a discussion of this problem see L. A. KECK, "The Poor among the Saints in Jewish Christianity and Qumran," *Zeitschrift für die neutestamentliche Wissenschaft* 57 (1966), pp. 54–78.

21. *New Heaven,* p. 147.

22. *Ibid.,* pp. 148f.

23. On this enormous subject see, L. FINKELSTEIN, *The Pharisees. The Sociological Background of Their Faith* (Philadelphia: Jewish Publication Society, 1962); M. SMITH, "Palestinian Judaism in the First Century," in *Israel: Its Role in Civilization,* ed. M. Davis (New York: Harper & Row, 1956), pp. 67–81; G. F. MOORE, *Judaism in the First Centuries of the Christian Era. The Age of the Tannaim* (Cambridge: Harvard University Press, 1927); and J. NEUSNER, *From Politics to Piety. The Emergence of Pharisaic Judaism* (Englewood Cliffs, N.J.: Prentice-Hall, 1973).

24. Acts 15:5 mentions "some believers who belonged to the party of the Pharisees." Whether or not we are to take this passage as a reliable report, it reflects Luke's distinctive attitude toward the Pharisees in the book of Acts. In contrast to the synoptic traditions, Acts portrays the Pharisees as occasional supporters of Jesus' followers; see the discussion in NEUSNER, *From Politics to Piety,* pp. 71f.

25. JOSEPHUS, *Antiquities,* 20.179–81.

26. On relationships between early Christianity and Qumran, see *The Scrolls and the New Testament,* ed. K. Stendahl (New York: Harper & Bros., 1957), and M. SIMON, *Jewish Sects at the Time of Jesus* (Philadelphia: Fortress Press, 1967), pp. 145–54.

27. On the importance of ritual hand-washing among the Pharisaic *ḥaberim* see J. NEUSNER, *Fellowship in Judaism. The First Century and Today* (London: Valentine, Mitchell, 1963), pp. 16f.

28. So G. F. MOORE, "The *am ha-areṣ* (the People of the Land) and the *ḥaberim* (associates)," in *The Beginnings of Christianity,* Part I: *The Acts of the*

Apostles, ed. F. J. Foakes Jackson and K. Lake, (London: Macmillan, 1920), 1:439–45.

29. The translations are MOORE's, *ibid.,* p. 444.

30. J. NEUSNER, *From Politics to Piety,* p. 77.

31. On the extent of Pharisaic influence in the early part of the first century see M. SMITH, "Palestinian Judaism," pp. 73–81; and NEUSNER, *From Politics to Piety, passim.*

32. On the inversion of the existing social order as a common motif in millenarian movements, see WORSLEY, *Trumpet Shall Sound,* pp. 251f.

33. TALMON, "Pursuit of the Millennium," p. 137 (her emphasis); see also D. ABERLE, "A Note on Relative Deprivation Theory As Applied to Millenarian and Other Cult Movements," in *Millennial Dreams* (above, n. 5), pp. 209–14 (Aberle's article is reprinted in *Reader in Comparative Religion,* pp. 537–41).

34. See the discussion in WORSLEY, *Trumpet Shall Sound,* pp. xxxvif.; and on early Christianity, S. WOLIN, *Politics and Vision. Continuity and Innovation in Western Political Thought* (Boston: Little, Brown, 1960), pp. 95–140.

35. Moore, among others, has emphasized that both *am ha-areṣ* and *ḥaber* are religious terms. As such they do not correlate with social or economic standing. Thus an observant priest or a student who abandoned his studies was considered an *am ha-areṣ.* On this issue see also E. E. URBACH, "Class-Status and Leadership in the World of the Palestinian Sages," in *Proceedings of the Israel Academy of Sciences and Humanities,* vol. 2 (Jerusalem, 1968), pp. 64–71.

36. *New Heaven,* p. 147.

37. TALMON, "Pursuit of the Millennium," p. 134.

38. So, for instance, M. WEBER, *Sociology of Religion,* pp. 2f. and 46f.

39. *Trumpet Shall Sound,* p. xii.

40. On the title "prophet" as applied to Jesus in early Christianity see O. CULLMANN, *The Christology of the New Testament* (Philadelphia: Westminster Press, 1959), pp. 13–50.

41. *New Heaven,* p. 95.

42. *Ibid.,* p. 155.

43. *Ibid.,* p. 141.

44. In *ibid.,* p. 150, BURRIDGE calls this the Brahman-Kshatriya relationship. He argues that a prophet is most likely to arise in conjunction with a transmission of power from "Brahman" to "Kshatriya," i.e., when a balance of power between the two groups has developed but the "Brahman" still maintains exclusive access to the rewards. This final condition might also apply to our case, but only if it could be shown that converts to Christianity and, say, Pharisees stood on roughly even terms in economics or some other equally important matter. It should also be noted that this final condition is tantamount to the idea of *relative* deprivation.

45. The "teacher of righteousness" clearly plays the same role in the Essene literature from Qumran. This obvious similarity no doubt underlies the efforts by various scholars to identify Jesus with the "teacher of righteousness."

46. On this point we should note that Jesus was in agreement with the Sadducees who, according to JOSEPHUS (*Antiquities* 13.297 and 18.16f.), also disregarded extra-biblical authority: "The Pharisees have transmitted to the people certain practices which are not recorded in the laws of Moses; for this reason the Sadducees reject them, saying that only the written regulations need to be honored. . . ." (*Antiquities* 13.297). On the issue of whether these extra-biblical materials were transmitted in written or oral form before 70 C.E., see J. NEUSNER, "The Rabbinic Traditions about the Pharisees before A.D. 70: The Problem of Oral Transmission," *Journal of Jewish Studies* 22 (1971), pp. 1–18.

47. On the parallels between this mode of scriptural interpretation and biblical exegesis as practiced at Qumran, see F. M. CROSS, *The Ancient Library of Qumran* (Garden City, N.Y.: Anchor Books, 1961), p. 218.

48. JOSEPHUS (*Antiquities* 18.17) comments that "whenever they [Sadducees] assume their priestly office, they submit, though unwillingly and of necessity, to the control of the Pharisees, for otherwise they would be unacceptable to the populace."

49. For a full discussion see CROSS, *Ancient Library*, pp. 127–60.

50. JOSEPHUS, *War* 4.151–57.

51. Mark's version reads, "I will destroy this temple that is made with hands, and in three days I will build another, not made with hands" (14:58). I accept R. BULTMANN's view (*History of the Synoptic Tradition* [New York: Harper & Row, 1963], p. 120) that Matthew's version is the more original one.

52. An interesting variant of the same pattern appears in Luke 10:16, where Jesus is addressing the disciples: "He who hears you hears me, and he who rejects you rejects me. . . ."

53. Chicago: Aldine, 1969.

54. R. K. MERTON states the same principle at a somewhat higher level of generalization: "Functional deficiencies of official structure generate an alternative (unofficial) structure to fulfill existing needs somewhat more effectively" (*On Theoretical Sociology*, p. 127).

55. *Ritual Process*, pp. 111f.

56. The address in Phil. 1:1 mentions "the bishops and deacons," but the primary addressees are "all the saints in Christ Jesus who are at Philippi." The bishops and deacons play no further role in the letter.

57. Compare a similar scene where, in denying a special request that James and John be allowed to sit at his right and left hand in the kingdom, Jesus explicitly contrasts hierarchical relationships among Gentiles with their absence among his followers: "But it shall not be so among you; but whoever would be great among you must be your servant, and whoever would be first among you must be slave of all" (Mark 10:35–45; cf. Matt. 20:20–28; Luke 22:24–27).

58. Matthew's version in 10:37 is considerably milder and thus probably later.

59. Luke's version in 8:19–21 is milder and probably later.

60. Compare BURRIDGE's comment in *New Heaven*: "It could be argued that orgies of sexual promiscuity . . . and the high idealism often connoted by the release from all desire, are polar opposites. But the fact remains that

both meet in precisely the same condition: that of no obligation" (p. 167, emphasis added).

61. For a discussion of the passage, see K. STENDAHL, *The Bible and the Role of Women* (Philadelphia: Fortress Press, 1966), pp. 32–35, and R. SCROGGS, "Paul and the Eschatological Woman," *Journal of the American Academy of Religion* 40 (1972), pp. 283–303. Scroggs argues convincingly that Paul's views in this regard are part of a widespread attitude in the earliest tradition (cf. 1 Cor. 12:12–13; Col. 3:1–11) and that they were part of an early baptismal liturgy (pp. 291–93).

62. In support of the view that Paul went a considerable distance toward embodying this ideal in his own congregations, see the persuasive arguments of W. A. MEEKS, "The Image of the Androgyne: Some Uses of a Symbol in Earliest Christianity," *History of Religions* 13 (1974), esp. p. 198.

63. MEEKS, *ibid.*, speaks of a "conservative reaction" (p. 206) that soon came to dominate the mainstream of the Pauline school (Ephesians, Colossians, 1 Timothy, etc.) and adds that if the passage in 1 Cor. 14:33b–36 is seen as Pauline, and not as a later interpolation, the reaction would have to be traced to Paul himself (p. 204).

64. Meeks remarks that "when Marcion permitted women to administer baptism and to conduct other official functions . . . he may have had better grounds than for his other innovations in thinking he was following the Pauline model" (*ibid.*, pp. 198f.). In his *Ecstatic Religion*, I. M. LEWIS treats the prominent role of women in possession cults like primitive Montanism as "thinly disguised protest movements directed against the dominant sex" (p. 31).

65. M. SMITH, *The Secret Gospel* (New York: Harper & Row, 1973), suggests two further explanations for the presence of these two opposing traditions in the early sources. First, he proposes that some of the legalist material is authentic and represents Jesus' teaching for those outside the law, although "he himself was free of the law, and so were those who had been baptized with his spirit" (p. 113). Second, he argues that the libertine side of primitive Christianity, amply attested in numerous texts that polemicize against it (Matt. 5:19; 7:15–27; Luke 7:36–50; Acts 20:29f.; Rom. 3:8; James 3:13–18, etc.) was deliberately concealed by more legalist groups who sought to persuade Roman readers "that Christianity was morally admirable and politically innocent . . ." (p. 124; cf. pp. 113–38).

66. *New Heaven,* p. 166.

67. In his letter to the Galatians, Paul argues at length that the old law is no longer binding on followers of Christ. But when he comes to specifying the content of the new law, he cites Lev. 19:18!

68. *New Heaven,* pp. 167f.

69. On the release of sexual energy and the role of promiscuity in millenarian cults see WORSLEY, *Trumpet Shall Sound, passim,* and R. KNOX, *Enthusiasm* (Oxford: Oxford University Press, 1950), pp. 566–77.

70. In seeking to explain Paul's restrictions on the attire of women in prayer and prophecy, Meeks argues that Paul can "insist on the continuing validity of the *symbolic* distinctions belonging to the humanity of the old Adam . . . ," while also maintaining that "in the present . . . *functional* distinctions which belong to that world may be disregarded" ("Image of the Androgyne," p. 202).

71. Compare 1 Cor. 6:12: " 'All things are lawful for me,' but not all things are helpful. 'All things are lawful for me,' but I will not be enslaved by anything."

72. In 1 Cor. 9:19 Paul applies the principle to himself: "For though I am free from all men, I have made myself a slave to all, that I might win the more [i.e., converts]."

73. JARVIE, for instance, describes BURRIDGE's *Mambu* as "in my view almost methodologically paradigmatic" (*Revolution*, p. 104). His one criticism, that Burridge nowhere sets out the interrelated problems of cargo cults, is more than satisfied in *New Heaven, New Earth*.

74. *The Jesus of the Early Christians. A Study in Christian Origins* (London: Pemberton Books, 1971). The publication of Wells's book created a considerable stir in Great Britain.

75. *Trumpet Shall Sound*, p. lxi.

76. In addition to the works of Harnack, Hahn, and Cullmann, noted below, see also J. JEREMIAS, *Jesus' Promise to the Nations* (London: SCM Press, 1958); D. GEORGI, *Die Gegner des Paulus im 2. Korintherbrief: Studien zur religiösen Propaganda in der Spätantike* (Neukirchen-Vluyn; Neukirchener Verlag, 1964), esp. pp. 83–218; and M. GREEN, *Evangelism in the Early Church* (London: Hodder and Stoughton, 1970).

77. See below, n. 78.

78. *Mission and Expansion*, 1:9; see also, pp. 15f. The missionary character of Judaism is also emphasized by GEORGI (*Die Gegner*, pp. 83–187), although both Harnack and Georgi recognize the differences between Jewish and Christian missions. I am rather inclined to agree with the observation of A. D. Nock that "we should be cautious in inferring widespread efforts by Jews to convert Gentiles. Individual Jews did undoubtedly try to 'draw men to the Law,' but in the main the proselyte was the man who came to the Law, and the duty of the Jew was to commend the Law by his example (cf. Deuter. 4:6) rather than by missionary endeavor" (from his review in *Gnomon* 33 [1961], p. 582 of H.-J. SCHOEPS, *Paul. The Theology of the Apostle in the Light of Jewish Religious History* [Philadelphia: Westminster Press, 1961]).

79. *Mission and Expansion*, 1:44.

80. *Mission in the New Testament* (Naperville, Ill.: A. R. Allenson, 1965), p. 51.

81. In his essay, "Eschatology and Missions in the New Testament," from *The Background of the New Testament and Its Eschatology* (Festschrift for C. H. Dodd), ed. W. D. Davies and D. Daube (Cambridge: The University Press, 1956), pp. 409–21.

82. Cullmann, p. 415.

83. Jointly authored by L. FESTINGER, H. W. RIECKEN, and S. SCHACHTER (New York: Harper & Row, 1956). See also FESTINGER's further elaboration of the theory in *A Theory of Cognitive Dissonance* (Stanford, Calif.: Stanford University Press, 1957).

84. *Theory*, p. 18.

85. *When Prophecy Fails*, p. 28 (their emphasis).

86. *Ibid.*, p. 4.

87. See E. R. DODDS, *Pagan and Christian*, pp. 120f.

88. It should be noted that *When Prophecy Fails* deals only with Jesus' death and that it ignores recent critical literature on the New Testament.

89. So, for instance, O. CULLMANN in *The Christology of the New Testament,* p. 60.

90. Mark's version (8:31) reads: "And he began to teach them that the Son of man must suffer many things. . . ." Mark's text can be interpreted to mean that Jesus is speaking of a person *other than himself.* In clarifying this ambiguity, by substituting "he" for "the Son of man," Matthew no doubt reflects the universal belief of early Christianity that Jesus was and understood himself to be the Son of man.

91. *When Prophecy Fails,* p. 24.

92. This is the view of most contemporary critics; see, for example, H. CONZELMANN, *An Outline of the Theology of the New Testament* (New York: Harper & Row, 1969): "These [sayings about the suffering Son of man] are all *vaticinia ex eventu:* not prognoses for the further development of the situation, but dogmatic assertions" (p. 133).

93. For a thorough discussion of the manner in which Christians used the Old Testament to support their views, see B. LINDARS, *New Testament Apologetic* (Philadelphia: Westminster Press, 1961).

94. 1 Cor. 1:23.

95. *Death of Peregrinus* 13.

96. ORIGEN, *Against Celsus* 2.39f.

97. *First Apology* 53.2.

98. FESTINGER, *Theory,* p. 248.

99. See N. PERRIN, *Rediscovering the Teaching of Jesus* (New York: Harper & Row, 1967), for a discussion of the central issues and a survey of recent literature.

100. For the contrary view that Jesus' sayings about the kingdom were intensified eschatologically by his followers after his death see E. STAUFFER, "Agnostos Christos. Joh.ii.24 und die Eschatologie des vierten Evangeliums," in *The Background of the New Testament and Its Eschatology* (above, n. 81), pp. 281–99.

101. In the second edition of his important work on responses to the delay of the kingdom (*Das Problem der Parusieverzögerung in den synoptischen Evangelien und in der Apostelgeschichte* [Berlin: Alfred Töpelmann, 1960], pp. 220–26), E. Grässer responds to his critics' charge that his false premise (Jesus expected the kingdom immediately) leads inevitably to false conclusions (the delay created difficulties because Jesus' words were disconfirmed). By insisting on his interpretation of Jesus, however, he fails to see that the results of his study would remain valid for Christian believers even if his reconstruction of Jesus cannot be sustained.

102. Compare also 2 Clement 11:2 (usually dated between 100 and 150 c.e.), which cites the same (unidentified) passage from Scripture ("Wretched are the double-minded . . ."), but concludes on a different note: "If we have done what is right before God's eyes, we shall enter his kingdom. . . ."

103. The translation is from *The Library of Christian Classics,* vol. 1: *Early Christian Fathers,* ed. C. C. Richardson (Philadelphia: Westminster Press, 1953), p. 55.

104. Grässer notes four types of material in the synoptics that reflect concern about the delay: first, expressions of uncertainty about precise chronology (Mark 13:32); second, commands and parables urging constant alertness in view of this uncertainty (Mark 13:33; Luke 12:35, 36–38); third, prayers and petitions that the kingdom come (Matt. 6:9–15; cf. Rev. 22:17; 1 Cor. 16:22); and fourth, direct expressions of concern (Matt. 24:45–51; 25:14–30; Luke 20:9). In addition, he details a series of texts that represent more far-reaching attempts to resolve the concern: statements of outright consolation (Luke 18:7–8; Mark 9:1; 13:30; Matt. 10:23); the so-called parables of contrast (e.g., Mark 4:30–32); and finally, actual changes in the timetable (Mark 13:10).

105. This verse is the key to Albert Schweitzer's interpretation of Jesus' ministry. In *The Quest of the Historical Jesus,* he argues that Jesus was distressed when his words remained unfulfilled and thus turned toward Jerusalem in an effort to force God's hand (pp. 358–60). Thus Jesus himself becomes the first to express concern about the delay of the kingdom. Schweitzer's views were later taken up and expanded by M. Werner, *The Formation of Christian Dogma* (New York: Harper & Bros., 1957). Werner argues that the delay was the single most important force in shaping the development of Christian doctrine.

106. One outstanding example is the Gospel of Luke; see H. Conzelmann, *The Theology of St. Luke,* pp. 95–136.

107. See the comment of P. Berger, *Sacred Canopy,* p. 195, n. 30: "The similarity of the phenomena analyzed in the case study [*When Prophecy Fails*] with what New Testament scholars have called *Parousieverzögerung* is astonishing and highly instructive."

108. "Eschatology and Missions" (above, n. 81), p. 409.

109. *When Prophecy Fails,* p. 27.

110. *Ibid.,* p. 23.

111. *Journal of Abnormal and Social Psychology* 65 (1962), pp. 136–41. For a more general critique of dissonance theory see R. Brown, *Social Psychology,* p. 601–8. It should be noted that on one particular issue, our analysis has endeavored to meet Brown's criticism. He notes that investigators have rarely made an effort, at the beginning of their studies, to determine whether a specific combination of ideas, beliefs, or actions is in fact dissonant for their subjects (p. 597). Throughout this section I have argued that the texts reveal just this awareness of dissonance.

112. *Ibid.,* p. 139.

113. *Ibid.,* p. 140.

114. *Ibid.,* p. 140.

115. *Ibid.,* p. 136.

116. I am indebted to my colleague, Alan Segal, for calling this further application to my attention.

117. *Theory,* pp. 32–83.

118. *Ibid.,* p. 83.

119. *When Prophecy Fails,* p. 28.

120. See below, pp. 83–85.

121. *Jewish Sects at the Time of Jesus,* p. 78.

122. Both concerns dominate the massive, and still indispensable commentary of R. H. CHARLES, *A Critical and Exegetical Commentary on the Revelation of St. John* (Edinburgh: T. & T. Clark, 1920), 2 vols.

123. Boston: Beacon Press, 1963.

124. "The Revelation to John: Its Dramatic Structure and Message," *Interpretation* 9 (1955), pp. 436–53; see also his article, "Revelation, Book of," *The Interpreter's Dictionary of the Bible,* vol. 4 (1962), pp. 58–71.

125. New York: Harper & Row, 1969, p. 16.

126. Especially in his essay, "The Effectiveness of Symbols," *Structural Anthropology* (Garden City, N.Y.: Anchor Books, 1967), pp. 181–201.

127. *Myth and Reality* (New York: Harper & Row, 1963) in a chapter entitled "Time Can Be Overcome" (pp. 75–91).

128. It is usually dated under the reign of Domitian, around the years 90–95 C.E.

129. See W. H. C. FREND, *Martyrdom and Persecution in the Early Church. A Study of a Conflict from the Maccabees to Donatus* (Garden City, N.Y.: Anchor Books, 1967), pp. 155–72.

130. *The Pursuit of the Millennium* (above, n. 5), p. 309. It should be noted that this particular passage does not appear in Cohn's second edition (1961) published as a Harper Torchbook by Harper & Row.

131. See above, pp. 25, 28.

132. Note also that the seven angels with the seven baleful trumpets are introduced in 8:2, then disappear in 8:3–5 (vision of the heavenly altar), and do not commence blowing until 8:6!

133. "Effectiveness," pp. 196f.

134. On transference see FREUD, "The Dynamics of Transference (1912)," *Collected Papers,* ed. Joan Riviere, vol. 2 (New York: International Psycho-Analytical Press, 1959), pp. 312–22.

135. The role of repetition or redundancy is stressed by LÉVI-STRAUSS, "Effectiveness," pp. 188, 190, and 193f.; and by E. LEACH, *Genesis as Myth* (above, p. 15, n. 1) pp. 8–9.

136. So also LÉVI-STRAUSS, "Effectiveness," pp. 193f.

137. *Ibid.,* p. 193f. (emphasis added).

138. *Ibid.,* p. 197.

139. So, among others, O. CULLMANN, *Early Christian Worship* (London: SCM Press, 1953), p. 7.

140. A. SCHWEITZER, *The Mysticism of Paul the Apostle* (New York: Seabury Press, 1968), pp. 239–72. The eschatological character of the Lord's Supper in early Christian tradition is clearly visible in numerous texts: "Truly, I say to you, I shall not drink again of the fruit of the vine until that day when I drink it new in the kingdom of God" (Mark 14:25; cf. Matt. 26:29); and "For as often as you eat this bread and drink this cup, you proclaim the Lord's death until he comes" (1 Cor. 11:26).

3

The Quest for Legitimacy
and Consolidation

If this [charismatic authority] is not to remain a purely transitory phenomenon, but to take on the character of a permanent relationship . . . it is necessary for the character of charismatic authority to become radically changed.

M. WEBER
The Theory of Social and Economic Organization

No human society can have permanence in history without regulations. Hence, it is self-explanatory that regulations gradually developed in the primitive Christian congregations. . . . [But] what if these regulations become regulations of law enforced by compulsion; what if their execution becomes the concern of an office? Will they not then directly contradict the nature of the Ecclesia?

R. BULTMANN
Theology of the New Testament

Strictly speaking, Weber is correct when he states that "in its pure form charismatic authority may be said to exist only in the process of originating. It cannot remain stable, but becomes either traditionalized or rationalized. . . ." [1] Various manifestations of attenuated charisma may survive the period of transition from no rules to new rules, but *if a movement is to survive and flourish* it must reach a settled state of one kind or another.[2] The primitive expectation of the End must be modified and the energies associated with it must be channeled in different directions—martyrdom, asceticism, bureaucracy, antiheretical activities, etc. In this transition from one stage to the other lies the key to survival for any religious community. And if we accept as a fundamental law the transformation from no rules to new rules, we may not at the same time lament the routinization of the primitive enthusiasm that characterizes all charismatic or millenarian movements in their second generation and sometimes even earlier. If, as Bultmann observes, "the word of the Spirit-endowed, being an authoritative word, creates regulation and tradition," [3] then he lacks all historical justification for his further statement that legal regulation, whether regulative or constitutive, "contradicts the Church's nature." [4] Bultmann's "Ecclesia as the eschatological Congregation guided by the Spirit's sway" is a time-bound phenomenon and must give way, indeed it prepares the way for a religious institution with fixed norms of legitimacy. By failing to pursue the full consequences of his own observation about the inevitability of regulations, he and numerous others have simply given up consistent historical analysis. Consequently, a good deal of nonsense has been written about the decline of primitive Christianity into "early Catholicism." [5]

Ironically, those most responsible for these misjudgments have failed to perceive that by pursuing a different line in their treatment of institutional development, they could have avoided this false dilemma altogether. For the routinization of charisma, as described by Weber, does not necessarily entail its extinction. In the case of early Christianity, a considerable body of literature survived the period of charismatic beginnings and became a part of the Christian Scriptures. In subsequent centuries, these writings served as models for repeated attempts—of which Bultmann's must be seen as one example—to infuse new life into the institution by appealing to the memory of its enthusiastic origins. Thus the simplistic model of charismatic beginnings (action) followed by consolidation (reaction) must be complemented by two further stages: first, a secondary action, or reaction, which is normally based on an idealized image of the original action; and second, a regular repetition of the entire cycle. From this perspective, the drive toward the revitalization of a moribund church must be seen as part of a recurrent pattern in which the prior stage of consolidation is an indispensable prerequisite.

THE QUESTION OF LEGITIMACY

According to Weber, the question of legitimate succession arises inevitably with the disappearance of the original charismatic leader. In theory, the problem arises because the leader has rejected traditional criteria of authority, so that his departure creates more than just a personal vacuum. Various solutions of the dilemma are usually available, often in competition with one another. These include appeals to various sources of authority—revelation, heredity, prior selection by the leader, special offices, etc. In practice, the initial stages of consolidation are characterized by intense conflict between competing forms of legitimacy (e.g., revelation as opposed to heredity) as well as between divergent interpretations of the same form (e.g., whose revelation is authentic? who stands in the line of apostolic succession?).

In trying to sort out the confusing and often contradictory picture of the quest for legitimacy in early Christianity, we will take as our starting point Weber's method of pure-type analysis.[6] In so doing, however, we must avoid the common error of substituting these pure types for specific historical situations. We may better understand the transition from enthusiastic beginnings to later consolidation by treating them as separate stages, but in any particular movement they will overlap and intertwine. Although Weber's three types of legitimate authority (charismatic, traditional, and rational-legal [7]) may never appear as pristine types in the real world, they remain indispensable keys to understanding the very complexity of that world. Weber himself has often been accused of oversimplifying the task of history through his use of pure-types, despite his insistence that they were merely analytical tools. The misuse of this approach is far better illustrated by the debate at the turn of the century involving Rudolf Sohm.[8] Against the established view, Sohm argued that ecclesiastical law by its very nature was antithetical to the self-understanding of the primitive church and that the intrusion of legal regulations signaled its demise as a pneumatic movement. Weber was directly indebted to Sohm for his use of the term "charisma," but unlike Sohm he recognized that charismatic authority does not normally occur as a pure form in historical cases.[9] But even with this important qualification, Weber's definition of charisma still fails to do justice to its social character. As we have seen in an earlier discussion, charisma involves more than a distinctive type of personality.[10] To quote Worsley,

> followers do not follow simply because of some abstracted "mystical" quality: a leader is able to magnetize them because he evokes or plays upon some strand of intellectual or emotional predisposition, and because —more than this—he purports to offer the *realization* of certain values in action. . . . The charismatic leader, more than other kinds of ruler, whose leadership may repose on quite different bases—patronage, force, constitutional authority, traditional right to rule, etc.—is singularly dependent upon being accepted by his followers.[11]

Charisma, Office, and Tradition[12]

One unusual aspect of early Christianity is that its antinomian energies persisted for as long as they did. Or to put the matter somewhat more cautiously, the process of consolidation did not set in with full vigor until the second half of the first century, and even then it was actively resisted by a number of individuals and communities. In this sense, one might even say that there were two outbursts of pure charismatic authority—Jesus himself *and* some of the early converts on Gentile soil.

Among those who had known Jesus personally, some seem to have established rather structured communities shortly after his death. The earliest community—or perhaps it would be better to say communities? —in Jerusalem may well have taken this route.[13] For them, discipleship of Jesus, that is, proximity to him during his lifetime, clearly served as a basic norm of legitimacy. Some have even suggested that a form of authority through familial kinship might explain the rise to prominence, at least in the written sources, of James the brother of Jesus, who had apparently not been a follower of Jesus before the crucifixion.[14] In these cases, charisma has given way to a traditional conception of authority, whether determined by age or heredity. But alongside this, we know that there were other forms of legitimacy which were wholly independent of heredity, age, or personal contact with Jesus. The figure of Paul—no relative of Jesus and certainly no lifetime disciple—conforms most readily to the type of pure charismatic successor whose authority rests on a personal revelation from the founder. In his role as community organizer, Paul fits the common pattern of second-generation leaders, but in addition his activity parallels that of an original charismatic prophet—he proclaims, he exhorts, he creates, and is subject to no earthly authority.

But here the paucity of our knowledge about the first century immediately raises certain questions. Was Paul a unique figure in his time, resisting the emergence of authority based on and legitimated by traditional criteria? Or does he embody a combination of charismatic and traditional roles that was rather widespread in the first generation of believers?

In answering these questions much will depend on the terms that are chosen to define the issues. If, for instance, we assume an initial opposition between charisma and office, it will be apparent that neither Jesus nor Paul based his legitimacy on any recognized or official status. But at the same time, their charismatic roles stood firmly within a line of *tradition*. Indeed, their charisma lay precisely in an authoritative reevaluation of traditional beliefs and institutions. For this reason, pure charismatic authority is both a theoretical impossibility and an historical fiction. Our earlier discussion of Burridge has shown that the successful prophet is one who brings into being a transformation of the old order and a vision of the new.[15] In other words, the authority of Paul rests on charisma rather than office, but its immediate context is a sense of tradition, both the old tradition that he reinterprets and the new one that his reinterpretation creates. To repeat Bultmann's formulation, "the word of the Spirit-endowed, being an authoritative word, creates regulation and tradition." [16] From the outset, then, charisma and tradition worked together, certainly for Paul and the other apostles, and most likely for Jesus himself. Thus the tension in the early communities is between charisma and office, not between charisma and tradition, and it is within this polarity that we must locate the process of routinization and consolidation.

Here again Paul will serve as a convenient starting point. The absence of established officials in Pauline congregations has long been noted. Paul's letters are always addressed to the entire community and his admonitions are never mediated by church authorities. This is not to say that he treated everyone uniformly or that he did not recognize the need for a distribution of functions within the community. In 1 Cor. 12:4–11 he differentiates explicitly between varieties of gifts (*charismata*), and elsewhere in the same chapter he recognizes, at least implicitly, a hierarchy among these gifts:

> And God has appointed in the church first apostles, second prophets,
> third teachers, then workers of miracles, then healers, helpers,
> administrators, speakers in various kinds of tongues. . . . But
> earnestly desire the higher gifts (12:28–31).

And even if he had not ranked apostles first on his list, it would be obvious from his dealings with his own congregations that he stood over them as their founder, so that his authority was metaphorically like that of a father over his children. But at the same time, the primary recipient of the Spirit was the entire congregation, the charismatic community, and Paul's own status as an apostle rested neither on a permanent office nor on a unique possession of the Spirit. It was not legally inherited or transferrable, nor did it depend on objective credentials. In terms of its basic structure, then, we must classify his authority as charismatic, even though it differs, in his own view, from that of Jesus in one important respect. Paul's status as an apostle rested exclusively on his vision of the risen Lord—"Am I not an apostle? Have I not seen Jesus our Lord?" (1 Cor. 9:1). To this extent, his legitimacy was derived from the greater authority of Jesus. Still, and this bears repeating, neither depended on a legally defined or inheritable office.

Paul knew, of course, that there were other varieties of apostles. Among these, he appears to have treated personal followers of Jesus with special respect—his visits to Jerusalem and his collection for the Jerusalem community indicate this. But all were apostles only insofar as they had known the risen Jesus. Apart from this and apart from loyalty to the gospel that he had received at the beginning, Paul admitted no other criteria of legitimacy. This does not mean that other criteria of apostleship were not current at the time. In fact, he confronts competing views in several passages, the most notable of which is 2 Cor., chapters 10–12. Against those who argued that he possessed no skill as a public speaker (10:10), i.e., that he lacked "personal charisma," he responds initially by conceding the point; but later he treats it as of little import in comparison with his superior knowledge and understanding. To the further charge that he was not strong and boastful, again presumably taken by his antagonists as signs of authentic apostleship,[17] he replies reluctantly and with deep ambivalence that he could point to such signs: he, too, was a Hebrew, an Israelite, a descendant of Abraham; he, too, could boast, but only in his apostolic frailty; he, too, had experienced visions and performed the requisite signs, wonders, and mighty works. But all of this turbulent rhetoric, he says, is merely a momentary and unwilling concession to his opponents, designed to prove that he could have been an apostle even on their terms. Fundamentally, he rejects their criteria. Whatever the roots of his own view—a tradition that emphasized Jesus' suffering and death as the path to salvation, a sense of living between the times, or even the lingering effects of his earlier career as a rabid persecutor of Christians—if he is forced to boast, he will glory only in his weakness (2 Cor. 12:7–10).

Two important observations may now be advanced on the basis of Paul's disputes with his opponents. In the first place, apostles embodied the paramount source of religious authority in the early decades; and to be an apostle, however one defined the criteria, was not to occupy an office. Although Paul and his opponents were sharply divided over the question of criteria for determining legitimacy, they nonetheless shared a common view that apostolic authority was charismatic and pneumatic rather than institutional or legal. The risen Lord, not an ecclesiastical functionary, had conferred this status. And in the second place, we are now in a position to understand the impetus toward institutional patterns of authority that dominates Christian writings of the late first and early second centuries. In addition to the obvious factors of growing numbers, geographic expansion, the need for administrators of community resources, the decline of End-time enthusiasm, and the inevitable instinct to preserve the ideal and material interests of the community itself—in addition to these factors, the primitive notion of apostolic authority carried within it the germ of its own undoing and the seeds of subsequent controversy. As those who had experienced the visions that constituted the basis of their calling began to disappear from the scene, it became necessary to regularize the basis of apostolic authority. By definition, it could not continue in its primitive form. The basic outlines of this process are well known and need only be summarized here. The category of apostles, which had extended originally to a large group whose function was primarily missionary, was fused with the idea of "the Twelve," a group that in the beginning had nothing to do with missions; the new institution of the twelve apostles then became the channel, at least in "orthodox" circles, through which all authority was transmitted and legitimated;[18] at first, local communities, usually through a group of ruling elders ("presbyters"), traced their lineage to the "original" twelve apostles;[19] at a later time, the figure of the local bishop came to represent, symbolically and legally, the legitimate line of apostolic succession; finally, authority and power came to rest exclusively on those who occupied the office of bishop and whose status in no way depended on personal qualification or charisma.[20] As early as 96 C.E., this scheme is articulated in 1 Clement:

> The apostles received the gospel for us from the Lord Jesus Christ;
> Jesus, the Christ, was sent from God. Thus Christ is from God and the
> apostles from Christ. . . . They preached in country and city, and
> appointed their first converts after testing them by the Spirit, to be the
> bishops and deacons of future believers (42). . . . Now our apostles,
> thanks to our Lord Jesus Christ, knew that there was going to be strife
> over the title of bishop. It was for this reason that . . . they later added
> a codicil to the effect that, should these [bishops] die, other approved
> men should succeed to their ministry (44).[21]

While the general contours of this transformation are clear enough, we should not assume that it happened without resistance at various points along the way. The image of an uninterrupted decline into a purely sacramental cultus is distorted in two fundamental ways: first, by failing to recognize the necessity of the transformation; and second, by ignoring the countermovements that accompanied it from the first. Various forms of reaction and resistance begin to appear in the generation immediately following Paul and the other apostles. Indeed, 1 Clement itself is directed at turmoil in Corinth, where a group of younger members had overthrown the established leaders of the community.[22] Within the New Testament, 3 John portrays a situation in which the writer's authority, like that of Paul, is not limited to any single congregation. The writer mentions a certain Diotrophes, described by H. von Campenhausen as the local bishop, whose primary concern was to defend his prerogatives against the authority of the author and other itinerant prophets.[23] If this reconstruction of the circumstances is at all accurate, we cannot avoid the irony of a situation in which a canonical author finds himself in serious opposition to a form of church order, namely the local episcopate, which was shortly to become normative throughout the Christian world. A similar situation underlies the noncanonical *Didache,* which probably reflects conditions in western Syria during the early part of the second century. As in the Pauline congregations, legitimate authority there still rested with the full community, although bishops and deacons exercised leadership in specific areas; charismatic leadership was still provided by itinerant teachers, apostles, and prophets (11:1–3). Toward the end of the writing, the author urges the readers not to scorn their local officials (bishops and deacons),

> for their ministry to you is identical with that of the prophets and
> teachers. You must not, therefore, despise them, for along with the
> prophets and teachers they enjoy a place of honor among you. (15:1–2) [24]

Without making too much of this exhortation, it would seem to imply that the congregation accorded greater authority to wandering prophets and apostles than to local functionaries. The author himself, in contrast to the "villainous" Diotrophes of 3 John, in no way impugns the legitimacy of these prophets, but simply urges the congregation to assign equal status to sedentary, noncharismatic leaders. In other words, the transition from charismatic to traditional forms of authority, which took place gradually and with frequent opposition, paralleled the replacement of itinerant prophets by local figures. Symbolically, this is just as it should be, for charismatic figures regularly appear as outsiders whose very itineracy calls into question accepted forms of authority.

Two examples from a later time may be cited to illustrate the continuing character of countermovements to consolidation. The Montanist controversy during the latter half of the second century can only be understood against the background of ecclesiastical authority as it had developed by that time. Doctrinally, little or nothing separated Montanism from second-century Christianity in Asia Minor and other regions of the West. Rather, the reaction that it provoked stemmed from its "opposition to the tradition-bound conventionality of Church life." [25] What offended the opponents of Montanism was not its beliefs but its ecstatic prophecy. What lay behind this resurgence of prophecy was an implicit challenge to institutional prerogatives. And what rendered it even more dangerous was that it appeared not as a radical innovation but as a return to the charismatic enthusiasm of the earliest decades, inspired perhaps by the Revelation of John. Finally, we might also make mention of the rise of monasticism in the fourth century. This, too, makes sense only as a reactionary movement against what M. Hill terms "the gradual concentration of power in a distinctly priestly hierarchy and an increasing accommodation to the norms of the previously hostile surrounding society." [26] But this outburst of charismatic energy came about not merely as a response to the increasing secularization of the church and the termination of state persecutions; it was also an effort to recover the radical enthusiasm of Christian beginnings. And here again, the written Scriptures played an important role. For in his life of Saint Antony, Athanasius reports that the great monk first entered the ascetic life after reading the command of Jesus, "Sell what you possess and give it to the poor" (Matt. 19:21).[27]

The Canon and the Preservation of Charisma

Among recent Protestant historians, the process of routinization has often been seen as leading to a static condition in which pneumatic or charismatic activity no longer had any place. In favor of this view, one could point out that the very idea of routinized charisma raises serious problems. Some critics, notably Worsley, have charged Weber with inconsistency on the grounds that charisma is precisely that which cannot be routinized:

> strictly speaking, charisma cannot, by definition, become routinized. It can be transformed, but then becomes something else. What it does become is *tradition,* insofar as the movement, once it persists long enough to pass from the hands of those directly designated by the prophet as his successors, now refers to the tradition established by the original leader." [28]

Other critics have advanced the quite different view that Weber failed to realize the full implications of his own insight. Edward Shils, for instance, argues that charisma, far from being limited to the initial stages of enthusiastic movements, is a fundamental component of all institutions at every stage of their existence. An "unintense" operation of charisma, he asserts, is present in all forms of rational-legal authority.[29] Other difficulties apart, Shils's contention is interesting in that it could be used to demonstrate that the picture drawn by Bultmann and others, in which institutionalization is seen as identical with fossilization, is fundamentally inadequate because it is based on an unnecessarily rigid understanding of charisma. But Weber might well have agreed with Worsley against Shils that a lack of intensity is not a characteristic of true charisma.[30] What does emerge from the polar positions of Worsley and Shils is the fact that there remains an unresolved tension in Weber's own thinking between his assertion that "in its pure form charismatic authority may be said to exist only in the process of originating" and his notion of routinized charisma.

In an effort to find a middle way between the hard-line view of Weber as inconsistent and a softer interpretation that sees a form of charisma in the very idea of organization, M. Hill has recently proposed a model of institutional development that attempts to account for routinization as well as later reactions against it. The process of institutionalization, he contends, involves not only "the development of more formalized roles and ideological definitions"[31] but also the creation of a set of shared values and symbols, what Berger and Luckmann call a symbolic universe.[32] Once established, these symbols serve to solidify the group, to stabilize its organizational structures and to legitimize those in control. But these same symbols may also, under certain conditions, become powerful instruments of conflict and change within the group.[33] Individual subgroups may arise whose commitment to the basic values of the larger group is quite tenuous. More commonly, a discontented subgroup will assert that it accepts the symbols, while insisting that "they (as against those who are actually placed in positions of power) are the true repositories of basic values."[34] This is most likely to occur, according to Hill, in an institution that claims a "charismatic pedigree."[35] Now if, as was the case in early Christianity, these normative symbols include a body of writings that preserve and even idealize an image of the group's charismatic origins, these writings themselves may become a recurrent focus of change and conflict. They maintain *in latent form* a source of charismatic authority for those who arise to challenge ecclesiastical routine. As we have seen, the history of Christianity is replete with examples of such revitalization movements, whose motto is almost always, "Back to the pure beginnings!" And were it not for the written Scriptures, such claims would have no serious legitimacy. In this sense, the formation of the New Testament produced a two-edged sword. On the one hand, it was an inevitable part of the effort "to maintain . . . the boundaries of the system, and to maintain the legitimacy of its values, symbols and norms." [36] It narrowed the range and type of literature that could serve as the final court of appeal in disputes about beliefs and practices. On the other hand, it also illustrates the principle that "the possibility of conflict and potential change is always present, rooted in the very process of crystallization." [37]

The ambiguity of the canon did not pass entirely unnoticed in early Christianity, for the canon was never allowed to serve as the sole bastion of orthodoxy. Acceptable interpretations of Scripture had to withstand the further test of conformity with the creeds as promulgated by the defenders of apostolic doctrine, primarily the bishops and church councils. Tertullian shows an acute awareness of the problematic character of Scripture in his *The Prescription against Heretics*. Here he argues that the apostolic rule of faith (*regula fidei*) is the norm against which all scriptural exegesis must be measured (14). Thus he urges orthodox believers not to dispute with heretics on scriptural grounds, not only because heretics are such clever exegetes (15), but more fundamentally because heretics, by virtue of their departure from the *apostolic* rule of faith, have relinquished all rights to the *apostolic* Scriptures. As a representative of emergent orthodoxy, Tertullian had experienced at first hand the abiding uncertainty of scriptural authority. He correctly recognized that if the opponents of Valentinus had based their case entirely on biblical grounds there would have been no satisfactory outcome whatsoever. For it was such figures as Valentinus and his school who produced the first biblical commentaries and elevated biblical authority to the highest level. In effect, the "orthodox" solution increasingly took the form of subordinating Scripture to the rule of faith (creeds) and to ecclesiastical control (the bishops and church councils). As von Campenhausen puts it, "the effect of the fight against the gnosis [of Valentinus and other pneumatics] was to intensify conservative trends and . . . the authority of church officials," [38] whereas "enthusiastic promptings, raptures, and visions are. in general forced out on to the periphery of the Church and into heresy, until monasticism creates a new home for them." [39]

ORTHODOXY AND HERESY

The Classical View and Its Critics

"All heretics at first are believers; then later they swerve from the rule of faith." [40] Origen's affirmation of the temporal priority of orthodoxy over heresy, with its corollary that heresy is a deliberate distortion of the true faith, is everywhere assumed in the early church. In support of this position, an "orthodox" image of early Christian history was developed very early and has persisted until quite recently. Essentially, it holds that Jesus revealed his true teaching to the apostles, who then preached it throughout the world; to protect their teaching from perversion at the hands of heretics, whose activity was anticipated from the beginning, the apostles entrusted the gospel to officially designated leaders in every city and town, further authorizing them to appoint successors, and so on.[41] In order to account for the departure of heretics from the true faith, various explanations were put forward, and primary among them was the influence of Greek philosophy.[42] Tertullian is typical of antiheretical writers in his claim that all heresies were instigated by philosophy.[43]

In contrast to this classical view, it now appears that the various mechanisms used to defend the orthodox party, as well as the orthodox consensus itself, were the products rather than the causes of the struggle over heresy. Originally, various "heretical" groups sought to authenticate their views by a variety of techniques: allegorical interpretation of Scripture; appeal to secret oral traditions delivered by Jesus to selected disciples and transmitted by them in an unbroken line of succession; and, with Marcion, the additional argument that the original apostolic teachings, particularly of Paul, had been corrupted by Jewish Christians who had tampered with his writings. In retrospect, however, it turns out that none of these devices was peculiar to heretical groups. Indeed, there is considerable evidence to suggest that the idea of a continuous apostolic tradition was first conceived in Gnostic circles and only later taken over by their orthodox opponents.[44] What we see, then, is a broad consensus among contending groups that apostolicity constituted the final ground of legitimacy, but radical disagreement as to who possessed the authentic tradition (secret as opposed to written teachings) and how it was to be interpreted (pneumatic exegesis as opposed to conformity with the rule of faith).

As mentioned earlier, the classical view of orthodoxy has held sway, even among modern historians, until quite recently. Its most serious challenge has come from Walter Bauer, whose *Orthodoxy and Heresy in Earliest Christianity* first appeared in 1934.[45] In essence, Bauer stood the traditional view on its head. Orthodoxy, rather than being the only party which preserved the apostolic teaching in its pure form, was the only party to survive the power struggles of the first several centuries. And to buttress its claim to legitimacy, it propagated the myth of its lineal descent from the original apostles. Heresy, far from being a deviation from apostolic truth, in many cases represented the earliest and often the only form of Christianity in numerous regions—Syria (Edessa), Egypt, and Asia Minor among others. These indigenous expressions of primitive beliefs and practices *became* heresies only at a later time, when Roman Christianity was able to exert its authority in these areas and to establish itself as the norm of true belief. In other words, according to Bauer, orthodoxy is largely an anachronistic value judgment in which the views of the victorious party were projected retroactively into the previous history of the group. Or to use the somewhat different formulation of S. J. Case, written a decade before Bauer, "heresy was fundamentally a social phenomenon. . . . Differences of opinion, that were always present even in the most peaceful community, never resulted in heresies until rival social attitudes crystallized around specific centers of interest." [46] According to this interpretation, heretics are nothing other than the losers in a prolonged struggle for power. Indeed, from a purely descriptive point of view, heresy represents the judgment, supported by institutional sanctions, that a person or group differs unacceptably from the beliefs of the dominant party. And without these accompanying sanctions, conflict between religious groups amounts to little more than innocuous name-calling.

Needless to say, Bauer's thesis has sparked widely divergent reactions and continuing discussion.[47] Among supporters, his original proposals have been refined at various points,[48] and even one of his staunchest detractors, H. E. W. Turner, was forced to admit that "the very diversity and variety of the thought of the Church tells against the adequacy of the classical view." [49] Beyond this, one other insight seems to have been accepted by most, namely, that full-blown orthodoxy was the end product rather than the starting point of a complex process and that the very idea of orthodoxy was subject to continuing modification.[50] Turner remarks, for instance, that "doctrinal tendencies which had passed as orthodox at an earlier stage were superannuated in the light of later developments." [51] Thus even according to Turner's more "orthodox" analysis, orthodoxy differs from its own professed ideology in that it must regularly abandon older, more primitive beliefs. Heresy, on the other hand, at least in some instances, is heretical for just the opposite reason, i.e., for adhering to beliefs and practices of unquestioned antiquity. This form of "archaizing heresy" may well underlie the increasingly hostile stance of Christianity in the West to the various "Jewish Christian" communities in Syria and Palestine. Here the irony of the orthodox position is most manifest, for it seems likely that these "Jewish Christian" groups preserved traditions that stemmed from the earliest communities in Jerusalem.

Although it cannot be denied that Bauer's treatment of heresy has forced a fundamental reexamination of the issue, recent discussion has nonetheless continued to emphasize the role of orthodoxy as the legitimate heir of the primitive gospel. Turner insists that only the orthodox tradition has remained loyal to the "religious facts" of the early church;[52] Marcel Simon and André Benoit criticize Bauer's approach because it ignores the doctrinal aspect of the issue and fails to ask whether heresy was really heretical;[53] and Helmut Koester proposes to use what "historically happened, i.e., in the earthly Jesus of Nazareth" as the criterion for evaluating "the orthodox and heretical tendencies of each new historical situation." [54] Clearly, such statements can only obscure the basic historical task. In dealing with a religious movement like early Christianity, where we confront diversity and disharmony from the very first, any effort to single out one point of view as more authentic than others will necessarily compromise a thoroughly historical orientation.[55] Such an approach may be justified in an ecclesiastical or theological setting, but it will not find, nor should it seek, any historical justification. Here again, the confusion of historical and theological categories has muddied the waters and blunted the initial impact of Bauer's thesis. In his concluding comments to the English edition of *Orthodoxy and Heresy*, Robert Kraft has stated the dilemma in its most succinct terms:

> Despite all the talk, especially by Bauer's Bultmannian heirs, of the unity of the historical and theological tasks, there is a strictly historical legacy left by Bauer. . . . The theological aspect is unavoidably present, but it concerns the "theology" of the participants, not of the investigator. If one then wishes to make theological judgments from his modern perspective . . . or in some other way to join the theological to the historical approach, that is his business, but it is not an inevitable or necessary adjunct to the descriptive historical task.[56]

The Positive Functions of Heresy

One unfortunate consequence of the debate surrounding Bauer's work has been a tendency to regard the phenomenon of heresy as a detour that deflected the churches' energies from more important matters. But if we examine it in the broader context of social conflict and institutional development, we may learn to appreciate it in a rather different light. Quite apart from the commonsense assumption that some amount of conflict is inevitable in any form of social existence, it is now possible to argue that conflict serves a positive function in solidifying social groups and in shaping the complex symbolic and institutional apparatus needed to sustain them. Put in its strongest terms, this means that if the church had not encountered heretics, it would have created them. And if our initial hypothesis should prove valid, we will do well to consider the likelihood that the tension between orthodoxy and heresy greatly exaggerates the "real" distance that separates them.

Among those who have studied the question of social conflict, Lewis Coser, in *The Functions of Social Conflict,*[57] comes closest to our present concern. Coser has distilled a series of propositions from the work of the German sociologist Georg Simmel [58] and applied them to the role of conflict in social settings. In general, he contends that *"conflict is a form of socialization,"* that "groups *require* disharmony as well as harmony," and that "far from being necessarily dysfunctional, *a certain degree of conflict is an essential element in group formation* and the persistence of group life." [59] More specifically, several of his propositions bear directly on the question of orthodoxy and heresy in early Christianity. For practical purposes, Coser treats the two basic forms of conflict, in-group and out-group, as separate categories. Properly speaking, in-group conflict involves heretics, whereas out-group tension focuses on Jews and pagans. In terms of early Christian literature, each type produced a distinctive literary form—*Apologies,* writings *Against the Pagans* and *Against the Jews* in the one case; and treatises *Against the Heretics* in the other. But in terms of their functional significance, they serve essentially the same purposes and thus belong together.[60]

Conflict Serves a Group-Binding Function[61]   The general formulation of this proposition draws an analogy from developmental psychology in positing that the search for identity is often reached through a process of rebellion against one's immediate parentage. Inevitably, this task of self-definition involves conflict in one form or another. Externally, this conflict took the form of dialogues with and diatribes against the Jewish and pagan background of nascent Christianity. The polemical tone of these interchanges reflects the urgency that often accompanies the efforts of young, minority communities to establish their own identity in the context of a larger world. Internally, according to Simmel, conflict also serves to strengthen group cohesion by reinforcing the inevitable divisions within increasingly complex organizations[62] and by ventilating feelings of hostility associated with these divisions.[63]

One clear example of this phenomenon is the crisis brought about by the increasing number of intellectuals who became believers in the second and third centuries.[64] The tension between "enlightened" and simple believers reached its fullest expression with Valentinus and his followers, who divided all believers into two distinct and irreconcilable categories, the "spirituals" who understood the deeper mysteries of the faith and enjoyed a higher level of salvation, and the "psychics" or ordinary Christians who remained at a lower level. But the same tendency manifests itself in non-Gnostic circles as well. Clement of Alexandria, for instance, complains that ordinary Christians are like the companions of Odysseus who deal with the dangerous Sirens "by stopping their ears because they know what would happen if they listened to the lessons of the Greeks; it would be impossible for them to return home." [65] Although we hear little from ordinary believers, who constituted a large majority in the church, their views found a powerful spokesman in the person of Tertullian. The charge that heresy resulted from the influence of philosophy pervades his *The Prescription against Heretics,* and his famous question, "What has Athens to do with Jerusalem?," reflects the same point of view. Although Tertullian himself was a highly educated intellectual, he appears to have shared a popular suspicion of "higher culture." In part, of course, his statements reflect the familiar postconversion process of defining oneself by turning against one's previous commitments. But when philosophers became Christians, the conflict was no longer merely external. Thus the negative assessment of philosophy in much of the antiheretical literature can be seen as a ventilation of hostility by the lower-class majority against the new class of intellectuals. These feelings were rooted in social facts, and the expressions of hostility on both sides made it possible for each group to maintain a distinctive position without abandoning the group altogether.

One further result of the debate over the value of philosophy was the establishment of limits beyond which philosophical speculation would no longer be tolerated. In the case of the Gnostics, the majority finally determined that the Gnostic synthesis of faith and speculative philosophy had taken them beyond the church altogether. As for individual intellectuals of a more "orthodox" bent, e.g., Clement and Origen, their difficulties with institutional conventions are well known. In the main, they seem to have operated on the periphery. Of Clement, von Campenhausen remarks that "it is therefore certainly no accident that [he] shows no more than a superficial interest in the 'official' and 'sacramental' Church in general." [66] And it is surely not amiss to see in his attitude a reflection of the "official" church's view of him. Eventually, the task of formulating doctrine was taken completely out of the hands of individual Christian philosophers, where it had quite naturally fallen from the start, and was placed under ecclesiastical control. All of this, I would suggest, is motivated in part by a tension *within* the church between a "populist" majority and an intellectual minority. Here again Tertullian offers confirmation of the tension, by revealing certain inconsistencies in his own thinking. For all of his professed antagonism toward Athens and the Academy, he was quite willing to utilize rhetorical and philosophical arguments against his enemies and to scorn "simple believers" for their ignorance on important matters of doctrine. In short, Tertullian exemplifies both sides of the conflict, for while he treats speculative theology as a potentially dangerous enterprise and emphasizes the higher authority of ecclesiastical offices on the one hand, he also marshals his own sophistication against ordinary believers and church officials when he thinks them mistaken.[67]

Finally, it cannot be taken as completely coincidental that the polemical literature against heretics and pagans flourished precisely in the second and third centuries. These years mark the beginning and the end of Christianity's cultural identity crisis in the Greco-Roman world. Throughout most of the first century, Christian communities had defined themselves by total opposition to the "world." By the end of the third century, however, they had created their own "world" and were ready to assume the role that Constantine would soon impose upon them. In between, they had experienced the internal and external conflicts that regularly accompany the creation of social worlds.

Ideology Intensifies Conflict[68]   Essentially, this proposition states that conflict will reach its most intense level when it involves competing ideologies or, better yet, competing views of the same ideology. When this happens, more than personal power or prestige is at stake. It is a matter of one's entire universe. For our purposes, this proposition applies to three critical moments in the history of early Christianity: the conflict with Judaism over the claim to represent the true Israel; the conflict with paganism over the claim to possess true wisdom; and the conflict among Christian groups over the claim to embody the authentic faith of Jesus and the apostles. The intensity of these struggles was a function of two separate factors: first, the degree to which individuals had defined themselves as members of the group, so that any threat to the group immediately became a threat to every individual, this being especially true of movements that presuppose a conversion; and second, the role of intellectuals, for as Coser observes, "intellectuals have contributed to the deepening and intensification of struggles by stripping them of their personal motivations and transforming them into struggles over 'eternal truths.' "[69]

Obviously, this proposition makes sense only if we assume that ideologies are more than mere projections of personal or material interests. S. J. Case remarks that "the zeal with which heretics were attacked found its principal incentive in a desire to . . . preserve intact the membership of the Christian groups whose unity was being endangered by the propagandist minorities."[70] In a limited sense, this observation is correct, but antiheretical writers seem less concerned with losing particular individuals than with refuting their opponent's ideology. Thus the threat touched the group as a whole rather than isolated members. Why this should be true lies partly in the fundamental importance for all religious groups of their ideology or symbolic universe and partly in the tenuous character of all ideologies, especially during their formative stages. For the institution, a symbolic universe serves to "integrate different provinces of meaning and encompass the institutional order in a symbolic totality." [71] For the individual, it "puts everything in its right place." [72] Thus any challenge to a group's ideology or symbolic universe will be treated as a threat to the existence of the group itself. For this reason, we must take seriously the theological debates of the early church and resist the temptation to reduce them to mere expressions of social, political, or geographical provinciality.[73] At the same time, however, we should not make the equally serious mistake of supposing that everyone found these debates to be stimulating or even intelligible.

Our discussion of this proposition also puts us in a better position to appreciate another aspect of the early resistance to speculative theology. We have seen that social tensions explain a good deal of this resistance, but we may also suspect the presence of a half-conscious instinct toward institutional self-preservation. By this I mean simply that ideological debates are notoriously divisive. Thus if we are correct in suggesting that Gnosticism as represented by Valentinus and Basilides was a movement among intellectuals, and if Tertullian and others were correct in presenting Gnostic groups as endlessly fissiparous, we will be in a better position to understand the relatively minor role given to intellectuals as expressing an instinctive desire to preserve the churches from internal dissensions at a time when they could least afford them.

The Closer the Relationship, the More Intense the Conflict[74] This proposition suggests a further source of anxiety about one's enemies, particularly those from within. The fact that the tension between Jews and Christians was most severe during the first century can be accounted for by acknowledging that resemblances between them were most pronounced during that time. Not only Roman officials, but many followers of Jesus were uncertain about what distinguished Jews from Christians. Thus it should cause no great surprise that one eventual resolution of this uncertainty was to relegate those who stood closest to Judaism, i.e., the various "Jewish Christian" sects, to the status of heretics. But on the particular issue of the parental relationship between Judaism and Christianity, there could be no permanent solution by the very nature of the case. Herein lay a potent source for the continuing conflict between the two groups in subsequent centuries. By the end of the first century, most Christian communities, at least outside of Syria and Palestine, were predominantly Gentile in their ethnic makeup and had no immediate sense of continuity with the Jewish people. This alone must have contributed to lessening the tensions that had characterized the early decades. Yet the underlying issue was kept alive through the formation of the New Testament, which not only preserved accounts of earlier hostilities but also perpetuated the consciousness of the church as the new Israel. To the degree that this memory of the church's origins remained alive, to the same degree the continued existence of the "old Israel" meant that the question of the church's legitimacy could never be permanently settled and that conflict was never far from the surface.

Turning from external to internal matters, the proposition also illumines the intense antagonism between emergent orthodoxy and Gnostic groups in the second and early third centuries. If we listened only to "orthodox" spokesmen, we might well conclude that an enormous gulf separated the two parties. In fact, however, quite the opposite is true. On this point, there has been a striking unanimity among modern scholars. In *Gnosticism and Early Christianity,* R. M. Grant stresses the point that Valentinus and Marcion were deeply disturbing precisely "because their systems were so closely related to Christianity, not because they were philosophical theologians." [75] And he adds that "it is an interesting question whether the teaching of the Gospels and the Epistles is more adequately interpreted by these Gnostic teachers or by such second-century 'orthodox' teachers as the apologists and Irenaeus." [76] Similarly, even Turner, who adamantly defends the historical continuity of triumphant orthodoxy with the faith of the primitive church, speaks of a penumbra between orthodoxy and heresy in the second century.[77] During this period, and especially in certain geographical areas, it was extremely difficult to draw clear lines between the two.

Finally, this proposition explains why the greatest amount of energy in the first few centuries was directed not at pagans but at heretics. In Coser's words, heresy "signifies and symbolizes a desertion of those standards of the group considered vital to its well-being, if not to its actual existence." [78] For this reason, it was never sufficient merely to refute the views of the heretics, because it was their very presence as professed believers that posed the greatest threat. Thus heresy had to be accounted for within a broad ideological framework.[79] This was accomplished in the first instance, as we can see from Tertullian's *Prescription,* by noting that heresy had been predicted by the Scriptures themselves (Matt. 7:15; 1 Tim. 4:13; etc.), but more importantly by the argument that heresy served the *positive function* of testing and purifying the true faith:

> We ought not to be astonished at the heresies which abound nor should
> their existence surprise us, for it was foretold that they would occur. . . .
> Their final purpose is, by affording a trial of faith, to give it the
> opportunity of being approved. (1.1)

And in the process, he appeals to the authority of Paul:

> for there must be factions among you in order that those who are
> genuine among you may be recognized. (1 Cor. 11:19)

In other words, a classic example of turning a vice into a virtue by accounting for it within one's own universe.

Conflict Serves to Define and Strengthen Group Structures[80]   At this point in our discussion we need to guard against exaggerating the positive functions of conflict. The controversies over Gnosticism were clearly dysfunctional in a twofold sense: first, in that the exclusion of Gnostic communities led to a momentary diminution of the total Christian population; and, second, from the point of view of Gnostics themselves, in that their exclusion brought about their eventual disappearance. And in other, less tangible ways, the victory of orthodoxy was bought at a price.[81] Still, because it is the positive contribution that historians have most neglected, we have emphasized the role of conflict in strengthening the organizational and ideological structure of the surviving party.

Here the example of Marcion is most instructive, for his decisive stand on numerous issues forced his "orthodox" opponents, by reaction, to adopt certain positions that they might otherwise not have chosen. By his rejection of the Old Testament, he gave impetus to the creation of a twofold Christian canon (Old *and* New Testaments).[82] By his drastic reduction of authoritative Christian writings to Luke and the letters of Paul, he prompted an inclusive attitude toward the scope of the New Testament. By his radical Paulinism, he encouraged the production of a pseudo-Pauline literature (1–2 Timothy, Titus) in which a "domesticated" [83] Paul regularly defends the concerns of orthodox Christianity.[84] On matters of doctrine, Marcion's relegation of the creator god to an inferior status led to a counteremphasis on the unity of creation and salvation in later theological formulations, and his docetic Christology contributed to an insistence on the reality of Jesus' birth and death in "orthodox" circles. In all of this I do not mean to imply that Marcion by himself was responsible for the shape of normative Christian theology, but that the controversy surrounding him illustrates the general principle in group formation that "the symbolic universe is not only legitimated but also modified by the conceptual machineries constructed to ward off the challenge of heretical groups within a society." [85]

Finally, we need to examine some of the ways in which external conflicts function to enhance a group's self-image and hence to strengthen its internal cohesion. We have earlier proposed that the written apologies of the second and third centuries were part of the process of drawing boundaries between the group and the outside world. At first, these boundaries were rather narrow and inflexible, but with time and an increased sense of the churches' identity, they became more fluid, much too fluid for some members. In dealing with these apologies, however, it has often been noted that they seem to have had little effect on those to whom they were addressed, i.e., various Roman emperors and governors. Pagan writers rarely show any knowledge of them,[86] and they certainly failed in their explicit goal of putting an end to persecution. One explanation for this apparent failure is to assume that they were never really intended for outsiders at all. V. Tcherikover has proposed such an interpretation for Jewish apologetic literature,[87] and there is no reason why it should not apply to Christian apologies as well. Tcherikover argues that the panegyric apologetics of pre-Roman times, extolling the wisdom of the Jews and the virtues of their law, was the product of "an inner need so characteristic of educated Jewish circles in Egypt . . . [who] found it easier to cling to Judaism as long as they knew that Judaism stood on an equal level with Hellenism." [88] It was thus an effort by those who understood themselves to be both Jews *and* Hellenes to counter the common charge that Judaism was directly inimical to Hellenistic civilization. At a later time, when confronted with a more aggressive anti-Semitism, Tcherikover contends that "the Jews found an everlasting source of consolation in the idea that their Law was pure and perfect" and in the conviction that a deep gulf separated "the pure doctrine of Moses and the pagan cults." [89] Inasmuch as Christianity in the early centuries found itself in exactly the same situation, it is not surprising to discover the same motifs in Christian apologetic literature: a rejection of pagan cults, together with an affirmation that the new faith offered the fulfillment of pagan philosophy.

In order to understand this position, however, we need to assume a deep-seated ambivalence on the part of the apologists toward pagan culture. As converts from cultivated backgrounds, they could deal with their ambivalence in one of two ways—either by scorning their pagan heritage, as Tertullian and others who equated heresy with philosophy sought to do, or by presenting their new religion as the perfection of what the pagan world had never fully comprehended. Beyond this, both of these responses served to reinforce internal cohesion, though in a less obvious manner. Whether or not the apologists persuaded pagan critics to revise their view of Christians as illiterate fools, they succeeded in projecting for the group as a whole a favorable image of itself as the embodiment of true wisdom and piety. The significance of this favorable image lies in the observation that there is a close connection between the internal cohesion of minority groups and their self-image. One formulation of this correlation is that "if the group is represented as having a high status, cohesion between the members becomes more closely knit. It begins to wane in a group which is accorded inferior status." [90] In light of the repeated charge by pagan critics that Christians occupied the lowest possible social and educational status in Roman society, we can now appreciate the purely social consequences of the counterassertion that Christians, and they alone, were truly wise. Whatever we may say about the expressed purpose of these apologies, their latent function was not so much to change the pagan image of Christians as to prevent that image from being internalized by Christians themselves. In this respect, it mattered little whether one scorned philosophy with Tertullian or embraced it with Justin. Both points of view terminated in a self-image of believers as the sole "lovers of wisdom" and thus contributed to strengthening their internal cohesion.

Conclusions

Our analysis of the quest for legitimacy and consolidation in the early church has suggested that some recent interpreters, by stressing the content rather than the form of institutional and theological development, have been misled by their own institutional and theological preoccupations. In particular, issues that have traditionally been treated as unrelated now appear as aspects of a single process: charismatic authority and the rise of institutional structures are complementary not antithetical movements; the struggle with heretics and the diatribes against pagans are but two aspects of the quest of identity. Each of these represents an indispensable phase in the birth and growth of any successful religious movement. As concerns what Weber called the routinization of charisma, the issue is not whether—again if the movement is to survive and flourish —pneumatic authority will give way to a rational-legal or a traditional conception of legitimate authority, but whether the institution will allow sufficient flexibility for periodic self-renewal by those who appeal to the movement's own charismatic pedigree. It is quite normal for new religious movements to show great rigidity in their formative stages. Typical of this stage is Ignatius' boast that "the greatness of Christianity lies in its being hated by the world, not in its being convincing to it" (Rom. 3:3).[91] In part, this is a defense against uncertainties within the group about its own standing and self-confidence. But there is also reason to believe that the response to diversity within is also a function of mutual relations with the outside world. Coser suggests that intolerance toward outsiders will produce a similar attitude toward internal dissension and that a more relaxed view of outsiders will be accompanied by greater internal tolerance.[92] The difference between the harsh treatment of Montanism in the second century and the more lenient approach to monasticism in the fourth no doubt mirrors the fact that Christianity was no longer under severe external constraint in the later period. It might also be interesting to ask whether the reaction to Marcion and Valentinus would have been appreciably different had they advanced their views in more settled times. In brief, the process of institutionalization is inseparable from the conflict between orthodoxy and heresy. The intensity of these struggles, as we have discovered, is very far from being an accurate measure of the "real" distance between the antagonists. Here we must emphasize, even more than Berger and Luckmann, the extent to which old symbols are transformed and new ones created as a result. The New Testament itself and a good deal of Christian doctrine owe their present form, and in some cases perhaps even their existence, to precisely these circumstances.

Inevitably these considerations raise the question of "good faith." If it is true that hatred of one's enemies is a powerful source of internal cohesion, can we be certain that movements do not in some sense create their own enemies as the need arises? The phenomenon of scapegoatism is familiar enough in the history of religious and political groups to suggest that it might also be present here. In terms of Christianity's early experience, the most obvious example of scapegoatism is the Roman accusation that the Christians, by their refusal to honor the traditional gods, were responsible for whatever ills befell the empire. On the Christian side, one is tempted to treat the opposition to pagan philosophy in similar fashion, inasmuch as Tertullian and others resort to philosophical arguments precisely when they attack heretics for consorting with philosophy. The same might be said of the opposition between the early church and Judaism. The intensity of this opposition as witnessed by Christian literature, e.g., the implacable hostility of Jewish leaders to Jesus in the Gospels, unquestionably distorts the "real" situation. If we could envisage the encounter from a Jewish perspective or as "neutral" outsiders, the conflict would no doubt appear less voluble. This is not to say that such enemies are created *ex nihilo*, but that the exaggeration of hostility, whether conscious or not, serves both to sharpen the group's identity and to strengthen its internal cohesion. At the very least, we may be certain that ideological struggles between kindred communities ought never be taken at face value and that such struggles play a role in the formation of ideological and institutional structures of which the participants themselves are but faintly aware.

NOTES

1. *The Theory of Social and Economic Organization* (New York: Free Press, 1964), p. 364; the passage occurs in a section that deals with the routinization of charisma.

2. In her essay, "Social Preconditions of Enthusiasm and Heterodoxy" (above, p. 18 n. 45), MARY DOUGLAS notes one important limitation to the scope of this "law." "The historical approach is misleading if it seems to imply that the stage of religious effervescence will always fizzle out whether or not it becomes a preliminary step to sectarian organization. For it can be sustained indefinitely. *Its only requirement is that the level of social organization be sufficiently low*" (p. 74; emphasis added). Thus the disappearance of enthusiastic behavior is not inevitable; but one must choose, as it were, between enthusiasm and growth.

3. *Theology of the New Testament*, 2 vols (New York: Charles Scribner's Sons, 1951), 2:98.

4. *Ibid.*, p. 97.

5. Compare the comments of H. CONZELMANN, *Outline*, pp. xvi and 289f.

6. For a recent discussion of Weber's pure-type analysis and of its value in historical research, see M. HILL, *A Sociology of Religion* (London: Heinemann Educational Books, 1973), pp. 147–51.

7. Discussed by WEBER in *Social and Economic Organization*, pp. 324–92.

8. SOHM expressed his views in his *Kirchenrecht*, vol. 1 (Munich: Von Duncker & Humblot, 1892). For further discussions, see A. HARNACK, *The Constitution and Law of the Early Church* (New York: G. P. Putnam's Sons, 1910); E. SCHWEIZER, *Church Order in the New Testament* (London: SCM Press, 1959); and CONZELMANN, *Outline*, pp. 41–46, 303–7.

9. See his remarks in *Social and Economic Organization*, pp. 328f.

10. See the discussion above, pp. 27f.

11. WORSLEY, *Trumpet Shall Sound*, pp. xii–xiii.

12. On this topic as a whole, see the important essay of J. SCHUTZ, "Charisma and Social Reality in Primitive Christianity," *Journal of Religion* 54 (1974), pp. 51–70.

13. See HARNACK, *Constitution and Law*, pp. 20–30; and H. VON CAMPENHAUSEN, *Ecclesiastical Authority*, pp. 70, 76–78.

14. On this subject see VON CAMPENHAUSEN's essay "The Authority of Jesus' Relatives in the Early Church," in *Jerusalem and Rome* (Philadelphia: Fortress Press, 1966).

15. See above, p. 32.

16. *Theology of the New Testament*, 2:98.

17. See in particular D. GEORGI, *Die Gegner des Paulus*, who stresses the point that Paul's apostolic opponents in 2 Corinthians represented a broad movement among the early missionaries, perhaps even a majority (p. 218).

18. On the origins of the idea of the "12 apostles," see VON CAMPENHAUSEN, *Ecclesiastical Authority*, pp. 14–19, and CONZELMANN, *Outline*, pp. 291f.

19. This method is clearly visible in Matt. 16:17–19 where Jesus is portrayed as bestowing great authority on Peter. This passage was no doubt used, perhaps even produced, by a community that traced its lineage to Peter.

20. This is particularly evident in the pastoral Epistles and the letters of Ignatius, all of which were written early in the second century.

21. The translation is from *Early Christian Fathers*, pp. 62–64.

22. On the controversy that prompted the letter, see VON CAMPENHAUSEN, *Ecclesiastical Authority*, pp. 84–95.

23. *Ecclesiastical Authority*, pp. 121–23.

24. The translation is from *Early Christian Fathers,* p. 178.
25. Von Campenhausen, *Ecclesiastical Authority,* p. 181.
26. *Sociology of Religion,* p. 143.
27. Athanasius, *Life of Saint Antony* 2.
28. *Trumpet Shall Sound,* p. xlix (Worsley's emphasis).
29. "Charisma, Order, and Status," *American Sociological Review* 30 (1965), pp. 199–213; a similar view is articulated by A. Etzioni, *A Comparative Analysis of Complex Organizations* (New York: Free Press, 1961), pp. 201–62 ("Compliance and Charisma").
30. *Trumpet Shall Sound,* pp. xlviiif.
31. *Sociology of Religion,* p. 172.
32. *Social Construction of Reality,* p. 92.
33. So S. N. Eisenstadt in his introduction to *Max Weber: On Charisma and Institution Building* (Chicago: University of Chicago Press, 1968), p. xliv.
34. Hill, *Sociology of Religion,* p. 142.
35. *Ibid.,* p. 172.
36. Eisenstadt, *On Charisma,* p. xliv.
37. *Ibid.,* p. xlv.
38. *Ecclesiastical Authority,* p. 186.
39. *Ibid.,* p. 191.
40. Origen, *Commentary on the Song of Songs* 3 (to 2.2).
41. Different variants of this scheme appear in 1 Clement 42; Tertullian, *Prescription* 20; and Eusebius, *Ecclesiastical History* 4.22.2–3 (quoting Hegesippus).
42. See the discussion in H. E. W. Turner, *The Pattern of Christian Truth. A Study in the Relations between Orthodoxy and Heresy in the Early Church* (London: Mowbray, 1954), pp. 7f., 216–31. We may also note that a similar evaluation of the influence of Greek philosophy on early Christian thought appears in several modern authors, e.g., A. Harnack, M. Werner, R. Bultmann, and P. Tillich.
43. *Prescription* 7.
44. The evidence is assembled and discussed by von Campenhausen, *Ecclesiastical Authority,* pp. 157–63.
45. The original German version, *Rechtgläubigkeit und Ketzerei im ältesten Christentum* (Tübingen: J. C. B. Mohr, 1934), was reprinted with an appendix by Georg Strecker in 1964; the English translation, produced by members of the Philadelphia Seminar on Christian Origins, appeared in 1971 (Philadelphia: Fortress Press).
46. *Social Origins of Christianity,* p. 199.
47. See in particular Strecker's second appendix, "The Reception of the Book," revised by R. A. Kraft, in *Orthodoxy and Heresy,* pp. 286–316.
48. See in particular H. Koester, "GNOMAI DIAPHOROI: The Origin and Nature of Diversification in the History of Early Christianity," in *Trajectories through Early Christianity* (above, p. 16, n. 25), pp. 114–57.
49. *Pattern,* p. 12.
50. *Ibid.*

51. *Ibid.*, p. 14.
52. *Ibid.*, pp. 26–35.
53. *Le judaisme et le christianisme antique* (Paris: Presses Universitaires de France, 1968), pp. 301–7.
54. "GNOMAI DIAPHOROI," p. 117.
55. See the comments of Strecker in BAUER, *Orthodoxy and Heresy*, p. 271, n. 83.
56. BAUER, *Orthodoxy and Heresy*, pp. 312f.
57. New York: Free Press, 1956.
58. The propositions are extracted from SIMMEL's *Conflict* (Glencoe, Ill.: Free Press, 1955).
59. *Functions*, p. 31 (emphasis added).
60. At least one ancient writer, Hippolytus, saw the issue in the same way. In his *Refutation of All Heresies* (c. 225 C.E.), he remarks that his work can serve not only to refute heresy but to enlighten pagans: "they [pagans] . . . will not despise our industry and condemn Christians as fools when they discern the opinions which they themselves have stupidly believed" (4.45).
61. COSER, *Functions*, p. 33.
62. Such divisions of labor had arisen as early as the time of Paul; in 1 Cor. 12:28 he lists the following functions: apostles, prophets, teachers, workers of miracles, healers, helpers, administrators, and speakers in various kinds of tongues.
63. Paul deals openly with such tensions at several points (e.g., 1 Cor. 12:31; 14:1–40) in an effort to prevent them from becoming too serious.
64. See the discussion in WEBER, *Sociology of Religion*, pp. 73f., and TURNER, *Pattern*, pp. 391–95.
65. *Stromata* 6.11.89.
66. *Ecclesiastical Authority*, p. 211.
67. See also R. M. GRANTS's comment in *Gnosticism and Early Christianity* (New York: Harper & Row, 1966), that the antiheretical writers regularly utilized circular reasoning in that "they appealed, at times, to Greek philosophy, especially Middle Platonism, in order to gain further support for their claims" (p. 141). Their claim, it will be recalled, was that heresy stemmed from the influence of Greek philosophy.
68. COSER, *Functions*, p. 111.
69. *Ibid.*, p. 116.
70. *Social Origins of Christianity*, p. 199.
71. *Social Construction of Reality*, p. 95.
72. *Ibid.*, p. 98.
73. So also A. H. M. JONES, *Were Ancient Heresies Disguised Social Movements?* (Philadelphia: Fortress Press, 1966).
74. COSER, *Functions*, p. 67.
75. P. 141.
76. *Ibid.*, p. 149.
77. *Pattern*, pp. 81–94.
78. *Functions*, p. 69.

79. BERGER and LUCKMANN describe this process as "nihilation" (*Social Construction of Reality*, pp. 114–16).

80. COSER, *Functions*, p. 72.

81. So GRANT, *Gnosticism and Early Christianity*, p. 199.

82. On Marcion's role in the formation of the Christian canon see VON CAMPENHAUSEN, *The Formation of the Christian Bible* (Philadelphia: Fortress Press, 1972), pp. 147–67.

83. So M. F. WILES, *The Divine Apostle: The Interpretation of St. Paul's Epistles in the Early Church* (Cambridge: The University Press, 1967), p. 139.

84. S. J. Case explains the relatively minor role played by Paul in the second and third centuries as due, in part, to the fact that "there was so little in Paul's work that lent itself to the service of Christianity in the hour of its need for social consolidation, and for the gradual upbuilding of a social structure" (*Social Origins of Christianity*, p. 164). For an interpretation of the pastoral Epistles as an attempt to reclaim Paul from the "heretics" see VON CAMPENHAUSEN, *Formation*, p. 181.

85. BERGER and LUCKMANN, *Social Construction of Reality*, p. 107; cf. also GRANT, *Gnosticism and Early Christianity*, pp. 198–200.

86. The one possible exception is the pagan polemicist Celsus, who may have known the works of Justin Martyr; see H. CHADWICK, *Early Christian Thought and the Classical Tradition* (New York: Oxford University Press, 1966), p. 22.

87. "Jewish Apologetic Literature Reconsidered," *Eos* 48 (1956), pp. 169–93.

88. Tcherikover, p. 180.

89. *Ibid.*, p. 181.

90. H. CARRIER, *The Sociology of Religious Belonging* (London: Darton, Longman and Todd, 1965), pp. 209f.

91. The translation is from *Early Christian Fathers*, p. 104.

92. *Functions*, p. 95.

4

Religion and Society
in the Early Roman Empire[1]

I believe that from the standpoint of strict interpretation, we are infinitely enriched when we attempt to understand the biblical sentence, "The last shall be first," as the psychic expression of the revolt of oppressed strata. . . . It is not irrelevant for an understanding of it to know that the phrase was not uttered by anybody in general and was not addressed to men in general, but rather that it has a real appeal only for those who, like the Christians, are in some manner oppressed and who, at the same time, under the impulse of resentment, wish to free themselves from prevailing injustices.

KARL MANNHEIM
Ideology and Utopia

Sometime in the 50s of the first century C.E., Paul addressed a series of letters to the Christian community in Corinth. In one of them he inadvertently provided a glimpse at the social constituency of earliest Christianity: "Not many of you were wise according to worldly standards," he says, "not many were powerful, not many of noble birth; but God chose what is foolish in the world . . . what is weak in the world . . . what is low and despised in the world" (1 Cor. 1:26–28). More than a century later the Christian apologist Minucius Felix replies to his pagan interlocutor: "That many of us are called poor is not our disgrace, but our glory" (*Octavius* 36). Roughly contemporary with Minucius was the pagan polemicist Celsus who characterized Christians as follows: "Their injunctions are like this. 'Let no one educated, no one wise, no one sensible draw near. For these abilities are thought by us to be evils.' By the fact that they themselves admit that these people are worthy of their God, they show that they want and are able to convince only the foolish, dishonorable, and stupid, and only slaves, women and little children" (Origen, *Against Celsus* 3.44).[2]

Even granting the exaggerated tone of Celsus' remarks and recognizing that Paul's statement implies that there were at least some Christians of wisdom, power, and noble birth, their comments point to a general conclusion concerning the social makeup of early Christianity: Christian communities of the first several centuries derived their adherents from the disinherited of the Roman Empire—slaves, freedmen, freeborn Roman citizens of low rank, and non-Romans (*peregrini*) of various nationalities. If true, this conclusion raises certain interesting questions. Was Roman society in the early Empire structured along readily identifiable class lines?[3] Was class status or affiliation a decisive factor in determining one's religious beliefs, activities, and associations? Was there any correlation between the religious character of early Christianity, its social constituency, and the attitude of "proper" Romans to it? And finally, what changes took place in the character of the Christian religion and/or in its social constituency and/or in the social structure of the Empire itself such that the Roman middle and upper classes eventually abandoned their resistance and embraced Christianity?

These questions raise once again a recurrent theme in our treatment of the social world of early Christianity, i.e., the correlation between religion and social class or status. M. Weber in particular argued the fairly straightforward view that class and status are important factors in shaping the religious propensities of any social group.[4] Obvious as it is, however, I. M. Lewis has found it necessary to reemphasize its importance in dealing with the case of religious ecstasy:

> Few of the more substantial works in this area of comparative religion pause to consider how the production of religious ecstasy might relate to the social circumstances of those who produce it; how enthusiasm might wax and wane in different social conditions; or what functions might flow from it in contrasting types of society.[5]

In terms of our present concern with the social constituency of early Christianity, this fundamental principle means that the tendency toward alienation from the established order of society, and thus toward new religious movements, will not be distributed evenly throughout any social system. As Burridge puts it, the one precondition of all regeneration movements is dissatisfaction with the current system, or "feeling oppressed." [6]

While it is undeniably true that millenarian or prophetic movements appeal primarily to the disprivileged, we need to avoid the unwarranted assumption that the condition of alienation, deprivation, or dispossession correlates exclusively with a narrow conception of social class, i.e., with the lowest socioeconomic strata. Dissatisfaction or deprivation may occur in several forms: certain social statuses (e.g., women and the aged) that cut across social classes;[7] a tribe or nation whose values are called into question by the presence of powerful foreign rulers; inhabitants of certain peripheral regions (e.g., Gailee) or provinces (e.g., the Eastern provinces of the Roman Empire) who feel themselves alienated from the centers of power; and most commonly, the lower-middle and middle classes in large urban settings.[8] By themselves, however, these conditions do not necessarily result in alienation from the established order. In addition, as Burridge[9] and Mary Douglas[10] have pointed out, there must be a weakening of the relevant social group and of its beliefs. Thus it is important to keep in mind that the category of disprivileged persons may well include individuals who are neither poor nor ignorant, e.g., intellectuals. This broader conception of deprivation, which we have called *relative deprivation,*[11] has a double advantage. It avoids reducing the explanation of new religious movements to a single factor, such as economics or politics, and it destroys the romantic image of early Christians as nothing but a collection of country yokels and impoverished slaves. At the same time, it puts us in a position to reconcile the view that Christianity was a religion of the disprivileged with Pliny's comment that the churches had attracted persons *"of every social rank."* [12] For according to our definition of what it means to be "disprivileged," Pliny's statement is entirely consistent with the view that Christianity was in fact a community of the dispossessed.

Finally, the correlation between religious and social factors should enable us to make certain general predictions about the development of religious communities whose social constituency is subject to constant change. As the social makeup changes, we would quite naturally expect concomitant changes of religious belief and practice. As the social constituency becomes increasingly diversified, the social world of the movement will move toward greater complexity. And as the various subgroups within the movement seek to legitimate their views by appealing to a common set of religious symbols or sacred writings, the issue of correct and acceptable interpretations must inevitably arise.

Unfortunately, this sort of approach has been quite rare among students of the early church. One result is that the initiative has often come from those whose interests have sometimes been less than purely historical. In a fascinating essay published in 1895, Friedrich Engels likened primitive Christianity to the modern proletariat. "The history of early Christianity," he said, "has notable points of resemblance with the modern working-class movement. Like the latter, Christianity was originally a movement of oppressed people: it first appeared as the religion of slaves and emancipated slaves, of poor people deprived of all rights, of peoples subjugated or dispersed by Rome." [13] Subsequent reactions to this Marxist view have been varied and often violent. Max Weber rejected the economic factor as of little significance and attempted instead to view the early churches in their relation to the social structure of the Empire. Ernst Troeltsch carried the reaction even further by claiming that the rise of Christianity was "a religious and not a social phenomenon" [14] and that the early communities "had very little to do with the most important socio-political events of the Imperial period." [15] It is only in recent years, and primarily among such classicists as A. D. Nock,[16] A. H. M. Jones,[17] and E. R. Dodds,[18] that the social constituency of early Christianity has again come into focus.[19] Among this limited circle, something approaching a consensus has emerged on two aspects of the social question: first, that for more than two hundred years Christianity was essentially a movement among disprivileged groups in the Empire; and second, that its appeal among these groups depended on social as much as ideological considerations.

THE ROMAN SOCIAL ORDER

Before proceeding to specific matters, we must say a word about the general question of social classes in Roman society. Unlike contemporary American society, where sociologists often disagree on whether clearly defined social classes exist at all, Roman society of the early empire presents a different picture.[20] In the period under discussion, from the last decades of the Republic through the end of the second century c.e., Roman society was characterized by readily distinguishable social classes. Contrary to what one might expect, the basic criteria for determining social class were birth and legal status, rather than wealth, education, or ethnic origin. Freedmen were sometimes wealthier than either equestrians or senators, but by law they could not become senators. Conversely, equestrians and senators were required to show fixed levels of capital in order to qualify for their respective classes. As for the noncorrelation of social class with either education or literary achievement, one need only mention Phaedrus, Livy, Terence, and Epictetus, all of whom were freedmen. Although the internal composition of classes varied in accordance with population shifts and economic trends, the classes themselves, as legally defined entities, did not change significantly from Republican to Imperial times. The one truly novel element in the class structure of the Empire was the immense social power of the emperor.[21] Beginning with Augustus, the emperors used their authority to regulate the financial requirements for senators and equestrians, to adjust the total number of senators, to delegate citizenship, to specify conditions under which an individual might pass from one class to another, and to introduce specific individuals into a higher class by nomination. All of these powers had long been exclusive prerogatives of the senate.

Senatorial Aristocracy

The social history of the senate in the first two centuries of the Empire is thus closely tied to the gradual demise of the old Roman aristocracy. Despite Augustus' efforts to avoid the outward signs of tyranny, the establishment of the principate, with enormous power vested actually, if not legally, in one man, led inevitably to bitter conflict between the emperor and the senate. The factors involved were many: traditional aristocratic opposition to tyranny, fostered in part by the influence of Stoicism and Cynicism; close family ties with the opponents of tyranny in the last decades of the Republic; reluctance to share in the Imperial cult; and loss of control over the army.[22] Still another factor was the general lack of administrative skills among senators, which meant that they often served merely as titular heads of their bureaus, leaving the administrative work to socially inferior but skilled freedmen and slaves. Ironically, this lack of administrative talent contributed eventually to the decline of the old aristocracy as the emperors were forced to promote men of skill to fill positions that normally required equestrian or senatorial status.

The result of this conflict was the eventual disappearance of the old Roman aristocratic families, largely as the result of purges under the Julio-Claudians (Tiberius, Caligula, Claudius, and Nero). The vacuum created by these bloody conflicts was filled by senators of non-Roman and ultimately of non-Italian origin. Tacitus writes that,

> after the merciless executions, when greatness of fame meant death, the survivors turned to wiser paths. At the same time, the self-made men [*novi homines*] repeatedly drafted into the senate from the municipalities and even from the provinces, introduced the plain living habits of their own hearths. Although by good fortune or industry many arrived at an old age of affluence, their previous attitudes persisted. . . .[23]

As Tacitus himself makes clear, the emergence of the *homo novus,* together with the progressive provincialization and de-Romanization of the senate, meant not simply new names and faces but new attitudes as well.[24] This emergent aristocracy of service, as M. Rostovtzeff calls it,[25] did not eschew entirely the old Roman virtues of liberality, equestrian skills, and reverence for the Roman deities, but their loyalties were often divided between Rome and their native lands. Apart from the simplicity in their life style, as noted by Tacitus, on simple matters such as place of domicile, financial contributions to civic functions, and support of religious activities, their devotion to Rome must have seemed deficient in the eyes of the old aristocrats.

In the religious affairs of the Empire it is difficult to specify a distinctively senatorial religion.[26] Naturally their basic instincts were conservative. They looked to the ancient Roman gods who had established and continued to support their privileged position in the social hierarchy. As part of his plan to restore the old order, Augustus had installed senators in the major priestly posts, with himself as *pontifex maximus.* But these ancient cults, like the more recent Imperial cult, were primarily sociopolitical in character, with only occasional evidence that their adherents regarded them as anything but routine civic institutions. For the most part, these priestly positions demanded no training or qualification beyond senatorial status, and in all respects senator-priests continued to lead a normal civil life. According to J. Beaujeu's study of senatorial religion, the literary and epigraphic evidence suggests that senatorial piety ranged from individual acts of deference (Pliny the Younger erected temples and statues to the gods) to reserve or even agnosticism (the same Pliny berated his uncle, Pliny the Elder, for his lack of religion), but rarely included strong religious sentiment.[27]

The case of the second-century rhetor Aelius Aristides, whose passionate devotion to the healing god Asclepius is chronicled in his *Sacred Tales,* is at once atypical of normal aristocratic religiosity and indicative of new currents in his day.[28] For it was in the second century that the emperors Hadrian and Marcus Aurelius became initiates of the Eleusinian mysteries, that Antonius Pius legalized the enthusiastic Phrygian cult of Cybele, and that senatorial participation in non-Roman (Mithras, Dionysus) or Greco-Roman (Isis-Diana, Serapis-Jupiter) cults increased markedly.[29] A particularly interesting case is the Dionysiac congregation at Tusculum, which numbered about four hundred members. From a social point of view the congregation is of exceptional interest because it shows the active participation in one cult of senators along with their clients, freedmen, and slaves.[30] Such cultic associations, especially those of Eastern origin, seem to have been the only areas in which social rank gave way to fellowship among different social groups. Even here, however, membership in the congregation included only the senators' immediate clients and households.

The conclusion to be drawn is that the new religious atmosphere of the second century, signaled by openness to non-Roman gods on the part of emperors and senators, resulted in large part from the provincialization of the senate itself.[31] Not only did the newly designated senators of non-Roman blood bring their native deities to Rome, but once there they exerted considerable influence on the Italian aristocracy. Traditional Roman conservatism continued to express its scorn for many Eastern *superstitiones,* especially those of recent origin, e.g., Christianity, but internal social changes had already given a new face to the religion of the aristocracy.

Equestrian Order

Just below the senate in social dignity and legal status came the order of equestrians or knights, although in terms of wealth and education the two orders were often indistinguishable.[32] Unlike senators, their number was not limited, their title was not restricted by heredity, and the emperor could designate as equestrian any citizen of free birth provided only that the census showed 400,000 sesterces (approximately $20,000).[33] The career of the equestrian, his *cursus honorum,* normally followed a fixed pattern of salaried positions: first, a series of modest commands in the army; second, procuratorial appointments involving financial administration; third, positions including responsibility for food distribution in Rome and for the imperial fleets; and finally, the highest posts open to equestrians, the prefectures of Egypt and of the Praetorian guard.[34] In addition, the administration of small provinces that did not require substantial troops was normally in the hands of equestrian procurators. Thus the province of Judea was governed by equestrians from 6 to 41 c.e. and again from 44 to 66 c.e. In time, this second aristocracy of service became an indispensable factor in the Imperial bureaucracy, and the emperors regularly chose new senators from eminent knights. But the solution of an administrative problem created a new social problem. However much these newcomers, most of whom were from the provinces, might seek to emulate the manners of the old aristocrats, their presence in positions of high responsibility was bitterly resented. The resultant tension was but one more element in the delicate social fabric that the emperors sought, ultimately in vain, to hold together.

On the matter of equestrian religion there is scanty information. In general, one would expect little difference from senatorial religion, with the one exception that knights could not hold the highest priestly posts in the public cults. Among those who aspired to the highest prefectures and eventually to senatorial status, there was undoubtedly dutiful adherence to the ancient gods, to the Imperial cult, and to the more respectable Oriental cults. Senators, equestrians, and the municipal aristocracies represented the established power in the Roman social order, and as such they showed little interest in religions that stood outside that order.

Municipal Bureaucracies

We must say a brief word about this important group, which, though not an official part of the Roman class structure, was nonetheless a crucial element in the unofficial aristocracy. From the time of the Republic, Rome had faced the problem of assuring good relations with its conquered peoples. These efforts generally took two directions: first, the enlistment of local politicians, rhetors, and philosophers as official advisers and emissaries; and second, strong support for local aristocracies.[35] With respect to the cities, the normal procedure was for the senate to approve municipal charters, taking account of local law and custom, and to allow the local citizens to elect municipal magistrates pretty much as they had in the past. Above these magistrates stood the council of decurions as the highest local authority.[36] In addition to their normal political duties, the decurions were expected to make regular contributions to local causes (spectacles, schools, temples, baths, libraries, etc.). As a reward for these often onerous services, the decurion could anticipate a series of honorific titles from the city; at a higher level, an appointment to the Roman equestrian order; and for the fortunate few, promotion to the rank of senator.

With certain notable exceptions, this system of local clients worked to the advantage of Rome. Only in the second century did relationships between Rome and the provincial cities begin to show signs of serious erosion.[37] Jealousies developed between cities over honors from Rome. From the beginning there were tensions between the cities and colonies of Roman citizens (normally retired soldiers), who begrudged the privileges granted to noncitizens in the cities; and many cities simply resented subjection to Rome. We should note, however, that this opposition rarely reached the level of outright revolt. Serious discontent, to the point of active resistance, arose primarily among peripheral groups. Such was certainly the case in Judea, where armed rebellion centered among the Zealots, whereas the aristocratic parties who dominated the city councils (*sanhedrin*) remained loyal to Rome. In Judea as elsewhere, the local aristocracy was the municipal equivalent of the Roman senate—conservative, wealthy, hereditary, and above all loyal to the purposes of the Empire.

No doubt this loyalty often included recognition of the Roman gods, but in the provinces its primary focus was the Imperial cult. Under Republican rule, the East had long been accustomed to honoring benefactors, whether local citizens or Roman governors, with official cults. Thus it was an easy transition when the Imperial cult supplanted the earlier benefactor cults as the chief sign of loyalty to Rome. Naturally the main proponents of these cults were the local, pro-Roman aristocracies. The title of *flamen Augusti,* designating the chief priest of the local cult,[38] soon became the most coveted honor that a city could bestow on a citizen and often led to the granting of Roman citizenship. Much has been said concerning the essentially political character of these cults. Bowersock, for instance, asserts that they reveal "little about the religious life of the Hellenic peoples but much about their ways of diplomacy." [39] Although it would be foolish to deny that the Imperial cult was essentially political in function, there are indications that at least some participants experienced something akin to religious sentiments. In a recent article, H. W. Pleket has discussed an inscription from Pergamum which shows an Imperial mystery cult, complete with a *sebastophant* who carried the emperor's image in a kind of sacred procession.[40] Although the evidence is not overwhelming, it does suggest that the Imperial cults and their aristocratic supporters could on occasion transcend their strictly political role.

Plebs

Having completed our survey of the aristocratic classes (*honestiores*), we come now to the amorphous category of lower-class freeborn citizens, both urban and rural.[41] Of the latter we know precious little. The situation with respect to the urban plebs is somewhat more favorable. In contrast to their rural counterparts, they benefited from the fact that the emperor assumed official responsibility for their physical needs. Inasmuch as this group numbered several hundreds of thousands in Rome alone, such imperial benevolence was no small consideration.

As citizens, the plebs enjoyed a social advantage over slaves, freedmen, and foreigners, but in the economic sphere citizenship often worked to their disadvantage. In business, commerce, and foreign trade they lacked the essential capital to compete with foreign entrepreneurs. In the labor market the availability of free slave labor hurt them considerably. So bad was their economic plight that Augustus had to restrict the number of citizens eligible for the grain dole to 200,000. Using Gagé's estimate of between 600,000 and 1,000,000 for the total city population, this means that one-third to one-fifth of the city was on relief.[42] Little wonder that Juvenal could summarize the salient features of life for the urban proletariat as bread and circuses. For them there was little else, and the endless rounds of public games and festivals provided a major source of release and fantasy. "In Juvenal's day and after," says Carcopino, "it indeed seemed a happier fate to be a rich man's slave than a poor, freeborn citizen." [43]

Finally, we must add a word about the religious practices of noncitizens in Rome.[44] From Republican times foreign groups had brought their cults to Rome. "I cannot abide," says Juvenal, "a Rome of Greeks; and yet what fraction of our dregs comes from Greece? The Syrian Orontes has long since poured into the Tiber, bringing with it its lingo and its manners. . . ." [45] Speaking of the Roman proletariat, Nock contends that "the Capitoline gods meant nothing to them, not even the patriotic emotion which they inspired in sceptical senators. They worshipped Isis and the Syrian goddess and were so lacking in any feeling of Roman propriety as to erect shrines to their favorite deities on the Capitol, which was like holding a Salvation Army meeting in the square before St. Peter's." [46] In short, there is solid evidence that foreign cults in Rome had a significant impact beyond their native devotees. Initially this impact was limited to the lower classes and to foreigners, but eventually, as we have seen, it reached to the emperor himself.

At this point in our discussion the question of urban religion naturally arises. Did urban dwellers also turn to religion for release and fantasy? If so, what kinds of religious communities were available to them? In seeking answers to these questions, we may turn again to Weber's analysis of religion and social stratification. According to Weber, the level of religiosity increases as one descends to a certain point in any social system.[47] Established groups, including the nobility, the professional military, and the various bureaucracies are past-oriented in religious belief and seldom become instigators of new religious movements.

At the opposite end of the social scale, neither slaves nor peasants, for different reasons, become religious reformers. In cities, this leaves the lower-middle and middle classes. These groups, says Weber, are privileged enough to recognize the potential benefits of higher social and economic status but are unable to attain this status. The result is a high degree of alienation from the social order and a consequent openness to religious movements that are future-oriented and congregational, especially if they offer some basis for future compensation. Thus far our analysis has borne out Weber's thesis.

Freedmen

We come now to the category of freedmen (*libertini*), i.e., slaves who had been released through the process of manumission.[48] In the late Republic manumission was a common practice. Wealthy aristocrats often freed their slaves out of charity or gratitude (especially toward nurses and tutors), but just as often they did so in order to increase their free clientele or even the size of their burial procession.[49] In fact, so common was manumission that the number of freedmen and their offspring created something of a social crisis in the early Empire.[50] The aristocracy became alarmed at the melting-pot character of their cherished city.[51] Consequently, Augustus established strict restraints on manumission by enforcing the tax on manumitted slaves, by sharply curtailing manumission by will, and by forbidding owners under twenty to manumit at all.

In religious matters freedmen show a remarkable, though understandable, diversity of interests. Augustus wisely sought to secure their loyalty by entrusting them with primary responsibility for certain offices in the civil religion. The emperor had reorganized the city of Rome by quarters, with images of the genius of the ruler (*Lares Augustes*) at a major intersection in each quarter. He then appointed officers from among the local residents, most of whom were freedmen, whose duty it was to oversee the local cult and to organize a calendar of festivals. Freedmen also served as priests in the non-Roman cults of Cybele and Mithras, and still others formed *collegia* under the patronage of Mercury, the god of merchants. In other words, those who had achieved some measure of success imitated the religions of their social superiors, whereas others remained loyal to what they knew of their native cults.

Slaves

Slavery was a prominent feature of the ancient world and reached its highest proportion in the first centuries B.C.E. and C.E.[52] Although controversies abound on the degree to which the Roman economy depended on slave labor,[53] there is general agreement that slaves constituted a significant segment of the Italian population in the early Empire.[54] We should not, however, regard slaves as a homogeneous group. They came from many national backgrounds[55] and served many different functions in the Roman economy. Their condition varied greatly according to such factors as geographical location (Egypt was notable for care and protection of slaves), individual skills, attitudes of owners, and political conditions. The slave revolts in Italy and Sicily in the late Republic attest to widespread discontent at that time, and this picture is reinforced by Cato's account of slave labor in the realm of agriculture.[56] Under Augustus the fate of slaves further declined as a result of the official policy to restore the Roman citizen to a preferred position vis-à-vis foreigners, freedmen, and slaves. By contrast, the period following Augustus saw a gradual improvement in slave conditions.[57]

In the second century, possession of slaves had become an important badge of social prestige, often purchased at great cost to the owner. Juvenal remarks that the rise to social prominence was difficult in Rome "where you must pay a big rent for a wretched lodging, a big sum to fill the bellies of your slaves and buy a frugal dinner for yourself." [58] But for the wealthy, slaves were no burden. Pliny the Younger owned at least 500; the freedman C. Caecilius Isidorus left 4,116 slaves at his death; and the emperor's retinue included at least 20,000.[59] If the emperor's household, with its extravagant system of specialized roles, is any indication, the life of the domestic slave cannot have been too rigorous.[60] This observation, taken with the fact that free citizens often competed with slaves for non-domestic jobs (in agriculture, mining, and pottery), would appear to support Carcopino's comment that "with few exceptions, slavery in Rome was neither eternal nor, while it lasted, intolerable." [61]

But we should not assume that the benevolence of owners like Pliny represents the norm. According to Roman law a slave was a thing (*res*), not a person, and instances of brutality are not uncommon in the literature of the time. Paul's first letter to the Corinthians (7:21) and his letter to Philemon reveal that escape from slavery was a common aspiration. Even the promulgation of humanitarian decrees, such as Claudius' edict granting freedom to sick slaves exposed by their masters, indicates that masters often exposed sick slaves. A similar judgment would have to apply to Seneca's magnanimous view that a soul might descend "into a Roman knight as well as into a freedman or a slave." [62] At the same time, the influence of men like Seneca and Pliny, especially among the aristocracy, should not be ignored as a factor in the gradual improvement of slavery in the Empire.[63] As for early Christianity, it never challenged the institution of slavery as such, nor did it exert any influence on Roman attitudes.[64] At their best, Christians accepted the Pauline idea that all believers were equal "in Christ" (1 Cor. 12:13; cf. Philem. 15f.), but here again Paul's letters themselves suggest that the best did not always prevail.

The picture of slave religion is at once puzzling and revealing. To begin with an apparent anomaly, we note that Paul's letter to the Philippians concludes with a greeting from "those of Caesar's household" (4:22). Although it is clear that the persons concerned were slaves and freedmen, not members of the imperial family, the presence of Christians among the emperor's slaves comes as something of a surprise. On the other hand, this bit of information suggests that the slaves were free in their religious life as long as it did not interfere with their official duties. Beyond this, F. Boemer has noted that Roman law granted slaves full legal standing in religious matters: their oaths were binding, their graves were sacred and could not be violated without penalty, and their curses were regarded as efficacious.[65]

In general, Roman slaves seem to have adopted traditional cults rather than forming a distinctively slave religion. Thus we find slave participation in almost every cult and *collegium* of the empire, with the natural exception of the official Roman cults. In certain *collegia,* notably those of Bacchus-Dionysus, they appear to have associated with freedmen and freeborn citizens as complete equals. The general pattern, no doubt encouraged by Rome, seems to have been one of accepting slaves into Roman cults and of allowing them to form their own associations under the patronage of Roman deities. In this respect the example of Christians in the imperial household constitutes something of an exception to the normal practice. They were not alone, however, for slaves were also active in propagating the *Dea Syria,*[66] and Tacitus records that a senatorial edict under Tiberius ordered the expulsion of four thousand slaves and freedmen "tainted" with the Egyptian and Jewish superstitions.[67] In short, it would appear that Weber's theory concerning slave religion is supported by the results of Boemer's study. In religious matters, slaves formed a microcosm that reflected the macrocosm of their masters. Weber had theorized that slaves as a group were almost never bearers of a distinctive type of religion.[68] Even the willingness of slaves to accept the religious forms of their owners, which one might regard as somewhat surprising, is accounted for by his theory. One factor was surely the ever-present possibility of release from slavery, which must have encouraged a superficial acceptance of traditional cults. Another is that the ambivalent attitude of depressed groups toward their social superiors always includes, along with hate and resentment, an element of admiration and an impulse toward emulation. Still another factor was the gradual improvement in the conditions of slavery in the early Empire, which reduced the social distinction between slaves and lower-class nonslaves and thereby impeded the emergence of a well-defined class consciousness among slaves. Finally, the fact that Rome allowed its slaves to find a degree of identity and solidarity in established *collegia,* whether the gods were Roman (Fortuna, Bona Dea, and Silvanus) or foreign (Mithras, Dea Syria, Bacchus, or Jesus) may also have contributed to the nonformation of a distinctive slave religion.

EARLY CHRISTIANITY
AND THE ROMAN SOCIAL ORDER

In returning to the questions raised at the beginning of this chapter, we must first take account of two apparent exceptions to the statement that early Christianity spread primarily among disadvantaged groups. These exceptions are wealthy believers such as Marcion and such highly educated figures as Valentinus and his followers.[69] In the first place we should recall that neither wealth nor education was a basic criterion in determining Roman social classes. From the lofty perch of the Roman senator, the dictum held true that "once a freedman, always a freedman." On the issue of wealth, we should also recall that from its inception Christianity had demonstrated a distinct bias against the rich. Thus when persons of wealth began to accept the new faith, the church was faced with a dilemma. Because the ideology of poverty had outlived the social conditions that had spawned it and because this ideology was too firmly imbedded in the sacred writings to be discarded altogether, it had to be reinterpreted to conform with a new set of social conditions.[70] In the case of the *Shepherd of Hermas,* the church reacted by insisting that God had provided wealth solely for the performance of his ministries (*Similitudes* 1.9), and Clement of Alexandria, in his treatise *Who is the Rich Man that Shall be Saved?,* sought to modify the tradition by showing that only the misuse of money, not money itself, constituted a barrier to salvation. Thus in terms of its ideology of poverty, Christianity underwent a dual modification that brought it closer to the social center of the empire. The influx of wealthy believers provided a new base of financial support and at the same time forced a reevaluation of the traditional deprecation of wealth.

The issues raised by the presence of educated believers lead in a rather different direction. Again we note that education was not a decisive factor in determining social status and that there is little evidence of highly educated Christians until well into the second century. Even more significant, however, is the fact that when men of culture began to appear in Christian communities they introduced a new and, for many, unacceptable version of the faith. The cases of certain Gnostics (Valentinus, Ptolemy, and Heracleon), of Marcion, and to a lesser extent of Clement and Origen are highly instructive. The distinctiveness of their religious views is as apparent to us as it was to their contemporaries, particularly in the West. Less apparent has been the observation that these views, when approached sociologically, appear as the inevitable product of a new intellectual class, a class whose pursuit of salvation regularly shows distinctive features: a disposition toward illumination-mysticism; a devaluation of the natural order; and a quest for the meaning of existence in theoretical and universal terms.[71] If we look at the bitter conflict between Gnostic and Roman Christianity from this perspective, it would appear that social differences were at least as important as, and probably supported the theological differences. In other words, the refusal of emergent orthodoxy to accept the Gnosticism of Valentinus and his school serves to corroborate other bits of evidence that point to the fundamentally nonintellectual, nonaristocratic character of Christianity in this period.

These considerations now bring us back to the basic issue: Is there a systematic correlation between the religious character and the social constituency of early Christianity at the various stages of its development? A. H. M. Jones has touched on the subject in his article on the social conflict between paganism and Christianity in the fourth century. He notes that the numerical strength of Christianity even at that time lay predominantly in Greek-speaking urban areas among the lower classes and that aristocratic aversion to the movement was still widespread.[72] In this connection we need to recall Weber's observation that the religion of nonprivileged classes bears three distinctive marks: a strong tendency toward congregational units; future-oriented systems of compensation (salvation); and a rational system of ethics. He further proposed that these are not accidental features, but that they derive directly from the particular position of disprivileged classes in an urban setting.[73] Their sensitivity to new religious movements is closely tied to the degree of their alienation from the immediate compensations of the socioeconomic order. In short, they look elsewhere for their rewards.

Earliest Christianity was just such a religious movement—congregational in structure, future-oriented with respect to promises of reward, and supported by a system of rational ethics.[74] Thus, according to Weber's thesis, it is no accident that early Christians came primarily from the urban populace. Before Christianity could and eventually did penetrate the official aristocracy, two significant developments had to occur. First, the religion itself underwent certain internal modifications (e.g., decline of eschatological emphasis and accommodation to classical culture), which rendered it more acceptable to the upper classes; and second, the aristocracy itself underwent a process of provincialization and democratization, which partly neutralized its aversion to non-Roman cults. As Jones puts it, the emergence of Christianity as a major force in the fourth century "coincided with a social change which brought to the front men from the middle and lower classes." [75] As much as any other factor, this coincidence made it possible for new aristocrats to embrace Christianity in a way that might well have been impossible for the upper classes in the immediately preceding centuries. At the same time, a variety of internal pressures had brought about a more positive attitude toward the values of traditional Greek and Roman culture. Ultimately these complementary developments had the effect of pulling church and empire toward a common middle ground; without them it is doubtful whether Christianity could have produced the institutional and ideological systems necessary for survival and success in the succeeding centuries.

NOTES

1. An earlier version of this chapter, "Religion and Social Class in the Early Roman Empire," appeared in *The Catacombs and the Colosseum: The Roman Empire as the Setting of Primitive Christianity*, ed. S. Benko and J. J. O'Rourke (Valley Forge: Judson Press, 1971), pp. 99–119.

2. The translation is from *Origen: Contra Celsum*, translated with an introduction and notes by H. CHADWICK (Cambridge: The University Press, 1965), p. 158.

3. In geographical terms this chapter will focus on the city of Rome, but with the assumption that conditions there prevailed more or less uniformly throughout the empire. In adopting this procedure I have followed the example of J. GAGÉ, *Les classes sociales dans l'empire romain* (Paris: Payot, 1964). Gagé notes (pp. 38f.) that the reforms of Augustus resulted in a uniform social structure in the empire and that local variations were relatively insignificant.

4. *The Sociology of Religion* (Boston: Beacon Press, 1964), esp. pp. 80–94 ("Castes, Estates, Classes and Religion").

5. *Ecstatic Religion. An Anthropological Study of Spirit Possession and Shamanism* (London: Penguin Books, 1971), p. 21.

6. *New Heaven, New Earth. A Study of Millenarian Activities* (New York: Schocken Books, 1969), p. 13.

7. The common attraction of women to enthusiastic cults is discussed by LEWIS, *Ecstatic Religion*, esp. pp. 30–35, and BURRIDGE, *New Heaven*, pp. 160–62. In *The Mission and Expansion of Christianity in the First Three Centuries*, 2 vols. (New York: G. P. Putnam's Sons, 1908), 2:73, A. Harnack states "that Christianity was laid hold of by women in particular and also that the percentage of Christian women, especially among the upper classes, was larger than that of Christian men."

8. See below p. 146, n. 75.

9. In *New Heaven,* p. 8, BURRIDGE speaks of "situations where the relevant assumptions about power are weakening and no longer enable individuals to perceive the truth of things."

10. *Natural Symbols,* p. 103.

11. In his essay, "On the Origin and Evolution of Religious Groups" (in *Religion in Sociological Perspective: Essays in the Empirical Study of Religion,* ed. C. Y. GLOCK [Belmont, Calif.: Wadsworth Publishing Co., 1973]), Glock treats deprivation as a necessary condition for the rise of new religious movements. He defines deprivation as referring to *"any and all of the ways that an individual or group may be, or feel disadvantaged in comparison either to other individuals or groups or to an internalized set of standards"* (p. 210; his emphasis). He further isolates five types of deprivation (economic, social, organismic, ethical, and psychic) and argues that the initial form and subsequent development of new religions will vary according to the type of deprivation.

12. Pliny, the Roman governor in the province of Bithynia, wrote to the emperor Trajan (c. 112 C.E.) about his dealings with Christians who were brought before him for condemnation. In his letter *(Epistle* 10.96), he describes his procedures as well as the spread of Christianity in his province; he states that believers represented "every age, social rank [*omnis ordinis*] and both sexes."

13. In the volume, *Marx and Engels on Religion* (above, p. 18 n. 47), p. 316.

14. *The Social Teaching of the Christian Churches,* 2 vols. (New York: Harper & Row, 1960), 1:43.

15. *Ibid.,* p. 41.

16. See especially the chapter entitled "The Spread of Christianity as a Social Phenomenon" in NOCK's *Conversion. The Old and the New in Religion from Alexander the Great to Augustine of Hippo* (Oxford: Oxford University Press, 1961), pp. 187–211.

17. "The Social Background of the Struggle between Paganism and Christianity," in *The Conflict between Paganism and Christianity in the Fourth Century,* ed. A. Momigliano (Oxford: Oxford University Press, 1963), pp. 17–37.

18. See the chapter entitled "The Dialogue of Paganism with Christianity," in DODDS's *Pagan and Christian,* pp. 102–38.

19. The only notable exception to this pattern is E. A. JUDGE, *The Social Pattern of Christian Groups in the First Century* (London: Tyndale Press, 1960).

20. In *Social Psychology* (New York: Free Press, 1965), ROGER BROWN devotes a section to "The Reality of Social Class." Brown remarks that the definition of socioeconomic classes in modern industrial societies is a highly arbitrary affair and that consciousness of class shows no consistent pattern in the United States. He establishes four criteria that must be met before one can use class distinctions as meaningful categories: "1) the population is conscious of classes, agreed on the number of classes and on the membership of them; 2) styles of life are strikingly uniform within a stratum and there are clear contrasts between the strata; 3) interaction is sharply patterned by stratum; 4) the boundaries suggested by these three kinds of data are coincident" (p. 114). On these rather hard criteria, it makes good sense to speak of social classes and class consciousness in Roman society.

Of the recent literature on the Roman social order see P. Garnsey, *Social Status and Legal Privilege in the Roman Empire* (Oxford: Clarendon Press, 1970), and the remarkable little book of R. MacMullen, *Roman Social Relations: 50 b.c. to a.d. 284* (New Haven and London: Yale University Press, 1974).

21. See the discussion in Gagé, *Les classes sociales,* pp. 71–77, 191–216; see also R. Syme, *The Roman Revolution* (New York: Oxford University Press, 1960), and G. Bowersock, *Augustus and the Greek World* (Oxford: Clarendon Press, 1965), esp. pp. 1–61.

22. See the excellent discussion in R. MacMullen, *Enemies of the Roman Order. Treason, Unrest and Alienation in the Empire* (Cambridge: Harvard University Press, 1966); on opposition to the principate in the Greek East see Bowersock, *Augustus,* pp. 101–11.

23. *Annals* 3.55.

24. The provincialization of the senate, although clear in its broad outlines, is vague on many points of detail. Gagé, *Les classes sociales,* p. 91, estimates that by 200 c.e. senators of provincial origin comprised one-half of the total body. Bowersock, *Augustus,* pp. 141f., cites the names of sixty-nine senators from Asia Minor down to the time of Commodus and notes that other senators came either from Greek colonies in Italy or from families of mixed Greek and Italian blood.

25. *Social and Economic History of the Roman Empire,* 2nd ed., rev. by P. M. Frazer (New York: Oxford University Press, 1957), p. 185.

26. See the extensive discussion in J. Beaujeu, "La religion de la classe sénatoriale à l'époque des Antonins," *Hommages à Jean Bayet,* ed. M. Renard and R. Schilling (Brussels: Latomus, 1964), pp. 54–75.

27. Beaujeu, *ibid.,* pp. 56f.

28. On Aristides' religion see Dodds, *Pagan and Christian,* pp. 39–45, and C. A. Behr, *Aelius Aristides and The Sacred Tales* (Amsterdam: A. M. Hakkert, 1968).

29. On the rise of foreign cults in the second century see Nock, *Conversion,* pp. 74–76, 122–37.

30. On the general issue of brotherhood in pagan religious associations see F. Boemer, *Untersuchungen über die Religion der Sklaven in Griechenland und Rom,* I: *Die wichtigsten Kulte und Religionen in Rom und im lateinischen Westen* (Wiesbaden: Steiner, 1957), pp. 172–79.

31. Carcopino, *Daily Life in Ancient Rome* (New Haven: Yale University Press, 1940), p. 56, notes that several emperors were also of provincial origin: Trajan and Hadrian were born in Spain, Antoninus Pius in southern France, and Septimius Severus from Semitic stock in North Africa.

32. On the equestrian order see the standard work of A. Stein, *Der römische Ritterstand* (Munich: C. H. Beck, 1927), and Gagé, *Les classes sociales,* pp. 107–22.

33. Equestrians were the capitalists in business, commerce, and industry, with regular responsibility for overseeing the financial management of the substantial imperial farms. In such capacities they acquired considerable wealth and administrative skills, both of which made them valuable in administering the empire.

34. The internal hierarchy of the equestrian order gave rise to a corresponding hierarchy of titles: *egregius, perfectissimus, eminentissimus.* Among equestrian procurators, it was customary to designate them according to the level of their salary: *sexagenarii* earned 60,000 sesterces, *centenarii* earned 100,000 and so on.

35. On the subject as a whole, see the extensive discussions in BOWERSOCK, *Augustus,* pp. 85–100, and GAGÉ, *Les classes sociales,* pp. 151–85.

36. It was probably by extending this general practice, which dated back to the republic, that Rome allowed Jewish residents in cities of the empire and in Jerusalem to elect their own officials and to live according to their ancient customs. The famous letter of the emperor Claudius to the Alexandrians and the many municipal decrees cited by Josephus, granting similar rights to Jewish residents of Roman cities, demonstrate the same basic principle; for a general discussion of the relevant issues see V. TCHERIKOVER, *Hellenistic Civilization and the Jews* (Philadelphia: Jewish Publication Society, 1961), pp. 296–332.

37. For discussions of the "municipal crisis" in the second century see GAGÉ, *Les classes sociales,* pp. 182, and BOWERSOCK, *Augustus,* pp. 101–11.

38. BOWERSOCK, *Augustus,* p. 117, suggests that the "Asiarchs" of Acts 19:31 were high priests in the imperial cult of the Asian provincial assembly; cf. also A. N. SHERWIN-WHITE, *Roman Society and Roman Law in the New Testament* (New York: Oxford University Press, 1963), pp. 89f.

39. *Augustus,* p. 112.

40. "An Aspect of the Emperor Cult: Imperial Mysteries," *Harvard Theological Review* 58 (1965), pp. 331–47.

41. For a more thorough discussion see Z. YAVETZ, *Plebs and Princeps* (London: Oxford University Press, 1969).

42. GAGÉ, *Les classes sociales,* p. 125; cf. CARCOPINO, *Daily Life,* p. 65.

43. CARCOPINO, *ibid.,* p. 64.

44. On the subject as a whole see G. LaPIANA, *Foreign Groups in Rome during the First Centuries of the Empire* (Cambridge: Harvard University Press, 1927); F. CUMONT, *Oriental Religions in Roman Paganism* (New York: Dover Publications, 1956); and NOCK, *Conversion, passim.*

45. *Satire* 3.60–63.

46. *Conversion,* p. 123.

47. WEBER, *Sociology of Religion,* pp. 80–117.

48. On the background and procedures of manumission, see the standard work on freedmen by A. M. DUFF, *Freedmen in the Early Roman Empire* (New York: Barnes and Noble, 1958), pp. 12–35. Although they almost always bear Greek or Latin names, Roman freedmen fall into the category of foreign groups in Rome because most Roman slaves came from outside Italy. Syria and Asia Minor gave the largest number, but Greece, Judea, Africa, and the western provinces contributed their share. JOSEPHUS (*War* 6.420) states that 97,000 Jews were taken captive by Titus in 70 C.E. Of these, the strongest were sent as slave laborers to Egypt (*War* 6.418).

49. Dionysius of Halicarnassus writes of cases in which dying aristocrats would free their slaves in order to increase the number of free persons attending their funeral (*Antiquities* 4.24).

50. DUFF, *Freedmen,* pp. 199f., suggests that as high as 80 percent of Rome's citizens were either freedmen or their descendants.
51. The historian LUCAN (*Pharsalia* 7.405) remarks caustically that Rome was "filled with the scum of the world" [*mundi faece repletam*].
52. On slavery in classical antiquity see W. WESTERMANN, *The Slave Systems of Greek and Roman Antiquity* (Philadelphia: American Philosophical Society, 1955).
53. See for instance the collection of essays edited by M. I. FINLEY, *Slavery in Classical Antiquity. Views and Controversies* (Cambridge: W. Heffer & Son, 1960). For a Marxist perspective see also K. KAUTSKY, *Foundations of Christianity,* esp. pp. 25–59 ("The Slave Economy").
54. See GAGÉ, *Les classes sociales,* pp. 43f.
55. See M. L. GORDON, "The Nationality of Slaves under the Early Roman Empire," *Journal of Roman Studies* 14 (1924), pp. 93–111; DUFF, *Freedmen,* pp. 1–11; and WESTERMANN, *Slave Systems,* pp. 96–102.
56. So WESTERMANN, *Slave Systems,* pp. 76f.
57. *Ibid.,* pp. 102f.
58. *Satire* 3.166f.
59. On these figures see CARCOPINO, *Daily Life,* pp. 69f.
60. Among the many official positions occupied by imperial slaves, Carcopino, pp. 70f., lists the following: bathers, masseurs, barbers, bakers, pastry cooks, wine tasters, and custodians for every conceivable public and private occasion.
61. CARCOPINO, *Daily Life,* p. 56. In a similar vein, R. MACMULLEN, *Enemies of the Roman Order,* p. 198, notes the scarcity of slave uprisings in the empire and cautions against regarding slaves as a clearly defined social class or interest group.
62. *Epistle* 31.11.
63. For a discussion of the factors behind the change in attitude and legislation concerning slavery in the first two centuries of the empire, see WESTERMANN, *Slave Systems,* pp. 113–17.
64. Eph. 6:5 and Titus 2:9f. enjoin slaves to be submissive to their masters; 1 Pet. 2:19 even demands obedience to cruel masters on grounds that the patient sufferer is pleasing to God. By contrast, only one passage, Col. 4:1, commands masters to treat their slaves fairly. Perhaps this discrepancy should be understood as reflecting the fact that there were more slaves than slave owners among early Christians.
65. BOEMER, *Religion der Sklaven,* pp. 184–86.
66. See F. CUMONT, *Oriental Religions,* p. 106.
67. *Annals* 2.85. CUMONT, *The Mysteries of Mithra* (New York: Dover Publications, 1956), pp. 63f., notes that slaves often participated in the cult of Mithras.
68. *Sociology of Religion,* pp. 99–101.
69. For a survey of the evidence on wealthy and educated Christians see HARNACK, *Mission and Expansion,* 2: 33–40.
70. One solution, of course, was to institutionalize the ideology in the form of the priesthood and the monastery.

71. See the discussion of intellectuals and their religion in WEBER, *Sociology of Religion*, pp. 123–25. For a more recent attempt at a sociological analysis of Gnosticism see E. M. MENDELSON, "Some Notes on a Sociological Approach to Gnosticism," in *Le origini dello gnosticismo*, ed. U. Bianchi (Leiden: Brill, 1967), pp. 668–75; H. G. KIPPENBERG, "Versuch einer soziologischen Verortung des antiken Gnostizismus," *Numen* 17 (1970), pp. 211–31; and P. MUNZ, "The Problem of 'Versuch einer soziologischen Verortung des antiken Gnostizismus,'" *Numen* 19 (1972), pp. 41–51.

72. "Social Background" (above, n. 17), pp. 17f.

73. See WEBER's discussion, *Sociology of Religion*, pp. 95–99. Weber relates the tendency toward congregational piety to the decline of blood groupings in the cities, with the result that urban dwellers sought and created substitute groupings through occupational organizations and religious associations (pp. 96f.). He explains the rise of a rational system of ethics in terms of the urban dweller's disassociation from the life of the peasant, which by and large follows the independent and nonrational course of nature. In contrast, the urban dweller must evolve his own rational order, based on "calculability and capacity for purposive manipulation," which culminates in a pattern of reward and compensation (p. 97). Concerning the future-oriented character of urban religion, Weber calls it a "theodicy of disprivilege" (p. 113). "What they cannot claim to *be,* they replace by the worth of that which they will one day *become,* to which they will be called in some future life or hereafter" (p. 106).

74. In the New Testament, the so-called "Haustafeln" or series of ethical commands directed to husbands, wives, children, and slaves (Col. 3:18–4.1; Eph. 5:22–6:9) would clearly fall into Weber's category of a rational system of ethics.

75. "Social Background," p. 37.

5

The Success of Christianity[1]

Modern social studies have brought home to us the universality of the "need to belong" and the unexpected ways in which it can influence human behaviour, particularly among the rootless inhabitants of great cities. . . . For people in that situation membership of a Christian community might be the only way of maintaining self-respect and giving their life some semblance of meaning. . . . Christians were in a more than formal sense "members one of another": I think that was a major cause, perhaps the strongest single cause, of the spread of Christianity.

E. R. DODDS
Pagan and Christian in an Age of Anxiety

THE PROBLEM OF PERSPECTIVE

The growth and transformation of Christianity in the years between the death of Jesus and the accession of Constantine, from roughly 30 to 312 C.E., cannot fail to evoke a reaction of one kind or another.

> Seventy years after the foundation of the very first Gentile Christian church in Syrian Antioch, Pliny wrote in the strongest terms about the spread of Christianity throughout remote Bithynia. . . . Seventy years later still, the Paschal controversy reveals the existence of a Christian federation of churches, spreading from Lyons to Edessa, with its headquarters in Rome. Seventy years later, again, the emperor Decius declared he would sooner have a rival emperor in Rome than a Christian bishop. And ere another seventy years had passed, the cross was attached to the Roman colours.[2]

Some see the success of Christianity—and I use the term in a strictly quantitative sense—as the work of divine providence, others as an unfortunate accident that contributed mightily to the demise of ancient Rome, and still others as the salutary blending of the best elements of Greco-Roman and Semitic civilizations. Unfortunately, these reactions tell us far more about their respective proponents than they do about the real factors behind the success of Christianity. In each case, the problem is that of perspective. Consider two examples. In the *Mission and Expansion of Christianity*, Adolf Harnack refuses even to treat the question as an open one. "Yes," he begins, "victory was inevitable." [3]

> Thus, in the first instance at any rate, our question must not run, "How did Christianity win over so many Greeks and Romans as to become ultimately the strongest religion in point of numbers?" The proper form of our query must be, "How did Christianity express itself, so as *inevitably* to become the religion for the world, tending more and more to displace other religions, and drawing men to itself as to a magnet?" [4]

How are we to reconcile this assumption with the words of Pliny, writing about 112 C.E. to the emperor Trajan on the subject of the spread of Christianity in the provinces of Asia Minor?

115

But I discovered nothing else than a perverse and extravagant superstition. I therefore adjourned the case and hastened to consult you. The matter seemed to me worth deliberation, especially on account of the number of those in danger; for many of all ages and every rank, and also both sexes are brought into present or future danger. The contagion of that superstition [Christianity] has penetrated not only the cities, but the villages and country as well. *Yet it seems possible to stop it and set it right. . . .*[5]

Are we to take Pliny's final words as nothing more than a diplomatic effort to allay the emperor's fears by downplaying the threat posed by Christianity? Or does it reflect the sober judgment of an intelligent Roman observer? If we must choose between the two, Pliny will be the wiser choice. In this case, Harnack has simply failed to extricate himself from the perspective of the fifth (and the twentieth) century and thus from the tacit assumption that because Christianity did eventually become the dominant religion of the West, its development in that direction must have been inevitable from the beginning. Apart from the obvious confusion of before and after, our earlier consideration of early Christianity as a millenarian cult should strengthen our confidence in Pliny's judgment that the future of the movement was very much an open question as late as 112 C.E.

A second example of perspectival distortion also involves Harnack. In answer to his own question whether Christianity's climb to the top could be called rapid, Harnack answers affirmatively. "Inconceivable rapidity"[6] and "astonishing expansion"[7] are the terms he uses. Ernest Renan, on the other hand, expresses no surprise at the eventual establishment of Christianity, but is amazed that the process took so long![8] In this instance, however, there is no possibility of adjudicating between the opposing views. Such judgments are entirely relative, and all the more so because, as Harnack himself admits, we lack comparable evidence for the expansion of other religions in the later Roman Empire.

Some Possible Solutions

In moving from questions of inevitability and rapidity to the more abstract level of evaluations and general theories of explanation, the problem of perspective looms more substantial than ever. Is it possible, or even desirable, to reconcile the traditional Christian answer in terms of divine providence with the antithetical view that holds that this new religion largely to blame for the fall of the glorious Roman Empire?

But when the time had fully come, God sent forth his Son, born of woman, born under the law, to redeem those who were born under the law, so that we might receive adoption as sons.

Gal. 4:5–5

Before the coming of the Lord, philosophy was necessary to the Greeks for righteousness. Even now it is useful for religion, serving as a kind of preparation for those who will come to full faith through demonstration. . . . Perhaps philosophy was given primarily to the Greeks until the time when the Lord would summon the Greeks. It served as an introduction to Christ for the Greeks just as the law did for the Hebrews. Thus philosophy prepared the way for him who comes to full perfection under Christ.

Clement of Alexandria,
Stromata 1.28.3

God was preparing the nations for his teaching, that they might be under one Roman emperor, so that the unfriendly attitude of the nations to one another . . . might not make it more difficult for Jesus' apostles to do what he commanded them when he said, "Go and teach all nations." . . . It would have hindered Jesus' teaching from being spread through the whole world if there had been many kingdoms. . . . Accordingly, how could this teaching, which preaches peace and does not even allow men to take vengeance on their enemies, have had any success unless the international situation had everywhere been changed and a milder spirit prevailed at the advent of Jesus? [9]

Origen, *Against Celsus* 2.30

Despite their varying emphases, these statements reflect a common belief that the pre-Christian world found its meaning and fulfillment in the coming of the Christ and his church. In retrospect it was argued that everything pointed to this momentous event; all previous history could be summarized in the title of Eusebius' treatise, *Preparation of the Gospel*. And as part of their endeavors to come to terms with Greek philosophy, the apologists held that the various philosophical schools had glimpsed selected aspects of ultimate truth. But these same apologists coupled this positive evaluation with two restrictions: first, that much of value in Greek philosophy had been plagiarized directly from Moses and the Old Testament, and second, that the philosophers were as often wrong as right.[10] The net result of this view was that the question of Christianity's victory was both answered and rejected. It had never really been a question at all, for divine providence had so ordained it from the beginning of time. Even Origen's recognition that political factors played a critical role in the process is merely an extension of divine providence to the arena of Roman history.

This theological solution has been remarkably persistent throughout succeeding centuries. Its influence appears directly in the concluding words to Edwyn Bevan's *Jerusalem under the High Priests*:

> But indeed the Christ whom the Christians worshipped was not the embodiment of any single one of those forms which had arisen upon prophetic thought; in Him all the hopes and ideals of the past met and blended; the heavenly Son of Man and the earthly Son of David, the suffering Servant of the Hebrew prophet and the Slain God of the Greek mystic, the Wisdom of the Hebrew sage and the Logos of the Greek philosopher, all met in Him; but He was more than all.[11]

Lest it be objected that Bevan's views are unrepresentative of modern scholarship, I would suggest that a less explicit form of the same approach still pervades much thinking about relations between early Christianity and its cultural environment. I have in mind a common structure which runs throughout numerous dictionaries, commentaries, and histories dealing with early Christianity: G. Kittell's *Theological Dictionary of the New Testament*;[12] H. Strack and P. Billerbeck's *Kommentar zum Neuen Testament aus Talmud und Midrasch*;[13] the monographs published in the series *Corpus Hellenisticum Novi Testamentum*;[14] and finally R. Bultmann's *Primitive Christianity in Its Contemporary Setting*.[15] In structure, and sometimes in explicit intent, these works treat the ancient world only insofar as it bears on, illuminates, and, by implication, culminates in the phenomenon of early Christianity. The main divisions of Bultmann's *Primitive Christianity* bear out this claim: The Old Testament Heritage—Judaism—The Greek Heritage—Hellenism—Primitive Christianity. Now it is not my contention that Bultmann or any of the others would advocate the paradigm of *praeparatio evangelica* as formulated by the early apologists and restated by Bevan. But the very structure of their approach is rooted historically in a similar ideology and to this extent serves to perpetuate it, perhaps unconsciously, in the minds of modern readers. Thus it operates as more than a mere vestige of a view no longer shared by critical historians, and as such it is subtly at odds with their stated methodology.

We should not suppose, however, that the solution inherent in the program of *praeparatio evangelica* is the only value-laden response to the rise of Christianity. From the moment when the pagan world first perceived the threat posed by Christian expansion, the church's enemies regularly cast it as the cancer, not the soul of ancient civilization. Galen, Celsus, and numerous others upbraided Christians for their preference of blind faith to sober reason.[16] The popular attitude is best expressed in the sarcastic words of Tertullian:

> If the Tiber reaches the walls, if the Nile does not rise to the fields; if the
> sky doesn't move or the earth does; if there is famine or plague, the cry
> goes up at once, "The Christians to the lion!" What, all of them to one
> lion? [17]

In other words, natural disasters were interpreted as vengeance from the
gods who were angry because Christians refused to worship them. Indeed,
Augustine's *City of God* is a massive rejoinder to pagan charges that
Christianity was to blame for the sack of Rome by the barbarian (but
Christian!) Alaric in 410 C.E. What separates Augustine from his pagan
antagonists is not any assessment of the facts—for both agreed in as-
sociating the rise of Christianity with the demise of pagan Rome—but
rather an evaluation of these facts. Cancer or cure? It depended on one's
perspective.

With the passing of time, the number of those in a position to brand
the church as the cancer of the empire diminished to the point of dis-
appearing. But the view attained a new dignity among a coterie of
modern critics. Among them the most vociferous and controversial has
been Edward Gibbon in *The History of the Decline and Fall of the
Roman Empire*.[18] His violent excoriation of Christian monasticism,[19]
for all of its intemperance, is nonetheless typical of a recurrent theme in
more recent historians of later antiquity—the decay of philosophy and
the rise of "superstition" as contributing factors in the success of Christianity. Gilbert Murray, in comparing the first Christian centuries with
the Athens of Sophocles and Aristotle, perceives a dramatic change of
tone:

> The new quality is not specifically Christian: it is just as marked in the
> Gnostics and Mithras-worshippers as in the Gospel and the Apocalypse, in
> Julian and Plotinus as in Gregory and Jerome. . . . There is an intensify-
> ing of certain spiritual emotions; an increase of sensitiveness, *a failure of
> nerve*.[20]

In short, Christianity was said to have triumphed over a corpse.[21] History, like nature, abhors a vacuum and the church was there to fill the
void.

To complete this sampling of traditional solutions, we may dwell
briefly on the unusual synthesis proposed by Arnold Toynbee in his
A Study of History.[22] After considering and rejecting Gibbon's view of
Christianity as a social cancer, Toynbee proceeds to revise his own
earlier interpretation of the church as a necessary but transitional stage
in the movement from one civilization (Roman) to another (modern
European). In the process of this revision, he arrives at a position in
which Gibbon's terms are completely reversed: religion is now seen as
"a higher species of society," [23] not an epiphenomenon of more basic

forces operating beneath the surface, and civilizations are understood as overtures to higher religions:[24]

> If we are looking for a social cancer, we shall find it, not in a church which supplants a civilization, but in a civilization which supplants a church. . . . If we take as a test case for the verification of this thesis, the genesis of the Christian Church, and cite the tenuous yet significant evidence afforded by the transference of words from a secular to a religious meaning and usage, we shall find this philological testimony supporting the view that Christianity is a religious theme with a secular overture, and that this overture consisted, not merely in the Roman political achievement of an Hellenic universal state, but in Hellenism itself, in all its phases and aspects.[25]

Two aspects of Toynbee's conclusions are especially relevant for our discussion. Though he deals essentially with the same facts known to Gibbon and Murray, he does not share their view of ancient history. Thus rather than eulogizing the age of the Antonines (96–169 c.e.) as the apogee of Roman political culture, he regards it as a last-ditch effort at self-preservation by a moribund civilization.[26] Our second observation is that Toynbee's perspective allows him to appreciate old facts in a new light. Nowhere is this more apparent than in his discussion of Christian asceticism. Here, it seems, is an aspect of the Christian movement on which earlier critics have been united in expressions of horrified indignation.[27] Here was the quintessence of Christian misanthropy that contributed so heavily to the collapse of the empire by capturing men just when they were most needed to maintain the machinery of empire.[28] "Where did all this madness come from?" asks E. R. Dodds.[29] And in his query we hear an echo of the pagan, Rutilius Namantianus, who returned from a voyage to Rome only to find once favorite islands occupied by monks:

> O foolish frenzy of a perverse brain,
> Trembling at ill, intolerant of good
> Tis conscience turns them executioners,
> Or dismal guts distended with black gall [30]
> . . . .
> Driven by the furies, out from men and lands,
> A credulous exile skulking in the dark,
> Thinking, poor fool, that Heaven feeds on filth.
> Himself to himself more harsh than the outraged gods.
> A worse creed this than ever Circe's poison,
> Men's bodies turned bestial, now their souls.[31]

By contrast, Toynbee's schema of historical development, moving from universal state to the higher level of universal church, creates an entirely different image of Christian monks and their role in civilization.[32] Now their withdrawal from the urban life of the empire becomes both prophetic and necessary:

> It is manifest that, in insulating themselves physically from their fellow men, these saints were entering into a far more active relation with a far wider circle than any that would have centered round them if they had remained "in the World" and had spent their lives in some secular occupation . . . This spectacle of their self-realization through self-surrender struck their contemporaries' imaginations and touched their hearts and thereby played its part in the forging of a social bond of a spiritual order which held firm when Society dissolved on the political and economic levels.[33]

To repeat what we have stated above, it is not a question at the moment of accepting or rejecting any of these solutions but of recognizing the extent to which a given perspective will shape our vision. Nor is it a matter, by way of reaction, of avoiding perspectives altogether. When Harnack boasts, in the preface to the fourth edition of *The Mission and Expansion of Christianity,* that "it contains virtually no hypotheses, but [only] assembles facts," [34] he is mistaken on two counts. First, in supposing that his work was or could be free of hypothetical constructs, and, second, in upholding this as a model of historical scholarship.

In sum, the problems raised in our discussion of traditional solutions suggest several items to be kept in mind in what follows. In the first place, we must treat the question of Christianity's success as a genuinely open one. It is difficult to avoid the suspicion that the neglect of this issue among students of early Christianity rests on the assumption, whether tacit or not, that there is no issue at all. Obviously, there came a time in the development of the movement when its fate was apparent to all. We need to seek after this point of no return, but with the knowledge that we are not looking for a fixed date. I have already proposed that the outcome was very much in doubt as late as 112 C.E.; it seems equally certain that it was no longer in doubt by the time (360–63 C.E.) of Julian's futile attempt to supplant the church with a revivified paganism. For certain major provinces, including Africa, Asia Minor, and Syria, Harnack would push the date back to the beginning of the fourth century:

> Between the reign of Gallienus and the year 303, the church in Africa must have increased by a process of geometrical progression. . . . But it is the Donatist movement which shows most plainly the extent to which the new religion had permeated the people, and even the Punic populations. People actually began to represent it as a national palladium.[35]

Harnack's last comment also points to the need for differential treatments of separate periods and geographical regions.[36] Christianity began in Palestine as a largely nonurban movement, but it had become an urban, non-Jewish, and increasingly middle-class religion by the mid-fourth century. Whereas Paul had exalted the contrast between pagan wisdom and Christian folly ("For since, in the wisdom of God, the world did not know God through wisdom, it pleased God through the folly of what we preach to save those who believe"—1 Cor. 1:21), the synthesis of Christian faith and Greek philosophy was all but complete by the same time.[37] But as Harnack's survey makes plain, the movement did not grow at a regular pace, nor was it of equal strength in the different provinces. Finally, it should be apparent that there can be no simple answer to the question "Why Christianity?" Many factors, some of them necessary but none of them sufficient, contributed to the final outcome. In an effort to assign a relative value to some of these factors, we must keep in mind two sorts of questions. What factors, internal as well as external, can we imagine as absent without materially affecting Christian expansion? In comparison with its chief competitors, what factors enabled Christianity to survive and flourish, while others either disappeared (e.g., Mithraism) or ceased to grow (e.g., Judaism)? Such questions are inevitably vague and subject to manipulation, but they may still perform a useful service if we treat them as general guides for inquiry and do not insist on definitive answers.

EXTERNAL FACTORS

The Empire[38]

Origen is surprisingly candid in his observation that the spread of Christianity was contingent on Augustus' creation of an ordered, unified, and reasonably peaceful empire. He appears even to intimate that it was an essential condition ("and how could this teaching . . . have had any success unless . . . ?"). Thus it is not surprising that he ascribes the reign of Augustus to divine providence. The restoration of peace, after decades of internal strife, and the extension of Roman rule throughout the Mediterranean basin did, in fact, create the political structure through which the international character of Hellenistic culture reached its fullest expression.[39] Ease of travel, which was essential for the administration of an empire, was also available to religious missionaries of all sorts. Communication was facilitated by the wide dissemination of Koinē Greek and, to a lesser extent, of Latin. As concrete manifestations of this unity, one could also point to Roman law and citizenship.[40] Although the granting of full citizenship to the provinces took place gradually, these two instruments were powerful symbols of cultural unity. In legal matters, Rome sought to recognize local customs everywhere, provided only that they were not in fundamental opposition to Roman interests. This is perhaps most evident in the broad privileges extended to Jewish communities, both in Palestine and in the diaspora:[41] exclusion from normal civic duties on the Sabbath, authority to establish independent Jewish courts for handling numerous internal matters, and freedom to maintain ancestral customs (food, worship, etc.) without interference from the state.

This basic attitude of toleration was no less evident in religious matters, though with important restrictions.[42] Private associations were always suspect and prohibited, except for such specific purposes as burial.[43] At the same time, religious belief was given free rein as long as it did not—and here Christianity was to encounter its gravest crisis—pit the believer against Rome's demand for outward conformity in religious acts, such as honoring the traditional gods, worshiping the emperor or his genius, participating in local ceremonies, and recognizing the symbols of Roman power. In this regard, the Cynics were the perfect models of patriotic atheism: scornful of the gods as agents in human history, yet punctilious in their observance of public rites. Finally, the international character of the Empire was reflected in the population of virtually every major city. Juvenal's renowned complaint that "the Syrian Orontes has long since poured into the Tiber, bringing with it its lingo and manners," [44] may be taken as evidence that large foreign settlements were to be found in most trading and commercial centers. Together with the people came their gods, to such an extent that they were impossible to control [45]—Isis, Cybele, Attis, Mithras, Moses, and Jesus. In many respects they were indistinguishable from one another, and the very fact of their existence in such large numbers must have facilitated the initial founding of Christian communities. They provided a kind of cover under which many churches existed unnoticed, in some areas for almost a century. By contrast, in areas where Christianity encountered a culture with a single, state-supported religion (Persia, China, etc.), it never enjoyed the luxury of relative calm during the initial period of foundation and consolidation.

Church and Empire in Conflict

Although the similarities between Christianity and other cults need to be emphasized, they should not blind us, nor did they blind the

Romans, to the obvious differences. Judaism and Christianity were the only cults in the empire that ran afoul of Rome's general policy of toleration. For a period of some two hundred and fifty years, the conflict between church and state took the form of intermittent persecution, sometimes official but mostly not.[46] To Roman eyes, the obstinate and incomprehensible intolerance of Christians made them appear not only foolish but treasonable. In many instances their beliefs seemed no different from those of many pagans; more often they were simply beneath contempt. Yet these people alone refused the command to put a pinch of incense before the altar, and these people alone died for their folly. Here the policy of toleration reached its limits. Whether we interpret the traditional belief in the *pax deorum*, i.e., the contractual agreement according to which the gods would protect Roman interests in return for the allegiance of her inhabitants, as sincere conviction, as sheer political expediency, or whatever, it was held by all to be inviolable. And the refusal of Christians to honor the agreement meant that its penalty clauses were invoked—either to appease the righteous anger of the offended gods or to punish the delinquent party.

We know that many Christians shared the official Roman view that offering the incense was no momentous affair and that it carried no religious conviction. For them, this empty ritual entailed no compromise of faith. Yet the church at large decided otherwise and enacted harsh sanctions against those who had thus secured their personal safety. In retrospect, we may well wonder whether this adamant stance was worth all the anguish.[47] Would Christianity have sacrificed anything of value by choosing the path of outward conformity? On the other hand, it is undeniable that the long-term consequences of this obstinacy worked to the benefit of the churches, and there is no real basis for rejecting the view of Christians themselves that the persecutions in some sense ensured their final victory. The *Letter to Diognetus* observes, no doubt accurately, that "the more of them are punished, the more do they increase" (7.8). And Augustine, in responding to the pagan Porphyry, notes that Porphyry "did not understand that these persecutions . . . tended rather to establish their religion more solidly and to commend it to others" (*City of God* 10.32). But why should this have been true? [48] In the first place, the martyrs were undeniable exemplars of human courage. And for pagan witnesses to these acts of public witness—indeed they were virtually the only public "activity" of the churches—the martyrs might be likened to their own heroes: the figure of Dionysus in the *Bacchae*, of Socrates in the *Apology* and *Crito*, or of Proteus Peregrinus in Lucian's *On the Death of Peregrinus*.[49] Still, no pagan, at least in the early decades, thought to compare Christian beliefs with Socratic wisdom. More illuminating is the suggestion of Dodds and A. D. Nock that Christian martyrdom also offered a respectable and profitable solution to a death wish that was widely current at the time.[50] Whether we regard this impulse toward self-destruction as perennial or episodic, there is firm evidence, to quote Dodds, that "in these centuries a good many persons were consciously or unconsciously in love with death."[51] To cite but one example from the pagan side, Seneca speaks in one of his letters of "a feeling which occupies many, a desire for death [*libido moriendi*]" (*Epistle* 24.25). On the Christian side, the phenomenon of voluntary martyrdom was quite common, so much so that it had to be curbed by ecclesiastical authorities.[52] One study has revealed, for instance, that as many as one-half of those who suffered death during the reign of Diocletian were either volunteers or in some fashion strove to bring attention to themselves.[53] And in the well-known case of Ignatius, we can witness his passionate plea to the community in Rome not to interfere in any way with his impending martyrdom:

> "I am writing to all the churches and instructing them that I am dying voluntary for God—unless, of course, you interfere. I beg you, do not do me a favor out of season. . . . (*Rom.* 4.1)
> For I am writing to you while I am alive, but I desire death. . . . (*Rom.* 7.2)

At this point one must ask how it is possible to understand the spectacular failure of persecution as a strategy for crushing or even neutralizing the Christian movement in the Empire. One basic reason is that in Roman eyes Christianity had come to be divorced from Judaism. Thus Rome misperceived the peculiar connection between belief and action which made it impossible for Jews and Christians, unlike other monotheists, to accept the Imperial political theology. An accommodation had been reached in the case of Judaism, partly to assure peace in the province of Judea and partly to honor its status as an ancestral religion. But once it became apparent that Christianity was more than a dissident Jewish sect, its roots in Judaism seem to have been forgotten altogether. The result was predictable: the more they tortured the alien body, the healthier it became.

The matter of martyrdom raises finally the question of how we are to assess the empire as a factor in the success of Christianity. Here I can only agree with Origen that it was a necessary condition. Without it, the movement would have developed in different and quite unpredictable directions. It is certainly not beyond imagining that less favorable conditions in the early decades might have snuffed out the movement completely. To illustrate the point, we may cite the example of Persia, where Christians never passed beyond the status of a minority community. The difference in political and religious circumstances between Persia and Rome are instructive in this regard.[54] Unlike Rome, which had no priestly caste and no single state religion, Persia was dominated, especially under Sassanian rule from the third century onward, by Zoroastrianism, whose priests were active in resisting Christianity from the first. And unlike the Roman Empire, where the proliferation of cults attested to the inadequacy of traditional institutions in a mass society, Persia reveals a more homogeneous society, in which new movements gained ground only against firm opposition. But we must also stop short of considering the empire as a sufficient factor for the simple reason that other cults, which benefited from the same conditions and were additionally exempt from persecution, failed to survive and prosper. This further suggests that the significance of Roman toleration in religious matters may have been overemphasized in recent discussion. At the start, Christianity was not really tolerated; it was simply unknown or thought to be a Jewish sect. Later on, it enjoyed a degree of toleration, but only so long as the internal stability of the empire was assured. In other words, toleration was a political luxury. Thus we hear nothing of systematic persecutions until the end of the second century, when they appear in tandem with the serious disorders, both internal and external, of the third century.[55] But by that time, the persecutions had the reverse effect of fostering rather than impeding the chances of final success. Ironically, then, it would appear that both phases of Christianity's encounter with Rome—the initial "toleration" and the subsequent persecution—worked in favor of its ultimate success.

Diaspora Judaism

In moving beyond the confines of its Palestinian cradle, Christianity enjoyed a second advantage which we can scarcely overestimate. Diaspora Judaism[56] provided a blueprint, precise to the finest detail, for the adaptation of Christianity to the Greco-Roman world. It is definitely not the case, as is sometimes imagined, that this outward expansion marked a departure from Judaism and Jewish influence. In leaving Palestine and embarking on the uncertain course of cultural accommodation, Christianity simply took as its model a different sort of Judaism. The literature, thought, and institutions of Hellenistic Judaism in the diaspora not only influenced their Christian counterparts; in a real sense, Hellenistic Christianity alone preserved the legacy of Hellenistic Judaism.[57]

Without belaboring this issue, let us survey some of the ways in which the churches followed in the footsteps of diaspora synagogues:

1. The sacred Scripture of early Christianity was the Jewish Bible in various Greek translations, primarily the Septuagint (LXX).[58] These

translations had been produced in previous centuries for the use of Greek-speaking synagogues in the diaspora, and Christian congregations simply adopted them, unaltered, for their own use—liturgical, apologetic, and otherwise. In fact, so thorough was this process of appropriation that it precipitated a crisis within Judaism. As Christians began to interpret the Septuagint in ways favorable to themselves (e.g., the term *parthenos* in Isa. 7:14 was cited in support of the virgin birth) and ·to press their interpretations against their Jewish opponents, arguing that they had failed to understand their own Scriptures, many Jewish communities felt the need for new translations.[59] Thus there came into being several new versions (Aquila, Theodotion).[60] Beyond the benefits already noted, the "Old Testament" provided Christianity with a sacred Scripture of divine origin and unparalleled antiquity. No pagan cult could make even a similar claim, and in "an age which turned its eyes to the ancients for wisdom and to heaven for a truth beyond the attainment of reason," [61] this was no small advantage.

2. To compound the insult in Jewish eyes, Christian interpreters took over not only the text of the Bible but Jewish methods of interpretation as well.[62] Typology, or the explanation of texts as predictions of events taking place in one's own time, runs throughout the biblical commentaries (*pesharim*) from Qumran, and it is also the basis of the Christian view that the Bible as a whole can only be understood as a prediction of the Christ. Similarly, the technique of allegory, whereby a "higher" level of meaning is discovered in otherwise straightforward texts, was borrowed directly from Jewish exegetes (Philo, etc.). And in the early years, one finds evidence that Christian exegetes were familiar with some of the more technical principles of rabbinic exegesis.

3. In addition to the Septuagint, Christians also took over and adapted numerous other Jewish writings.[63] In fact, Christian recensions of Jewish documents constitute an important segment of early Christian literature: several books of the Sibylline Oracles, the Testaments of the Twelve Patriarchs, the Fifth and Sixth Books of Ezra (additions to the Jewish Fourth Ezra), the Ascension of Isaiah, etc. In a somewhat different category are the writings of Philo. Apart from a single passage in Josephus, Philo's immense corpus of exegetical and apologetic works passes without the slightest mention in subsequent centuries of Jewish history. With the disappearance of Alexandrian Judaism in the second century c.e., Philo's works seem to have been preserved and copied by Christian hands. In any case, his influence was felt exclusively in Christian circles, among such figures as Clement of Alexandria, Origen, and Eusebius.[64]

4. The significance of Philo and other Jewish apologists goes well beyond their individual writings. One of the major tasks confronting Christianity as it moved into the pagan world was that of coming to terms with a new culture. Too much accommodation and the movement would

have become one more syncretistic cult among others (the case of Christian Gnosticism?); too little and it would have atrophied (the case of "Jewish Christianity"?). In seeking a middle way, the Christian apologists were able to follow the models created by their Jewish predecessors. Indeed, the basic themes of Jewish apologetic literature recur constantly in Christian texts: pagan cults and deities were utterly foolish, but Greek philosophy, and particularly Plato, had often come close to the truth; the best of Greek philosophers were both monotheists and opponents of idolatry; Greek philosophers had plagiarized their wisdom from Moses, the first and greatest of all sages; the Scriptures are not to be read literally, and when understood properly, i.e., allegorically, are entirely consonant with philosophy; and Jews (or Christians) are not haters of mankind, as pagan critics charged, but models of perfect virtue and piety. Finally, the steps toward a broader intellectual synthesis of Christian tradition and Greek thought were equally dependent on the example of Philo. On various theological issues, including creation, the nature of virtue, divine attributes, Christology, and even the Trinity, Philo's reflections paved the way for later Christian formulations.[65] In this regard, we must also remember that the emergence of a systematic rapprochement between Christianity and Greek thought became an important factor in attracting the intelligentsia of the later empire. Celsus, writing around 170 C.E., was no doubt justified in his assertion that most believers were uneducated. But one hundred years later, when Porphyry produced his *Against the Christians,* such charges were no longer entirely valid. Thereafter, Christians could reasonably argue that a new cultural system had emerged and that the center of intellectual creativity had shifted from paganism to Christianity.[66]

5. Equally important as these literary and theological influences is the purely institutional aspect of diaspora Judaism. The book of Acts, our only early witness, indicates that missionary activity took place in and around synagogues. Many early converts—how many is not certain— must have come from such Jewish communities. Some of these were probably Jews by birth, but most were probably full (proselytes) or partial (god-fearers) Gentile converts to Judaism. Internally, Christian congregations adopted the basic structure of synagogue communities:[67] meetings at least once a week in addition to an annual calendar of holy days; worship services consisting of set prayers, Scripture readings according to fixed cycles, exhortations, and psalmody; communal care for the sick, elderly, etc.; authority vested in a ruling council, with a single figure as titular leader; and regular contacts with other synagogues through designated emissaries who regulated matters of liturgical calendar, financial

contributions, and heretical teachings. As a direct result of this strong institutional apparatus, members of Jewish and Christian congregations developed a double sense of community: first, within the local community, which symbolized and reinforced their distinctive values; and, second, as part of an international network of communities, which served to counterbalance their sense of isolation in times of uncertainty or open hostility. Thus, in a special sense, one might argue that the availability of the synagogue as a model for the religious community helped to preserve primitive Christianity from extinction. As the initial impetus for the formation of community, namely the expectation of the End, began to fade, it is quite conceivable that the energies of the movement could have dissipated for want of communal structure. This surely would have happened if the churches had adopted the institutional pattern of the so-called mystery cults. By following instead the pattern of the synagogue, the early enthusiasm was redirected toward the community itself and historical continuity was ensured. In brief, it seems difficult to find fault with S. Baron's judgment that "it was Hellenistic Jewry which . . . decided the struggle in favor of Christianity." [68]

INTERNAL FACTORS

The preceding discussion has produced the following results: The peaceful conditions prevalent in the early decades of the Roman empire, together with the existence of Hellenistic Judaism in the diaspora, were necessary and essential preconditions for the expansion of Christianity outside of Palestine. Without them, it would certainly not have reached the pinnacle of power as and when it did. Indeed, it might never have reached it at all. Still, these external factors alone will not explain why Christianity "made it" whereas others did not. Consequently, we must look within, to internal factors.

One element that is less important than one might imagine is missionary activity proper.[69] In the early years, when missions concentrated primarily around Jewish communities, there must have been considerable overt proselytizing. The book of Acts, corroborated by Paul's letters, portrays the apostles as speaking openly in synagogues. There is no reason to doubt that this was a common practice in the first decades. Beyond this, Acts also presents Paul, and here Paul's letters are silent, as addressing pagan audiences in public settings, e.g., he speaks to a group of Athenians in Acts 17. Later on, however, there is little evidence of public speeches or other forms of large-scale propaganda. Unlike Judaism with its official synagogues, Christianity had no identifiable places of assembly for at least two hundred years. And unlike various pagan cults, it had neither a distinctive priesthood nor public processions. As for the written apologies, most of which are addressed to pagan notables, there is little evidence that they were read outside of Christian circles, except by such figures as Celsus, who used them as material for anti-Christian polemic. In general, then, we must imagine Christian missions as rather quiet and unobtrusive, depending heavily on personal contact within closely defined social circles. Even at a later time, when Christian schools developed in Alexandria and other cities, interest seems to have been aroused by word of mouth rather than by public announcements. Initially, it might seem surprising that this form of mission proved so fruitful, yet on closer analysis the very opposite turns out to be true. In his *Doomsday Cult. A Study of Conversion, Proselytization, and Maintenance of Faith,* John Lofland contends that traditional explanations of cult formation have overstressed the role of "hard times" (deprivation).[70] As a complement, he proposes "pre-existing friendship nets" as a universal factor in all types of cult formation.[71] Whether in contemporary America or in the early Roman Empire, families, friends, and fellow workers provide a ready social basis for converts to new religious cults.[72] This need not mean that entire families were always converted together—though this sometimes happened (e.g., Acts 11:14; 16:15; 18:8)—but that such restricted social units supplied a convenient means of communication as well as the rudiments of social relations (Lofland calls them "affective bonds") that could be carried over into the new group.

For all of its success as a missionary cult, however, the winning of converts cannot be regarded as the key to the continued growth of the Christian movement. In a world that offered an unlimited variety of religious options, there needed to be something further to retain the loyalty of converts through time. This something was the sense of community. With but one major exception (Judaism), no other cult engaged its adherents at so many levels or covered so wide a range of human activities. Dodds's observation, cited at the head of this chapter, is supported not only by the evidence from Christian sources, but by an acute observation from one of its most knowledgeable and severe critics. The emperor Julian, who had been raised as a Christian but later converted to a form of Neoplatonism, wonders in one of his letters,

> Why do we not observe that it is their benevolence to strangers, their care
> for the graves of the dead, and the pretended holiness of their lives that
> have done the most to increase atheism [Christianity]?

And he adds,

> It is disgraceful that when no Jew ever has to beg, and the impious Galileans [Christians] support not only their own poor but ours as well, all men see that our people lack aid from us.[73]

Essentially the same picture emerges from Lucian of Samosata's equally unfriendly, but nonetheless revealing, account of the outpouring of support for an imprisoned Christian leader. The evidence is thus overwhelmingly against Ernst Troeltsch's assertion that "the rise of Christianity is a religious and not a social phenomenon." [74] On the contrary, it was neither totally religious, as were many pagan cults that met only for ritual activities, nor totally social, as were numerous voluntary associations. The key to its success lay precisely in the combination of the two. The sense of community that pervades early Christian literature also fits closely with the social status of most early converts. As we have seen in our earlier discussion, the need for community is greatest among "outsiders" or liminal groups. In this light, it can come as no surprise to discover that as late as the early fourth century, Christianity was still found primarily in urban areas and that its adherents there were drawn largely, though not exclusively, from the lower-middle and middle classes.[75]

One further characteristic of the movement had the effect of strengthening its sense of community. It has often been observed that Christianity, together with Judaism, was the only exclusivist cult in the ancient world and that conversion had serious consequences for domestic life. The statement that Jesus had come "to set a man against his father, and a daughter against her mother. . . ." (Matt. 10:35; cf. Luke 12:53), proved to be remarkably accurate for more than two hundred years. Pathetic scenes like that between the martyr Perpetua and her pagan father must have been rather common.[76] We can glimpse something of the outrage that these conversions produced among pagans in Celsus' indignant tirade against Christian teachers who turn children against their parents and in the wounded pride of Thamyris whose fiancée Thecla abandoned him forever in response to Paul's gospel of chastity.[77] But if conversion often proved disastrous for the family unit, by the same token it tended to strengthen the converts' dependence on their newly chosen focus of identity and thus to reinforce its all-embracing character. Something of the same effect probably resulted from the death of Christian martyrs. Those who were left behind, and they constituted the great majority, must have experienced a heightened sense of obligation not only to sustain their own loyalty but to support fellow believers at moments of crisis. Finally, the simple fact of frequent meetings served the same end.

By contrast, the cult of Demeter at Eleusis met just once a year and entailed no association among initiates. The moment of initiation itself may have been laden with emotion, as with Lucius' mystic journey through the universe during his acceptance into the cult of Isis,[78] but such "peak experiences" rarely bore fruit in subsequent communal activities. Indeed, much of this initial impact must have been diluted by the knowledge that one's loyalty to Isis in no way prevented further initiations into other cults. In this sense, the exclusivism of Christianity, which was the source of persecution, was also one of its greatest strengths. In Dodds's words,

> there were too many cults, too many mysteries, too many philosophies of life to choose from; you could pile one religious insurance on another, yet not feel safe. Christianity made a clean sweep: . . . one choice, one irrevocable choice and the road to salvation was clear. Pagan critics might mock at Christian intolerance, but in an age of anxiety, any "totalist" creed exerts a powerful attraction. . . .[79]

CHRISTIANITY AND ITS COMPETITORS

At this point in our discussion, we must accept the obligation of measuring our results against some test cases. It is not enough to designate a combination of external and internal factors as an adequate explanation unless we can also demonstrate that these same factors were lacking in other cults of the time. If, for instance, it should turn out that some other religious community met all of the conditions stipulated thus far, we would have no choice but to look for additional factors or, failing that, to renounce any pretense of having provided an adequate explanation of the success of Christianity. For purposes of carrying out this test, I have selected three examples—the cult of Mithras, the philosophical schools, and Judaism. Not only do we possess more information about these, by far, than other groups, but they are also the competitors about which Christians themselves expressed the greatest concern.

Mithras

Of all the pagan cults in the late empire, Mithraism[80] stood closest to Christianity and furthest from other mysteries. Both religions were Oriental in origin and both transmitted an ancient tradition (Jewish and Persian) in a new form (Christian and Mithraic). Both demanded a serious commitment from their adherents; in Mithraism, the initiate was required to repent and be baptized on entering the cult and then to advance slowly through seven successive grades. Both set high moral standards for all believers, and both centered on a cultic hero whose own career was symbolized by a victory achieved through struggle. So close were the similarities in certain areas that various Christian writers felt the need to account for them. After describing the rite of the Lord's Supper, Justin Martyr goes on to remark that

> this also the wicked demons do in imitation handed down as something to be done in the mysteries of Mithra; for bread and a cup of water are brought out in their secret rites of initiation.[81]

Tertullian explains the resemblances in a similar fashion:

> He too [the devil] baptizes some of his believers and faithful followers, promising the forgiveness of sins after a washing. And if memory serves me well, he puts a mark on the forehead of his soldiers. He also celebrates an offering of bread, introduces an image of resurrection and under a sword puts on a crown.[82]

He also describes a rite in which the initiate is threatened with a sword if he does not accept a crown; but when the crown is placed on his head, he must remove it while saying, "Mithras is my only crown." [83] Tertullian calls this rite an "imitation of martyrdom [*mimum martyrii*]."

As Justin's comment suggests, Mithraism was in fact Christianity's most serious competitor during the critical years of the third century. In this period, Mithras became attached to the cult of the sun (*sol invictus*), which in turn was quite popular in aristocratic and philosophical circles, reaching its apogee as the quasi-official religion of the Empire under Aurelian, Galerius, and Julian.[84] For all its popularity, however, the demise of the cult was just as dramatic as its ascent. For our purposes, the significant question is whether we can attribute its "failure" to factors that transcend the similarities noted above. One fact seems clear. By virtue of its adoption into the state religion, it was guaranteed both momentary victory and ultimate defeat. As Harnack notes,

> the state [under Constantine] withdrew its state-religion, and this meant the downfall of every religion which had hitherto been protected. . . . All that was left was the religion which hitherto had neither been a state-religion nor enjoyed the protection of the state. . . .[85]

Two further characteristics of Mithraism contributed to its eventual disappearance. First, women were excluded; probably, as one recent critic has suggested, "as an extreme effort to ensure ritual purity." [86] By thus eliminating one-half of the total population, the cult precluded any possibility of achieving the status of a world religion. Such pagan antagonists as Celsus could accuse the churches of catering to women,[87] but in so doing they failed to perceive that most pagan cults offered little to other than aristocratic women. Beyond this, the evidence from the inscriptions and Christian sources indicates that Mithraism was found largely in the army.[88] This not only placed a further restriction on its social appeal, a restriction that was exacerbated by tensions between the army and the general populace in the third century, but it points to an even more fundamental difference between the two cults. In his study of the social sources of Mithraism, R. L. Gordon concludes that "there is no possibility of discussing Mithraism as a response to some form of deprivation: we find simply a confirmation or reiteration of ordinary social experience." [89] "The Mithraist of the sacred paintings," he adds, "is young, strong, unbearded, the image of social conformity, not of marginality." [90] Herein lies not only a basic distinction but a decisive element in Christianity's favor. We should not lose sight of the fact that Christianity was moving in the same direction, and that from Constantine on it too was to become an agent for maintaining social control. But it was still very much a community of the dispossessed in the third century. Contrariwise, Mithraism appealed to established sectors of society and thereby proved quite unacceptable to a large majority of the urban population among whom Christianity flourished. Thus we must finally reject E. Renan's view that Mithraism would have conquered if Christianity had fallen. Its practice as well as its basic ideology narrowed its social base to the point at which it could no longer stand. By contrast, Christianity remained open to all. Unlike the cult of Isis, it did not require large sums of money for initiation garb, priestly fees, and sacrificial offerings. Even when the movement began to attract the wealthy, it never entirely lost its attractiveness among the disinherited.

Philosophical Schools

In taking up the issue of competition between philosophy and Christianity, we should not imagine that it was exclusively, or even primarily, a matter of contending ideologies. In the later empire, the philosophical schools,[91] and most notably Neoplatonism, functioned very much like religious communities; from the beginning this had been true of Epicureanism. Furthermore, by that time there were few matters of intellectual substance separating Christian from pagan intellectuals. Not only did apologists and theologians from Justin Martyr onward contend that the true philosopher would naturally embrace the new faith, but increasingly this wish became reality. As Dodds notes, the debate was neither between monotheism and polytheism, nor between ethical rigorism and laxity.[92] By implication, then, the question "Why Christianity rather than philosophy?" poses a false dichotomy. Unlike Mithraism, the Neoplatonic schools never really disappeared; they simply continued in a Christian guise. Thus the relevant question becomes "Why were intellectuals increasingly drawn to Christian rather than to pagan Neoplatonism?" And once the question is put in this form, it is no longer germane to the issue of Christianity's final success in the empire. In other words, the victory was assured long before the last remnants of pagan intellectual resistance faded away, and nothing would have changed the outcome even if a vocal minority had persisted.

Still we need to examine briefly why it is that the philosophical schools never became widely popular.[93] In a sense, the answer becomes obvious as soon as one poses the question. However much the Platonic tradition succeeded in "popularizing" itself in the late empire, by the inclusion of magic and a conscious effort at syncretizing, it remained a philosophy and thus limited in its social appeal. All the major schools, including Stoicism, Epicureanism, and Platonism, demanded some degree of education. Thus they could never have become popular religions, just as Christianity, had it begun with a figure like Origen, would never have become a popular religion. This point was well understood and emphasized repeatedly by Christian writers. Justin Martyr concludes his discussion of Platonism with the observation that

> among us you can hear and learn these things from those who do not even know the letters of the alphabet—uneducated and barbarous in speech, but wise and faithful in mind—even from cripples and the blind.[94]

Similarly, Augustine caps his critique of the Neoplatonist Porphyry with the argument that although Christianity and Platonism pursue the same goal, namely a universal means of liberating the soul, Christianity alone makes this liberation available to all people and to all nations.[95] In the final analysis, it was able to offer the best of both worlds, philosophy and popular appeal. There can be no doubt that popular support was the more important element in its final victory, but the gradual appropriation of philosophy made that victory complete.

Judaism

In turning to Judaism, we face the most difficult and least studied aspect of Christian expansion in the ancient world.[96] Thus far we have argued that the development of early Christianity at two decisive stages

—its formation in Palestine and its outward movement into the Greco-Roman world—was critically determined by the experience of Judaism. Now we must seek to explain how it happened that, in the words of Renan, Christianity and not Judaism reaped the fruits of that experience. Once again the alternatives are reasonably clear: either we must revise our earlier conclusion that the Jewish synagogue served as the model for the Christian congregation, or we must search for additional factors. If, as we have argued, *communitas* was the decisive element that favored Christianity in comparison with other cults, and if this sense of *communitas* derived from the synagogue, why was the copy more successful than the model?

Lest there be any thought that the issue as stated is really a false one, requiring no explanation at all, we should take note that before the war of 70 c.e. Judaism was a widely disseminated and expanding movement in the empire. The factors behind its growth have been endlessly debated—some emphasizing natural proliferation, others missionary success—and various population figures have been estimated, but with few reliable data and no conclusive results.[97] But whatever the causes, and whether one characterizes Jewish proselytizing as active or passive, many synagogues included numerous converts. The conversion of the royal house of Adiabene in Mesopotamia[98] and the sentencing of Flavius Clemens and his wife Falvia Domitilla, both relatives of the emperor Domitian, on charges of atheism (that is, Judaism)[99] demonstrate that Jewish sympathizers were to be found at every level of pagan society. Indeed, the attractions of Judaism were both numerous and appropriate to the time: an ancient heritage, preserved in written form (no pagan cult had the equivalent of the Jewish Scriptures); an uncompromising monotheism, combined with serious moral standards; a belief that basic religious truths had been revealed directly by the divinity and thus were beyond dispute; a strong sense of community; and finally, a conviction that Judaism represented the religious destiny of all humanity. Of course not all Jews shared these views, but if we examine the apologetic literature of Judaism, these themes will be found to recur constantly. Together they constitute the program of Judaism as a universal religion, and not coincidentally they were to constitute the program of universal Christianity at a later date.

To complete this picture, however, we must also take account of tensions between Jews and pagans. But here we must take care not to fall prey to common misconceptions. The earliest and predominant relationships between Jews and Gentiles were positive.[100] The two focal points of genuine hostility—Alexandria[101] and Rome—which are often taken as normative, are more like exceptions. In Alexandria, despite sporadic tensions and despite the unsympathetic role played by Egypt in the Jewish Scriptures, serious hostilities did not arise until Rome appeared on the scene in the first century B.C.E. From that moment on, the Jews were trapped inescapably between their own allegiance to Rome and the violent anti-Romanism of Egypt. The notorious *Acts of the Pagan Martyrs* show with remarkable clarity that the Alexandrian aristocracy vented its anti-Roman wrath on the Jews and used the occasion in part to recover and in part to invent the repertory of classical anti-Semitism.[102] And in similar fashion, the diatribes of such Roman writers as Tacitus and Quintilian reflect more the bitter aftermath of the Jewish wars than traditional anti-Jewish sentiments.[103] Even the level of popular animosity has sometimes been exaggerated. The distinctive aspects of Jewish life (food regulations, Sabbath observances, circumcision) may have offended some, but as Baron rightly comments, they "seem to have attracted the Gentiles more than did Jewish monotheism and ethics." [104] In the major centers of the diaspora, there is simply not sufficient evidence to substantiate the claim that such practices, by themselves, were primarily responsible for tensions between Jews and Gentiles. This is not to deny that the distinctiveness of these customs attracted the curiosity and sometimes even the indignation of "nativistic" non-Jews. But on balance they seem to have been the pretext rather than the root cause of ancient anti-Semitism.

Quite apart from these preliminary remarks, in one sense the answer to our question is perfectly straightforward. Judaism ceased to be a major religious alternative as a direct consequence of the armed conflicts of 70, 115, and 135 C.E. Thus by the time Christianity began to assert itself as a cultural force, Judaism had been relegated to and in large measure had accepted the status of a minority community.[105] In purely chronological terms, this answer is impeccable; at a deeper level it begs the important questions. Were the conflicts of 70, 115, and 135 C.E. inevitable, i.e., did they express some perennially unresolved conflict within Judaism? If they were not inevitable, would diaspora Judaism have continued to develop as a universal religion? Why did the aftermath of these struggles lead to the disappearance of Hellenistic Judaism in the one instance but to the strengthening of Hellenistic Christianity in the other? Although each of these questions involves a distinctive set of issues, they are fundamentally variants of a single problem—the reconciliation of ancient tensions between nationalist and universalist tendencies within Judaism.[106] Thus when Baron speaks of the traumatic events between 70 and 135 C.E., he can conclude: "Sudden, and yet inherent in the situation." [107]

To ask whether these conflicts and their final resolution in favor of a more particularist view of Judaism were inevitable is to indulge in speculation. More interesting is the question about what would have become of the universalist tendencies in Hellenistic Judaism if they had not fallen victim to the wars. Some have interpreted the local incidents that preceded the wars as evidence that no form of Judaism could have become a universal religion. Yet in later years, Christianity suffered the same insults and persecutions. In most essential respects ancient anti-Semitism parallels anti-Christianism and thus cannot by itself account for the different fate of the two movements. Or one might, as we have mentioned above, regard the ritual obligations of the Law as hindrances to the development of Judaism as a mass religion. To a degree this was a factor in Christianity's favor, in that converts were promised the full advantages of Judaism without having to assume the whole burden of the Law. For many Gentile sympathizers and god-fearers, Christianity no doubt offered a solution to a real dilemma: how to separate the distinctively religious elements of Judaism from their nationalistic setting. Still, this factor should not be overemphasized. In the first place, the ritual obligations of full conversion had not deterred many Gentiles from taking this step. At the same time, it is not clear how far these obligations were observed in Hellenistic Jewish communities. Most of the evidence comes from rabbinic sources, and as a general rule it is wise not to transpose rabbinic regulations from the third century back to the first or from Palestine to the diaspora. Josephus, moreover, provides important evidence that cannot be ignored. In his narrative of the conversion of Helena and the royal court of Adiabene, he reports a dispute about whether Helena's brother, Izates, needed to be circumcised. Ananias, the Jewish merchant responsible for Izates' conversion, insisted that it was not necessary, whereas Eleazar ("who had come from Galilee and was known as a rigorist in matters concerning traditional practices") took the opposite view.[108] In the end, Izates was circumcised, but the very possibility of the dispute points to differing attitudes toward the observance of ritual laws. The testimony of Philo is equally illuminating in this respect. Personally, he was opposed to Jewish interpreters of the Law who held that those who understood its spiritual meaning were no longer obligated to follow it in a literal sense.[109] But although Philo insisted on full obedience to the Law among proselytes, he also argued that the Mosaic Law embodied the perfect expression of divine wisdom for all humanity and for all time.[110] Finally, we need to remember that in the eyes of pagan critics, Christian customs were every bit as repugnant as those of the Jews—indeed Celsus preferred Jewish customs because they at least preserved ancestral practices, whereas Christian customs were both antisocial and recent!—and that conversion to either group involved the breaking of hallowed traditions.

In view of these considerations, the critical problem now is to account for the total demise of Hellenistic Judaism by the middle of the second century c.e. That it collapsed and that rabbinic Judaism emerged as the dominant force both in Palestine and in the diaspora is undeniable; it is symbolized by the complete absence of Philo's name in Talmudic literature. One possible explanation for this sudden reversal would be to admit that previous generations have overestimated the significance of Hellenistic influences in diaspora communities. The sheer bulk of Philo's writings and the extent of his influence on later Christian theologians may have led us to assume that he was more representative than was really the case. If this is so, the lack of Hellenizing literature from other centers of diaspora Judaism (Rome, Antioch, etc.) may not be entirely coincidental. It is often overlooked that Philo's work is characteristic, at best, of a small aristocratic minority even among diaspora Jews and that he may well have had no impact at all on the populous majority. The "literalists" whom Philo opposes in many passages may have been in command all along.[111] Beyond all of these conjectures, however, the wars themselves dealt the final blow. Initiated on the Jewish side by those who would tolerate no accommodation with the pagan world, whether religious or political, they failed to attract support from the diaspora and thus ended in a series of crushing defeats. As a result, any return to the optimistic program of Philo was out of the question. The wars had generated considerable anti-Jewish sentiment throughout the Empire, and this factor alone put a drastic limit on the number of potential converts. In Jewish circles, the process of turning away from a rapprochement with Greco-Roman culture was further encouraged by several factors: first, Rome, together with its culture, was now the despised enemy who had visited great suffering on the nation of Israel; and second, the mantle of cultural accommodation had in the meantime passed to Christianity,[112] thus making it unlikely that many Jews would choose to pursue this course.

In the final analysis, the question of Christianity's competition with Judaism can be reduced to two essential factors. The first is that direct competition never occurred, because of external and purely contingent causes. Had the resolution of the conflict between nationalist and universalist forces within Judaism taken a different course, and had the wars of 70, 115, and 135 c.e. never taken place, there are no grounds, based on prior history, to assume anything other than that diaspora Judaism would have continued to expand and flourish throughout succeeding centuries. As a major universal religion, it would have offered the kind of serious competition that Christianity never found in Mithraism or the philosophical schools. This prospect is even more intriguing when we consider that these same wars also tipped the balance within Christianity, consigning the various forms of "Jewish Christianity" to ultimate oblivion and hastening the emergence of "Hellenistic Christianity" as the dominant force within the movement. This form of Christianity preserved all of the advantages of its Jewish heritage but without the only two factors that might otherwise have inhibited its growth—the obligations of the ritual law and the close connection between religion and national identity. By proclaiming that the Christ was "the end of the Law" and by presenting itself to the world as "the new, spiritual Israel," Hellenistic Christianity was able to reap the political and social fruits that had been sown by three centuries of Hellenistic Judaism.

RESULTS

The distinctive factors that can be cited as facilitating the ultimate triumph of Christianity are twofold: a series of *external* circumstances that were completely beyond its control (the organization of the empire under Augustus; the experience of Hellenistic Judaism; the series of armed conflicts between Rome and Judaism; and the internal crisis of the empire in the third century) and a single, overriding *internal* factor, the radical sense of Christian community—open to all, insistent on absolute and exclusive loyalty, and concerned for every aspect of the believer's life. From the very beginning, the one distinctive gift of Christianity was this sense of community. Whether one speaks of "an age of anxiety" or "the crisis of the towns," Christian congregations provided a unique opportunity for masses of people to discover a sense of security and self-respect.

By thus emphasizing the importance of community, I do not intend to deny numerous other factors.[113] The answer to the question "Why Christianity?" must of necessity be complex. But if we search for an internal aspect—because all cults were subject to the same external conditions—that is not to be found in any other cult, we will have no choice but to isolate it as the decisive element in our final explanation of the success of Christianity. Conversely, those aspects of belief and practice that were clearly common to Christianity and its pagan competitors cannot qualify, by themselves, as decisive factors in Christianity's favor. For just this reason we cannot accept Peter Brown's contention that "however many sound and cultural reasons the historian may find for the expansion of the Christian Church, the fact remains that in all Christian literature from the New Testament onwards, Christian missionaries advanced principally by revealing the bankruptcy of men's invisible enemies, the demons, through exorcisms and miracles of healing." [114] So did Apollonius of Tyana and the anonymous exorcists who produced the host of magical papyri. And the exultant prayer of Lucius to the goddess Isis,

> Thou art she that puttest away all storms and dangers from men's life by stretching forth thy right hand, whereby likewise thou dost unweave even the inextricable and tangled web of fate, and appeasest the great tempests of fortune, and keepest back the harmful course of the stars. The gods supernal do honour Thee; the gods infernal have Thee in reverence. . . .[115]

though spoken by a pagan, could have been pronounced by a Christian with very few changes.

Finally, we must consider the argument that the figure of Jesus as presented in the Gospels exerted a powerful attraction. S. Angus and K. S. Latourette recognize that communal organization played an important role in ensuring Christianity's survival, but they insist that the underlying cause of its success was the figure of Jesus himself.[116] C. G. Jung presents a variant of the same idea:

> The Christ-symbol is of the greatest importance for psychology in so far as it is perhaps the most highly developed and differentiated symbol of the self, apart from the figure of the Buddha. . . . This is probably one of the reasons why precisely those religions founded by historical personages have become world religions, such as Christianity, Buddhism and Islam. The inclusion in a religion of a unique human personality—especially when conjoined to an indeterminable divine nature—is consistent with the absolute individuality of the self, which combines uniqueness with eternity and the individual with the universal.[117]

Surely it is more than coincidental that these three religions focus on a historical founder-figure. At the same time, however, Jung's hypothesis is untestable because we know very little about the role that the Gospels played in attracting new converts. In reacting to this sort of proposal, Nock goes so far as to treat any appeal to the figure of Jesus as "a product of nineteenth-century idealism and humanitarianism" and adds that in early Christian literature "all the emphasis is on the superhuman qualities of Jesus . . . not on his winning humanity." [118] But we should recall that in Jung's formulation it is precisely the combination of human and divine elements that is psychologically significant. The later christological and trinitarian controversies turned on just this issue, and the widely popular infancy gospels propagated the image of Jesus as a "divine-man" throughout succeeding centuries. Although the Gospels and their picture of Jesus may have played a relatively minor role in attracting new members, they were a central component of the members' experience *after* conversion. Whether through homilies, Scripture readings, or artistic representation, the Christ-symbol must have touched religious sensibilities in many ways that we can no longer measure. But to assert that it was the major cause of Christianity's success is to claim more than the available evidence will allow.

At this point we may return to a question raised at the beginning of this chapter. At what stage can we say with reasonable confidence that the progress of Christianity was irreversible, both in the sense that it could no longer be eradicated and that it would eventually "conquer" the empire? Surely not before 112, when Pliny reassured Trajan that its growth could be arrested, and just as surely, long before Julian sought in vain to replace Christianity with his version of Neoplatonism. The critical turning point probably came a century earlier, toward the middle of the third century. By the early third century, Christianity had survived its most serious obstacles, both internal (the "heresies" of Marcion, the Gnostics, and Montanus) and external (including the first official persecution under Decius); had implanted itself in every significant locality of the empire;[119] and had developed the institutional and intellectual apparatus to withstand any further onslaught. Writing around 245 C.E., Origen admits that Christians represented "just a few" of the total population.[120] But by the end of the fourth century, Lucian the Martyr could affirm that "almost the greater part of the world is now committed to this truth, even whole cities. . . ."[121] In terms of sheer numbers, then, the greatest increase appears to have taken place between 250 and 300 C.E. But the issue is not simply one of statistics. Even with respect to Origen's statement, it must be remembered that the majority of Christians were to be found in the cities and towns, whereas the majority of the total population lived in the country. As a result, the statistical influence of Christians in the population was quite disproportionate to their absolute number. Thus when Constantine finally seized control of the more heavily Christianized Eastern provinces in 324 C.E., his public recognition of Christianity was in large measure a matter of shrewd political judgment.[122] From that moment on, Christianity alone could serve as the religious basis of the far-flung Empire.

NOTES

1. In addition to the literature cited in this chapter, see S. J. Case, *The Social Origins of Christianity*, pp. 208–53; S. Angus, *The Mystery-Religions and Christianity* (New York: Charles Scribner's Sons, 1925), pp. 271–314 (discusses numerous factors, but locates the key element in the "Personality of

Jesus"); G. LaPiana, *Foreign Groups in Rome* (above, p. 111 n. 44), pp. 398–403 (emphasizes Christianity's appeal to lower as well as upper social groups; in both instances, says that this was made possible by the factor of organization); and K. S. Latourette, *A History of the Expansion of Christianity*, vol. 1: *The First Five Centuries* (New York: Harper & Bros., 1937), pp. 162–70 (also stresses the need for doing justice to the complexity of causes; like Angus, locates the underlying, but not in itself sufficient cause in the "vast release of energy [which] . . . happened to the men who associated with Jesus" [p. 167]).

2. Harnack, *Mission and Expansion*, 2:335f.

3. *Ibid.*, 1:513.

4. *Ibid.*, p. 512.

5. Pliny, *Epistle* 10.96.8–9. The translation is from *A New Eusebius*, ed. J. Stevenson (London: SPCK, 1965), p. 14.

6. Harnack, *Expansion*, 2:335.

7. *Ibid.*, p. 336.

8. *Histoire des origines du christianisme*, 7 vols. (Paris: Calmann-Lévy, 1902), 7:585.

9. The translation is from H. Chadwick, *Origen: Contra Celsum*, p. 92.

10. On the subject as a whole, including the accusations of plagiarism, see H. Chadwick, *Early Christian Thought*, pp. 13–15, 173.

11. London: E. Arnold, 1924, p. 162.

12. The first German volume appeared in 1933; the first volume of the English translation appeared in 1964 (Grand Rapids: Eerdmans). The set has been completed with the publication of the ninth and final volume (Stuttgart: W. Kohlhammer, 1973).

13. Munich: Beck, 1922–61; the full set includes six volumes. A revised edition has been anounced.

14. Initiated by Georg Heinrici in 1915 and carried forward by Ernst von Dobschütz, Adolf Deissmann, Hans Lietzmann, and others. The project is currently responsible for a series of volumes published by Brill in Leiden.

15. Cleveland and New York: Meridian Books, 1956.

16. See the discussion in Dodds, *Pagan and Christian*, pp. 120f.

17. *Apology* 40.2. The translation is from *Tertullian*, ed. T. R. Glover (Cambridge, Mass.: Harvard University Press; Loeb Classical Library), p. 183.

18. The first volume, with its two chapters on the progress of Christianity (chaps. 15, 16) appeared in 1776. On the subsequent controversy, see S. T. McCloy, *Gibbon's Antagonism to Christianity* (London: Williams and Norgate, 1933), and D. P. Jordan, *Gibbon and His Roman Empire* (Urbana: University of Illinois Press, 1971).

19. Chap. 37.

20. *Five Stages of Greek Religion* (Garden City, N.Y.: Doubleday, 1951), p. 119.

21. Compare the surprisingly strong words of Dodds, *Pagan and Christian*, p. 132: "One reason for the success of Christianity was simply the weakness and weariness of the opposition. . . ."

22. Toynbee's views are spelled out at length in volume 7 (London: Oxford University Press, 1954), which deals with "universal states" and "universal churches."

23. *Study,* 7:420–525.

24. *Ibid.,* pp. 526–33.

25. *Ibid.,* p. 526f.

26. For a critical assessment of Toynbee's general conclusions, see ARNOLDO MOMIGLIANO, "Christianity and the Decline of the Roman Empire," in *The Conflict between Paganism and Christianity in the Fourth Century* (above, p. 109 n. 17), pp. 1f. In particular, Momigliano notes that Toynbee's attempt to date the decline of Rome to the year 431 B.C.E. is not an original theory but rather echoes earlier Marxist views of ancient history.

27. See the brief discussion in HELEN WADDELL's introduction to *The Desert Fathers* (Ann Arbor: University of Michigan Press, 1957), pp. 4–13.

28. For a recent and more sophisticated approach to the same issue see MOMIGLIANO, "Decline," pp. 7–12. He views Christianity in the fourth century as more a competitor than an antagonist of the state. As such, it offered new access to sources of power and social mobility; by the fourth century, the company of bishops had become a powerful new aristocracy with the empire. T. A. KOPOČEK, "Curial Displacements and Flight in Later Fourth Century Cappadocia" (forthcoming in the journal *Historia*), illustrates this position by demonstrating that certain candidates for municipal offices "fled" into ecclesiastical roles in order to escape the onerous burdens of public service.

29. *Pagan and Christian,* p. 34.

30. RUTILIUS, *On His Return,* lines 439–52. The poem is usually dated around 415 C.E. This free translation is from WADDELL, *Desert Fathers,* p. 8.

31. *Ibid.,* lines 519–26.

32. For a superbly revisionist treatment of the same subject, see PETER BROWN, "The Rise and Function of the Holy Man in Late Antiquity," *Journal of Roman Studies* 71 (1971), pp. 80–101.

33. *Study,* vol. 7, pp. 388f.

34. Cited on p. vii of J. PELIKAN's introduction to volume 1 of *Mission and Expansion* (New York: Harper & Row, 1961).

35. *Mission and Expansion,* 2:284f.

36. Emphasized also by MOMIGLIANO, "Decline," pp. 5f.

37. On the subject as a whole, see CHADWICK, *Early Christian Thought,* and W. JAEGER, *Early Christianity and Greek Paideia* (Cambridge: Harvard University Press, 1965).

38. Compare HARNACK, *Expansion,* 1:19–23.

39. On Roman power in the Greek East, see G. W. BOWERSOCK, *Augustus and the Greek World.*

40. See the complete discussion in A. N. SHERWIN-WHITE, *The Roman Citizenship* (Oxford: Clarendon Press, 1939).

41. See V. TCHERIKOVER, *Hellenistic Civilization and the Jews,* pp. 296–332.

42. On Roman policy concerning religious matters, see W. H. C. FREND, *Martyrdom and Persecution,* pp. 77–93.

43. The example most often cited concerns a group of firemen in Nicomedia; in reply to Pliny's request for advice, Trajan answers that "whatever we call them, and for whatever reason, men who have gathered together will soon become a political organization" (*Epistle* 10.34).

44. *Satire*, 3.60–63.

45. See, especially, A. D. NOCK, *Conversion*, pp. 99–137.

46. So G. E. M. DE STE. CROIX, "Why Were Christians Persecuted?," *Past and Present* 26 (1963), pp. 1–38.

47. See, for instance, the poignant plea of a pagan father to his recently converted Christian daughter in the *Passion of Perpetua*, 1.2 and 2.1–2.

48. D. W. RIDDLE has treated this issue in his important, and neglected, *The Martyrs. A Study in Social Control* (above, p. 17 n. 41). By understanding the phenomenon of martyrdom in terms of conflict between loyalties to opposing groups, Riddle is able to demonstrate that Christian communities developed and applied effective techniques for controlling the attitudes and behavior of prospective "confessors." These techniques included: the promise of specific rewards in the age to come; the threat of sanctions for those who "denied"; communal support and veneration for those on trial or in prison; the glorification of martyrs as heroes of the faith; the rehearsal of set answers to Roman magistrates; and finally, the creation of a martyrological literature (acts, exhortations, etc.).

49. See NOCK, *Conversion*, pp. 193f.

50. *Ibid.*, pp. 197–202; compare DODDS, *Pagan and Christian*, pp. 135f.

51. *Pagan and Christian*, p. 135.

52. Compare FREND, *Martyrdom and Persecution*, pp. 216f. and 263f.

53. G. E. M. DE STE. CROIX, "Aspects of the 'Great' Persecution," *Harvard Theological Review* 47 (1954), pp. 101–3.

54. See LATOURETTE, *The First Five Centuries*, pp. 103, 163f., and 226–31.

55. See G. E. M. DE STE. CROIX, "Christianity's Encounter with the Roman Imperial Government," in *The Crucible of Christianity*, ed. A. Toynbee (New York and Cleveland: World Publishing Co., 1969), p. 348.

56. On Judaism in the diaspora, see H. LEON, *The Jews of Ancient Rome* (Philadelphia: Jewish Publication Society, 1960); V. TCHERIKOVER, A. FUKS, and M. STERN, *Corpus Papyrorum Judaicarum*, 3 vols. (Cambridge: Harvard University Press, 1957–64); and J. JUSTER, *Les juifs dans l'empire romain*, 2 vols. (Paris: P. Geuthner, 1914).

57. See, in particular, the work of S. BARON, *A Social and Religious History of the Jews*, vols. 1 and 2 (New York: Columbia University Press, 1952). In vol. 2, pp. 162–69, Baron speaks of Christianity as "Hellenistic Jewry's new religion."

58. On the Bible of the earliest Christians, see H. VON CAMPENHAUSEN, *The Formation of the Christian Canon*, p. 103.

59. On the Septuagint and later Greek versions, see S. JELLICOE, *The Septuagint and Modern Study* (Oxford: Clarendon Press, 1968).

60. On Aquila, see JELLICOE, *Septuagint*, pp. 76–83.

61. G. F. MOORE, *History of Religions*, vol. 1 (New York: Charles Scribner's Sons, 1949), p. 532.

62. On the general subject of biblical interpretation in the early churches, see B. LINDARS, *New Testament Apologetic*; R. P. C. HANSON, "Biblical Exegesis in the Early Church," in *The Cambridge History of the Bible*, vol. 1 (Cambridge: The University Press, 1970), pp. 412–53; J. BONSIRVEN, *Exégèse rabbinique et exégèse paulinienne* (Paris: Beauchesne, 1939); and

R. M. GRANT, *A Short History of the Interpretation of the Bible* (New York: Macmillan, 1963).

63. See the discussion in J. DANIÉLOU, *The Theology of Jewish Christianity* (Chicago: Henry Regnery, 1964), pp. 11–19.

64. For Philo's influence on the early fathers, see CHADWICK, *Early Christian Thought*, pp. 44–46, 55–57, 140–43, 150–52.

65. So especially, H. A. WOLFSON, *Philo: Foundations of Religious Philosophy in Judaism, Christianity and Islam,* 2 vols. (Cambridge: Harvard University Press, 1968), and *The Philosophy of the Church Fathers* (Cambridge: Harvard University Press, 1970); and E. R. GOODENOUGH, *An Introduction to Philo Judaeus* (New York: Barnes and Noble, 1963), pp. 24f., 73f., 115f., and 158f.

66. So DODDS, *Pagan and Christian,* pp. 121–23.

67. On the influence of synagogue tradition on the development of Christian worship, see W. O. E. OESTERLEY, *The Jewish Background of the Christian Liturgy* (Oxford: Clarendon Press, 1925); F. GAVIN, *Jewish Antecedents of the Christian Sacraments* (London: SPCK, 1928); C. W. DUGMORE, *The Influence of the Synagogue upon the Divine Office* (London: Oxford University Press, 1945); and E. WERNER, *The Sacred Bridge* (New York: Columbia University Press, 1959).

68. BARON, *Social and Religious History,* 2:151.

69. So also HARNACK, *Mission and Expansion,* 1:512, and NOCK, *Conversion,* p. 192.

70. Englewood Cliffs, N.J.: Prentice-Hall, 1966, pp. 60–62.

71. *Ibid.,* p. 61.

72. *Ibid.,* p. 60.

73. *Epistle* 84a (in the edition of J. BIDEZ and F. CUMONT; *Epistle* 22 in the edition of W. C. Wright in the Loeb Classical Library), 429D and 430D. The practice of support for the poor was present from the beginning, but by the third century it had become a major enterprise requiring full-time administration. Eusebius quotes Bishop Cornelius (c. 250 C.E.) as claiming that the Roman church alone supported some 1,500 widows and poor members of the church; for a complete discussion of Christian philanthropy and social services, see HARNACK, *Expansion,* 1:147–98.

74. *The Social Teaching of the Christian Churches,* 1:43.

75. For a discussion of the same phenomenon in a contemporary urban setting, see R. POBLETE and T. F. O'DEA, "Anomie and the 'Quest for Community': The Formation of Sects among the Puerto Ricans of New York," *American Catholic Sociological Review* 21 (1960), pp. 18–36.

76. *Passion of Perpetua,* 3 and 5f.

77. *Acts of Paul and Thecla,* 7–19.

78. APULEIUS, *Metamorphoses* 11.23.

79. *Pagan and Christian,* pp. 133f.

80. On Mithraism in general, see HARNACK, *Mission and Expansion,* 2:317–23; F. CUMONT, *The Mysteries of Mithra;* A. D. NOCK, "The Genius of Mithraism," *Journal of Roman Studies* 27 (1937), pp. 108–13; M. J. VERMASEREN, *Mithras, The Secret God* (New York: Barnes and Noble,

1963); and R. L. GORDON, "Mithraism and Roman Society: Social Factors in the Explanation of Religious Change in the Roman Empire," *Religion* 2 (1972), pp. 92–121.

81. *First Apology*, 66; the translation is from *Early Christian Fathers*, pp. 286f. In his *Dialogue with Trypho* (chap. 70), Justin further accuses the Mithraists of borrowing the motif of Mithras' birth from a rock from Dan. 2:34 ("As you looked, a stone was cut out by no human hand. . . .").

82. *Prescription*, 40.3–4.

83. *On the Crown*, 15.

84. See CUMONT, *Mysteries of Mithra*, pp. 83–103.

85. *Mission and Expansion*, 2:323.

86. GORDON, "Mithraism and Roman Society," p. 98.

87. So ORIGEN, *Against Celsus*, 3.44.

88. GORDON ("Mithraism and Roman Society," p. 98) relates this fact to the exclusion of women by noting that the Roman army refused to recognize the legal marriage of a soldier until about 195 C.E.

89. "Mithraism and Roman Society," p. 95.

90. *Ibid.*, p. 101.

91. See the discussion in NOCK, *Conversion*, pp. 164–86 ("Conversion to Philosophy"); on Neoplatonism as a religious school, see also DODDS, *Pagan and Christian*, pp. 122f.

92. *Pagan and Christian*, pp. 116–20.

93. *Mission and Expansion*, 2:322f.

94. *First Apol.* 60; the translation is from *Early Christian Fathers*, p. 281.

95. *City of God* 10.32.

96. The only extended discussion known to me is that of S. BARON, *Social and Religious History*, 2:129–71.

97. See the discussion in *Social and Religious History*, 1:171–79.

98. The story is recounted by JOSEPHUS, *Antiquities* 20.17–53.

99. On the case of Flavius and his wife, see LEON, *Jews of Ancient Rome*, pp. 33–35.

100. See J. GAGER, *Moses in Greco-Roman Paganism* (Nashville: Abingdon Press, 1972), pp. 162–64.

101. On Egypt, see TCHERIKOVER, *Corpus Papyrorum Judaicarum* (above, n. 56), 1:1–111.

102. See the edition of H. MUSURILLO, *The Acts of the Pagan Martyrs* (Oxford: Clarendon Press, 1954); see also *Corpus Papyrorum Judaicarum*, 2:25–107.

103. The one exception to this picture is Cicero. In his speech delivered in defense of Flaccus (accused of misappropriating Jewish funds), he cites Judaism as a *barbara superstitio* (*Pro Flacco* 67). But in assessing the social significance of Cicero's unfriendly remarks, we should keep in mind his normal technique of maligning his opponents; see LEON, *Jews of Ancient Rome*, pp. 5–9.

104. *Social and Religious History*, 2:149.

105. Baron speaks of the process as "closing the ranks" (2:129–71).

106. Compare Baron, 2:87f. and the more extensive treatment in W. Bousset, *Die Religion des Judentums im späthellenistischen Zeitalter* (Tübingen: J. C. B. Mohr, 1966), pp. 53–96.

107. *Social and Religious History*, 2:87.

108. Josephus, *Antiquities* 20.38–45; see the discussion in L. H. Feldman's translation of Josephus' *Jewish Antiquities* (Cambridge: Harvard University Press, 1965; Loeb Classical Library), 9:410, note a. Feldman cites a similar controversy in the Babylonian Talmud (*Yebamot* 46a), in which Rabbi Joshua argues that only baptism (i.e., not circumcision) was necessary for converts, whereas Rabbi Eliezer required circumcision.

109. Philo, *The Migration of Abraham* 98f.

110. Emphasized by Goodenough, *Introduction*, pp. 34–36, and by numerous others.

111. See especially *On the Confusion of Tongues*, 191f.

112. In speaking of the years between 300 and 363 c.e., Peter Brown, *The World of Late Antiquity: From Marcus Aurelius to Mohammad* (London: Thames and Hudson, 1971), uses the phrase "the conversion of Christianity" (p. 82).

113. One factor that I have not emphasized is Christian doctrine itself. Harnack (*Mission and Expansion*, 1:85) notes that doctrine gradually became an important missionary attraction, but not before the mid-third century.

114. *World of Late Antiquity*, p. 55.

115. Apuleius, *Metamorphoses* 11.26; the translation is from C. K. Barrett. *The New Testament Background: Selected Documents* (New York: Harper & Row, 1961), p. 99.

116. See above, n. 1.

117. "Introduction to the Religious and Psychological Problems of Alchemy," in *Psychology and Alchemy* (Princeton: Princeton University Press, 1968; vol. 12 of Jung's collected works), p. 19.

118. *Conversion*, p. 210.

119. See Harnack's summary in *Expansion*, 2:324–37.

120. *Against Celsus* 8.69.

121. Cited in Rufinus' Latin version of Eusebius' *Church History* 9.6.3.

122. For a contrary view, see A. H. M. Jones, "The Social Background of the Struggle between Paganism and Christianity," in *Paganism and Christianity* (above p. 109 n. 17), pp. 33f.

Index

Abel, E. L., 16 n. 27
Aberle, David, 59 n. 33
Abreaction, 55, 56
Acts, Book, 25, 31, 34, 37, 61 n. 65, 128, 129
Acts of Paul and Thecla, 146 n. 77
Acts of the Pagan Martyrs, 137
Adiabene, 136, 138
Aelius Aristides, 98
Africa, 20, 28, 111 n. 48
Against the Heretics (writings), 80
Against the Jews (writings), 80
Akiba, Rabbi, 26
Alexandria, 130, 136
Allegory, 127
Allport, G., 16 n. 24
Am ha-areş, 26, 27, 28
Analysis, pure-type, 68
Ananias (Jewish merchant), 138
Ancestors, and sacred order, 10
Angus, S., 141, 143 n. 1
Anti-Christianism, 138
Antioch, 139
Anti-Romanism, 137
Anti-Semitism, 86, 137, 138
Antonines (emperors), 120
Antoninus Pius, Emperor, 99, 110 n. 31
Antony, Saint, 74, 90 n. 27
Apollonius of Tyana, 140
Apologies:
    Christian, 80, 85, 86, 87, 130
    Jewish, 86
    latent function of, 87
Apologists:
    Christian, 84, 117, 128
    Jewish, 127 f.
Apostles, 70, 71, 77
    "The Twelve," 72

Apostolic succession, 72
Applebaum, S., 57 n. 14
Apuleius, 146 n. 78, 148 n. 115
Aquila, 127
Aristotle, 119
Ascension of Isaiah, 127
Asceticism, 67, 120
Asclepius, 99
Asia Minor, 51, 56, 78, 111 n. 48
Asiarchs, 111 n. 38
Associations, private, 123
Athanasius, 74, 90 n. 27
Attis, 123
Augustine, 119, 124, 135
Augustus, Emperor, 97, 102, 104, 122
Aurelian, Emperor, 133
Authority:
    charismatic, 69
    scriptural, 76
    sources of, 30, 68

Bacchus, 106
Bacchus-Dionysus, 105
Banton, M., 17 n. 33
Baron, S., 129, 137, 145 n. 57, 147 notes 96, 97, 104, and 105, 148 n. 106
Barrett, C. K., 148 n. 115
Barth, G., 16 n. 29
Basilides, 83
Bauer, W., 15 n. 11, 77, 78, 79, 91 n. 56
Baur, F. C., 14
Beaujeu, J., 98, 110 notes 26 and 27
Behr, C., 110 n. 28
Believers, economic status of, 24
Bellah, R., 17 n. 33
Benko, S., 108 n. 1
Benoit, André, 79

Berger, Peter, 9, 10, 15, 17 n. 35, 18 n. 49, 64 n. 107, 75, 88, 92 notes 72 and 85
Bergson, H., 17 n. 42
Bevan, E., 118
Bianchi, U., 113 n. 71
Bible:
   formation of Christian, 11
   Jewish versions of, 126 f.
Billerbeck, P., 118
Bishop, 72, 73, 76
Bithynia, 115
Boemer, F., 105, 110 n. 30, 112 n. 65
Bona Dea, 106
Bonsirven, J., 145 n. 62
Bornkamm, G., 16 n. 29
Bousset, W., 16 n. 17, 148 n. 106
Bowersock, G., 101, 110 notes 21 and 22, 111 notes 35 and 38, 144 n. 39
Bowman, J. W., 50
Braden, Marcia, 46
Brandon, S. G. F., 57 n. 14
Brown, P., 140, 144 n. 32, 148 n. 112
Brown, R., 64 n. 111, 109 n. 20
Bultmann, R., 7, 16 n. 17, 60 n. 51, 66, 75, 90 n. 42, 118
Bureaucracies, municipal, 100
Bureaucracy, Christian, 67
Burridge, K. O. L., 1, 2, 10, 20, 24, 29, 32, 35, 36, 37, 59 n. 44, 60 n. 60, 62 n. 73, 70, 95, 108 n. 7, 109 n. 9

Cadbury, H. J., 17 n. 29
C. Caecilius Isidorus, 104
Caligula, Emperor, 98
Campenhausen, H. von, 18 n. 48, 73, 76, 81, 89 notes 13 and 22, 90 n. 44, 92 notes 82 and 84, 145 n. 58
Canon, Christian, 11 f., 76, 85
   conflicting views of, 11
   as product of later centuries, 4
Carcopino, J., 102, 104, 110 n. 31, 111 n. 42, 112 n. 59
Carrier, H., 92 n. 90
Case, S. J., 12, 78, 82, 142 n. 1
Catholicism, early, 67
Cato, 104
Celsus, 43, 94, 128, 131
Chadwick, H., 92 n. 86, 108 n. 2, 143 n. 9–10, 144 n. 37

Charisma, 67, 68, 69, 70, 75
   interactionist model, 28 f.
   latent form, 75
"Charismatic pedigree," 75
Charles, R. H., 65 n. 122
"Chicago School" 12, 17 n. 41
China, Christian development of, 123
Christian beginnings, orthodox image of, 4
Christianity, triumph of, 140–42
Christians, like companions of Odysseus, 81
Christological controversies, 28
Christology, 85, 128
   docetic, 85
Cicero, 147 n. 103
Citizens, Roman, 94, 101
Citizenship, Roman, 123
Class status (*see* Social class)
Claudius, Emperor, 98, 111 n. 36
Clement of Alexandria, 80, 81, 106, 107, 117, 127
Clients, Roman, 100
Cognitive dissonance:
   and Christian missions, 37–49
   and conversion, 48 f.
   criticism of theory, 64 n. 111
   modification of theory, 46–48
Cohn, Norman, 20, 51
Colossians, Letter to, 61 n. 63, 113 n. 74
Communities:
   Christian sense of, 140
   disaffected, 14
   Jewish Christian, 77, 78, 83
   liminal, 33
Conflict:
   between Church and Empire, 123–26
   positive function of, 79–88
Consolation as purpose of book of Revelation, 50, 51
Consolidation, Christian, 68, 69
Constantine, Emperor, 115, 142
Conversion:
   and dissonance, 48 f.
   to Judaism, 128, 136–38
Converts, Jewish, 29, 41
Conzelmann, H., 16 n. 29, 63 n. 92, 64 n. 106, 89 n. 5
Coponius (Roman governor of Judea), 23
Corinth, 94

Corinthians, 36
Coser, Lewis, 80, 87, 91 notes 61, 68, and n. 74, 92 n. 80
Councils, church, 76
Creeds, 76
Cross, F. M., 60 n. 47
Crucifixion, 23, 41
Cullmann, O., 7, 38, 58 n. 16, 59 n. 40, 63 n. 88, 65 n. 139
Cult, imperial, 98, 101, 111 n. 38
Cults:
  cargo, 21
  millenarian, 20 f.
  pagan, 48
  peripheral, 2
Culture, pagan, 86
Cultures, non-Western, 14
Cumont, F., 111 n. 44, 112 n. 66, 146 n. 80, 147 n. 84
Cursus honorum, equestrian, 99
Cybele, 99, 103
Cynicism, 97
Cynics, 123

Daniel, Book of, 50
Daniélou, J., 146 n. 63
Daube, D., 62 n. 81
Davies, W. D., 62 n. 81
Davis, M., 58 n. 23
Dead Sea Scrolls, 6 (*see also* Essenes, Qumran)
Dea Syria, 105, 106 (*see also* Syrian goddess)
Death wish, 125
Decius, Emperor, 115, 142
Decurions, 100
Deissmann, Adolf, 143 n. 14
Demeter, 132
Deprivation, 23, 27, 51, 95, 130, 134
  relative, 27, 59 n. 44, 95
Diaspora, Jewish, 123, 126, 128, 137, 139
Dieterich, A., 12
Diocletian, Emperor, 125
Diognetus, Letter to, 124
Dionysius of Alexandria, 4
Dionysius of Halicarnassus, 111 n. 49
Dionysus, 99, 124
Diotrophes, 73
Disciples, authority of, 8
Disconfirmation, of beliefs, 40, 43, 44, 46

Disputes, with Jewish opponents, 11
Dobschütz, Ernst von, 143 n. 14
Dodd, C. H., 62 n. 81
Dodds, E. R., 17 n. 38, 96, 109 n. 18, 114, 120, 124, 125, 130, 132, 143 notes 16 and 21, 146 notes 66 and 79, 147 n. 92
Domitian, Emperor, 65 n. 128, 136
Douglas, Mary, 15 n. 1, 18 n. 45, 89 n. 2, 95
Duff, A. M., 111 n. 48, 112 notes 50 and 55
Dugmore, C. W., 146 n. 67
Durkheim, E., 17 n. 42

"Early Catholicism," 67
Early Christianity:
  as millenarian movement, 20–37
  relation to Judaism, 5, 135–40
  relation to paganism, 5
  as *the* religion, 6
  as social cancer, 120
  social constituency of, 5, 94, 106–8
  as social world, 2, 11
  study of, 3, 4 f., 13
  and syncretism, 6
  transformation of, 21, 115
Early Christians, pagan views of, 40
Ecstasy, religious, 76, 95
Edessa, 78
Egypt, 78, 99, 104, 111 n. 48
Eisenstadt, S. N., 90 notes 33, 36, and 37
Eleazer (convert to Judaism), 138
Eleusinian mysteries, 99
Eliade, Mircea, 50
Eliezer, Rabbi, 148 n. 108
Emperor, social power of, 97
Engels, F., 14, 96
Ephesians, Letter to, 61 n. 63, 112 n. 64, 113 n. 74
Epictetus, 97
Epicureanism, 135
Equestrian order, 97, 99–100, 110 n. 33
Eschatology, 38, 40, 44, 45, 46
Essenes, 25, 31, 38
Ethics:
  early Christian, 50
  millenarian, 32–36
Etzioni, A., 90 n. 29

Eusebius, 90 n. 41, 117, 127, 146 n. 73, 148 n. 121
Exclusivism, in Christianity, 132
Exegesis, 11, 29, 77 (*see also* Allegory, Typology)
Exorcism, 140
Ezekiel, Book of, 50
Ezra, Fifth and Sixth Books of, 127

Farmer, W., 57 n. 14
Farrer, Austin, 50
Feldman, L. A., 148 n. 108
Festinger, L., 39, 45, 46
Finkelstein, L., 58 n. 23
Finley, M. I., 112 n. 53
1 Clement, Letter of, 44, 45, 72, 73, 90 n. 41
1 Corinthians, Letter to, 33, 36, 61 n. 63, 62 notes 71 and 72, 65 n. 140, 70, 71, 104, 105
1 Peter, Letter of, 112 n. 64
1 Thessalonians, Letter to, 44
1 Timothy, Letter to, 61 n. 63, 84, 85
Flaccus, 147 n. 103
Flavia Domitilla, 136
Flavius Clemens, 136
Foakes Jackson, F. J., 17 n. 41, 59 n. 28
Form criticism, and sociology, 7
Fortuna, 106
Frazer, P. M., 110 n. 25
Freedmen, 94, 97, 99, 102, 103
Frend, W. H. C., 65 n. 129, 144 n. 42, 145 n. 52
Freud, S., 65 n. 134
Fuks, A., 145 n. 56

Gagé, J., 102, 108 n. 3, 110 notes 21, 24, and 32, 111 notes 35, 37, 42, 112 n. 54
Gager, J., 16 n. 21, 147 n. 100
Galatians, Letter to, 35, 48, 61 n. 67
Galerius, Emperor, 133
Galilee, 23
Gallienus, Emperor, 121
Garnsey, P., 110 n. 20
Gavin, F., 146 n. 67
Geertz, C., 17 n. 33, 20
Georgi, D., 62 n. 76, 89 n. 17
Gerhardsson, B., 16 n. 27
Gibbon, E., 119, 120

Glock, C. Y., 109 n. 11
Gnosticism, 83, 85
Gnostics, 36, 81, 119, 142
  social status of, 106 f.
God-fearers, 128, 138
Goodenough, E. R., 146 n. 65
Gordon, M. L., 112 n. 55
Gordon, R. L., 134, 147 notes 80, 86, and 88–89
Gospels:
  apocryphal, 7, 9
  "distortions" in, 8
  as models, 9
  production of, 8, 26
  as religious charters, 8
  sources for Christian communities, 7, 9
  sources for Jesus, 7
  synoptic, 33, 45
Grant, F. C., 58 n. 19
Grant, R. M., 91 n. 67, 92 notes 81 and 85, 146 n. 62
Grässer, E., 63 n. 106, 64 n. 104
Greece, 111 n. 48
Greek, Koinē, 122
Green, M., 63 n. 76

Hadrian, Emperor, 99, 110 n. 31
Hahn, F., 38
Hahn, H. F., 15 n. 1
Hand-washing, ritual, 26
Hanson, R. P. C., 145 n. 62
Hardyck, Jane Allen, 46
Harnack, Adolf, 38, 40, 89 notes 8 and 13, 90 n. 42, 108 n. 7, 112 n. 69, 115, 116, 121, 122, 133, 143 notes 2 and 6–7, 146 n. 69, 148 notes 113 and 119
Harrison, J., 12
Harvey, Van, 16 n. 22
Healings, 26
Heinrici, Georg, 143 n. 14
Held, H. J., 16 n. 29
Helena of Adiabene (convert to Judaism), 138
Hellenism, 86
Hellenistic Christianity, 137, 139 f.
Hellenistic Judaism, 126, 129, 137, 138, 140
Hengel, M., 57 n. 14

Heracleon, 107
Heresies, 78
Heresy, 35, 49, 76–81, 84, 88
Heretics, 76
High priest, Jewish, 25, 31
Hill, M., 74, 75, 89 n. 6, 90 n. 34–35
Hillel, Rabbi, 26
Hippolytus, 91 n. 60
Historians of religion, 5, 6, 15 n. 16
Hollinger, D. A., 18 n. 50
Honestiores, 101
Hymenaeus, 44

Ideology, and conflict, 82, 83
Ignatius, 87, 89 n. 20, 125
Insider-outsider, category of, 30
Intellectuals, 80, 82, 95
Irenaeus, 84
Isaiah, Book of, 127
Isenberg, S. I., 57 n. 1
Isis, 102, 123, 132, 134, 141
Isis-Diana, 99
Izates (brother of Helena of Adiabene), 138

Jaeger, W., 144 n. 37
James (brother of Jesus), 69
James, Letter of, 24, 61 n. 65
Jarvie, I. C., 21, 57 n. 6–8
Jellicoe, S., 145 n. 59–60
Jeremias, J., 62 n. 76
Jerome, 119
Jerusalem, 25, 71
Jesus, 5, 23, 26, 69, 106, 123
    authority of, 8, 28
    death of, 38, 40, 41–43, 45
    images of, 22, 28, 141 f.
    as millenarian prophet, 22, 28, 29
    quest for historical, 7
    resurrection of, 38
Jewish Christianity, 139
Jewish Christians, 49, 77, 78, 83
John (*see* Revelation, Book of)
John, Gospel of, 6, 8, 17 n. 32, 31, 33
John of Gischala, 57 n. 13
John the Baptist, 58 n. 15
Jones, A. H. M., 91 n. 73, 96, 107, 108, 148 n. 122
Jordan, D. P., 143 n. 18

Josephus, 25, 57 n. 11–13, 58 notes 18 and 25, 60 n. 46, 111 n. 48, 138, 147 n. 98, 148 n. 108
Joshua, Rabbi, 148 n. 108
Judaism, 26, 86, 88, 122, 124, 125, 130, 131, 132, 135–40
    apocalytic, 27, 43
    missionary zeal, 38, 62 n. 78
    Rabbinic, 139
    relation to early Christianity, 11
Judas the Galilean, 23
Judea, 100, 101, 111 n. 48
Judge, E. A., 109 n. 19
Julian, Emperor, 119, 120, 130, 133, 142
Jung, C. G., 141
Justin Martyr, 43, 87, 92 n. 86, 132, 135
Juvenal, 102, 104, 123

Kaminsky, H., 57 n. 9
Kautsky, K., 18 n. 47, 112 n. 53
Keck, L. A., 58 n. 20
Kingdom (*see* Eschatology)
    delay of, 43–45
Kinship ties, 34
Kippenberg, H. G., 113 n. 71
Kirk, G. S., 17 n. 42
Kittell, G., 118
Knox, R., 61 n. 69
Koester, Helmut, 7, 16 n. 25, 79, 90 n. 48
Kopoček, T. A., 144 n. 28
Kraft, Robert, 79, 90 n. 47
Kuhn, T. S., 2, 3, 18 n. 50
Kümmel, W. G., 4, 6, 7, 15 notes 10 and 16, 18 n. 46

Lake, K., 17 n. 41, 59 n. 28
Lake City (group), 39, 47
Language, as social construction, 9
LaPiana, G., 111 n. 44, 143 n. 1
Latin, 122
Latourette, K. S., 141, 143 n. 1, 145 n. 54
Law, Jewish, 138
Leach, E., 15 n. 1, 65 n. 135
Legitimacy:
    criteria of, 30, 71
    of social worlds, 12
Leon H., 145 n. 56, 147 n. 103

Lessa, W., 15 n. 4
Lévi-Strauss, Claude, 50, 51
Leviticus, Book of, 61 n. 67
Lévy-Bruhl, L., 17 n. 42
Lewis, I. M., 61 n. 64, 95, 108 n. 7
Lietzmann, Hans, 143 n. 14
Lightfoot, R. H., 16 n. 29
Lindars, B., 63 n. 93, 145 n. 62
Literalists, Jewish, 139
Liturgy, Christian, 56, 128
Livy, 97
Locke, John, 5
Lofland, J., 130
Lord's Supper, 56
Lucan, 112 n. 51
Lucian of Samosata, 43, 131
Lucian the Martyr, 142
Lucius (devotee of Isis), 141
Luckmann, T., 15 n. 14, 17 n. 35, 75, 88, 92 n. 85
Luke, Gospel of, 8, 24, 26, 27, 30, 31, 32, 34, 42, 60 notes 52 and 57, 61 n. 65, 131

McCloy, S. T., 143 n. 18
MacMullen, R., 110 n. 22, 112 n. 61
Magical papyri, 141
Malinowski, B. K., 12
Manumission, 103
Marcion, 61 n. 64, 77, 84, 85, 88, 92 n. 82, 106, 107, 142
Marcus Aurelius, Emperor, 99
Mark, Gospel of, 24, 26, 27, 30, 31, 32, 34, 38, 42, 45, 60 n. 57, 63 n. 90, 64 n. 104, 65 n. 140
Marriage, 35
Martyrdom, 50, 67, 125, 132
Martyrs, 124, 131
Marx, K., 14
Marxists, on early Christianity, 14, 18 n. 47
Marxsen, W., 16 n. 29
Matthew, Gospel of, 8, 24, 26, 27, 30, 31, 32, 35, 37, 60 notes 51 and 57, 61 n. 65, 65 n. 140, 74, 84, 89 n. 19, 131
Meeks, W. A., 17 n. 32, 61 n. 62
Melanesia, 21
Mendelson, E. M., 113 n. 71
Merton, R. K., 57 n. 8, 60 n. 54

Messiah, 41
  suffering, 41, 42
Middle Platonism, 91 n. 67
Millenarian movements, 14, 22
  descriptions, 20 f.
  emotional energy, 35
  ethics, 32–36
  explorations of, 21, 36 f.
  and moral regeneration, 29, 32
  prepolitical character, 27
Millennium, 49
Millerite movement, 39
Minucius Felix, 94
Mishnah, 26
Missionaries, competition between, 26
Missions, 130
  Christian, 37–49, 62 n. 76
  Jewish, 38, 62 n. 78
Mithraism, 122, 132–34, 139
Mithras, 99, 103, 106, 119, 123
Models (*see also* Paradigms, Perspectives)
  comparative, 2, 3, 13
  explanatory, 2
  Gospels as, 9
  theoretical, 2, 3, 12, 14
Mohammedanism, 20
Momigliano, A., 109 n. 17, 144 notes 26, 28, and 36
Monasticism, 74, 76, 87, 119
  as reactionary movement, 74
Money, 24
Monotheism, Jewish, 137
Montanism, 21, 35, 45, 74, 87
Montanus, 142
Moore, G. F., 58 n. 23, 59 notes 29 and 35, 145 n. 61
Morgan, R., 15 n. 12
Mosaic Law, 48
Moses, 30, 31, 117, 123, 128
Munz, P., 113 n. 71
Murray, G., 119, 120
Musurillo, H., 147 n. 102
Myth:
  in Book of Revelation, 50
  Christian, 52
  and psychoanalysis, 55
  therapeutic, 51, 54, 55

Namantianus, Rutilius, 120
Neill, S., 15 n. 8

Neoplatonism, 130, 134, 142
Nero, Emperor, 98
Neusner, J., 58 notes 23 and 27, 59
  n. 30, 60 n. 46
New Testament, 88 (*see also* Canon,
  Christian)
  as problem, 4
  as sacred scripture, 7
Niebuhr, Reinhold, 18 n. 47
Nock, A. D., 62 n. 78, 96, 102, 109 n. 16,
  124, 141, 145 notes 45 and 49, 146
  n. 80, 147 n. 91
Non-citizens, Roman, 102

Oceania, 20, 29
O'Dea, T. F., 146 n. 75
Odysseus, 81
Oesterley, W. O. E., 146 n. 67
Office, ecclesiastical, 69, 70
Old Testament, 85
Oral tradition, 77
  anthropological studies of, 7
  function of, 8
  and gospels, 7
  origin of, 8
  among Pharisees, 60 n. 46
  in preliterate societies, 7
  reconstruction of, 8
Origen, 76, 81, 90 n. 40, 94, 107, 117,
  122, 125, 127, 135, 142, 147 n. 87
O'Rourke, J. J., 108 n. 1
Orthodoxy, 49, 76, 77, 78, 80, 84, 88

Palestine, 23, 78, 83
Paradigms (*see also* Models, Perspec-
  tives)
  anthropological, 3
  problems of 13 f.
  sociological, 3
Paradigm-shift, in study of early Chris-
  tianity 2, 3, 13, 14
Paranoia, and apocalyptic mentality, 51
Parsons, T., 14 n. 1
Parusieverzögerung, 64 n. 107 (*see also*
  Kingdom, delay)
Passion of Perpetua, 145 n. 47, 146 n. 76
Paul, 5, 25, 33, 34, 35, 37, 43, 45, 48, 49,
  69, 70, 73, 77, 85, 94, 104, 122, 129
  authority of, 28

Paul (*cont.*)
  as prophet, 28
  his school, 61 n. 63
  significance in early Christianity, 4
Pax deorum, 124
Pelikan, J., 144 n. 34
Pergamum, 101
Perpetua, 131
Perrin, N., 16 n. 29, 63 n. 99
Persecution, 50, 51, 55, 124
Persecutions, 124, 126
Persia, 123, 125, 126
Perspectives (*see also* Models, Para-
  digms)
  historical, 3
  literary-historical, 3
  theological, 3
Pesharim, 127
Peter, 41f., 89 n. 19
Phaedrus, 97
Pharisees, 26, 29, 31, 58 n. 24, 60 notes
  46 and 48, 48
Philadelphia Seminar on Christian Ori-
  gins, 90 n. 45
Philanthropy, Christian, 146 n. 73
Philemon, Letter to, 104, 105
Philetus, 44
Philippians, Letter to, 60 n. 56, 105
Philo, 127, 138, 139
Philosophical schools, 134 f., 139
Philosophy, 81, 86
  Greek, 77, 117, 122, 128
  pagan, 86, 88
Plato, 128
Pleket, H. W., 101
Pliny the Elder, 98
Pliny the Younger (Roman governor),
  51, 95, 98, 104, 109 n. 12, 115, 116,
  142, 144 n. 43
Plotinus, 119
Poblete, P., 146 n. 75
Polemic, 48, 49
Pontifex maximus, 98
Pontius Pilate, 24
Porphyry, 124, 128, 135
Postman, L., 16 n. 24
Poverty, ideology of, 24, 106
Praeparatio evangelica, 118
Praetorian guard, 99
Predictions, in gospels, 8, 44
Prefect, 23 (*see* Procurator)

Presbyters, 72
Procurator, 23 (*see* Prefect)
Propaganda, 130
Prophecy, 74
Prophet, 28–31, 70
  symbolic function, 28
Proselytes, 128, 138
Proselytism, 39, 47, 48
Proteus Peregrinus, 124
"Psychics," 80
Psychoanalysis, 50, 51, 54
  and myth, 55
  and shamanism, 55
Ptolemy (Gnostic writer), 107
Pure-type analysis, 68

Quintilian, 137
Qumran, 38, 49, 59 n. 45, 127 (*see also* Essenes)

Rationalization, 45, 47, 49
Redaction criticism, 8
Redemptive media, 29, 30
  law of Moses, 29 f., 32
  temple cult, 30 f., 32
Regula fidei (*see* Rule of faith)
Religion:
  equestrian, 100
  of non-privileged classes, 107
  non-Western, 2
  and sacred cosmos, 9
  senatorial, 98
  as social construction, 9, 10
  and social status, 2, 93–113
  as social world, 9
Renan, E., 116, 134
Renard, M., 110 n. 26
Resentment, 26
Revelation, Book of, 4, 49–57, 64 n. 104, 74
  use in liturgy, 56 f.
Revitalization movements, 12, 20, 75
Richardson, C. C., 63 n. 103
Riddle, D. W., 17 n. 41, 145 n. 48
Riecken, H. W., 62 n. 83
Rituals, new, 11
Riviere, Joan, 65 n. 134
Robinson, J. M., 16 notes 25 and 29
Rohde, E., 12

Roman Empire, 94, 129
Roman Law, 123
Romans, Letter to, 61 n. 65
Rome, 11 n. 36, 126, 136, 139
Rostovtzeff, M., 98
Routinization, 67, 74, 87
Rufinus, 148 n. 121
Rule of faith, 76
Rumor, formation and transmission of, 7

Sabbatai, Zevi, 40
Sabbath, 26, 123
Sacred cosmos (*see* Social world)
Sacred scripture, 127
Sacred time, permutations of, 11
Sadducees, 34, 60 n. 46
Ste. Croix, G. E. M. de, 145 notes 46, 53, and 55
Samaritans, 37
Sanhedrin, 101
Satan, 42
Scapegoatism, 88
Schachter, S., 62 n. 83
Schilling, R., 110 n. 26
Schoeps, H.-J., 62 n. 78
Schubert, P., 4
Schutz, J., 89 n. 12
Schweitzer, A., 7, 9, 17 n. 31, 56, 64 n. 105, 65 n. 140
Schweizer, E., 89 n. 8
Scroggs, R., 61 n. 61
Sebastophant, 101
2 Clement, Letter of, 63 n. 102
2 Corinthians, Letter to, 71 f.
2 Peter, Letter of, 44, 45
2 Timothy, Letter to, 85
Segal, Alan, 64 n. 116
Seneca, 104, 125
Septimius Severus, Emperor, 110 n. 31
Septuagint, 127
Serapis-Jupiter, 99
Sex:
  continence, 34
  liberality, 34
  strictures, 35
Shamanism, and psychoanalysis, 55
Shepherd of Hermas, 106
Sherwin-White, A. N., 111 n. 38, 144 n. 40

Shibutani, T., 16 n. 24
Shils, Edward, 74, 75
Sibylline Oracles, 127
Sicily, 104
Simmel, Georg, 80, 91 n. 58
Simon, M., 49, 58 n. 26, 79
Simon the Zealot, 23
Sitz im Leben, social dimensions of, 10, 17 n. 37
Slave conditions, 104
Slave labor, 102, 104
Slave religion, 105
Slave revolts, 104
Slavery, 103
Slaves, 94, 99, 102
   possession of, 104
Smith, J. Z., 3, 17 n. 37
Smith, M., 16 n. 27, 57 n. 14, 58 n. 23, 59 n. 31, 61 n. 65
Social anthropology, 12, 20
Social class, 24, 95, 97, 106
Social classes, Roman, 93–106
   legal status, 97
Social psychology, 12
Social sciences,
   and ancient Israel, 14 n. 1
   and early Christianity, 3, 12, 13 f.
Social status (*see* Social class)
Social stratification, 14
Social world, 10
   changes in, 96
   complexity of, 96
   diversified, 96
   legitimacy of, 12
   precarious, 12
Sociology, 12
   and form criticism, 7
Socrates, 124
Sohm, Rudolph, 68, 69, 89 n. 8
Son of Man, 42, 45
Sophocles, 119
Spencer, R. F., 18 n. 45
"Spirituals", 82
Status distinctions:
   abolition, 33
   minimization, 33
Stein, A., 110 n. 32
Stendahl, K., 16 n. 20, 58 n. 26, 61 n. 61
Stephen, 31
Stern, M., 145 n. 56
Stoicism, 97, 135

Strack, H., 118
Strecker, G., 91 n. 55
Structure, key to Book of Revelation, 50
Succession, 68
   apostolic, 72
Suffering, 8
Symbolic universe, 83, 85
Symbols, 75
   in myth, 51, 55 f.
   new, 11
Syme, R., 110 n. 21
Synagogue, 127, 128, 129, 130, 136
Syria, 73, 78, 83, 111 n. 48
Syrian goddess, 102 (*see also* Dea Syria)
Syrophoenician woman, 37

Tacitus, 98, 105, 137
Talmon, Yonina, 15 n. 4–6, 20, 28, 57 n. 6, 59 notes 33 and 37
Talmud, Babylonian, 26, 148 n. 108
"Tax collectors and sinners," 30
Tcherikover, V., 111 n. 36, 144 n. 41, 147 n. 101
Teacher of righteousness, 59n. 45
Terence, 97
Tertullian, 45, 76, 77, 81, 83, 84, 86, 87, 90 n. 41, 118, 133
Testaments of the Twelve Patriarchs, 127
Thamyris, 131
Thecla, 131
Theodotion, 127
Theology, 83
   and historical methodology, 5, 6, 7, 12
   of New Testament, 5
3 John, 73
Thomas, Gospel of, 8
Thrupp, Sylvia, 57 n. 5
Tiberius, Emperor, 98, 105
Tillich, P., 90 n. 42
Titus, Emperor, 111 n. 48
Titus, Letter to, 85, 112 n. 64
Toleration, Roman, 124, 126
Torah, 32
Toynbee, A., 119, 120
Tradition, and authority, 69, 70, 74
Trajan, Emperor, 51, 110 n. 31, 115, 142

Transference, 54, 55
Trinity, 128
Trobriand Islanders, 12
Troeltsch, E., 96, 130
True Word (group), 46 f.
Turner, H. E. W., 78, 84, 90 notes 42 and 49, 91 notes 64 and 77
Turner, Victor, 33, 34
Tusculum, Dionysiac congregation at, 99
"The Twelve" (apostles), 72, 89 n. 18
Typology, 127

Urbach, E. E., 59 n. 35
Urban proletariat, 102
    religion of, 102

Valentinus, 5, 76, 80, 83, 84, 88, 106, 107
Vansina, J., 16 n. 23, 17 n. 30
Vermaseren, M. J., 146 n. 80
Virgin birth, 127
Vogt, E. (*see* Lessa, W.)

Waddell, Helen, 144 notes 27 and 30
Wallace, A. F. C., 20
Wealth, 34, 106
Weber, Max, 18 n. 48, 37, 59 n. 38, 66, 67, 74, 75, 87, 89 n. 6–7, 91 n. 64,

Weber, Max (*cont.*)
    95, 96, 102, 103, 105, 107, 113 notes 71 and 73
Wells, G. A., 37
Wendland, P., 15 n. 11
Werner, E., 146 n. 67
Werner, M., 64 n. 105, 90 n. 42
Westermann, W., 112 notes 52 and 55
Willoughby, H. R., 15 n. 9
Winch, P., 9
Wolfson, H. A., 146 n. 65
Wolin, S., 59 n. 34
Women, 35, 95, 134
    excluded from Mithraism, 133, 134
World-construction, 9, 10, 11 f.
World-maintenance, 9, 10, 12
Worsley, Peter, 5, 20, 23, 28, 29, 37, 57 n. 10, 59 n. 32, 74, 75, 89 n. 11
Wrede, W., 4, 5, 6
Writings:
    Against the Heretics, 80
    Against the Jews, 80
    Against the Pagans, 80
    noncanonical, 102

Yavetz, Z., 111 n. 41

Zealots, 23, 24, 31, 101
Zechariah, Book of, 50
Zoroastrianism, 126